Advance Praise for *Don't Blow Yourself Up*

"West Virginia's favorite son is also its most beloved writer, the *Rocket Boys*' Homer Hickam. In the summer after he graduated from high school, he realized he had forgotten to apply to a college. Not to worry, his mother did it for him…and got him admitted too. Hmm. This boy was obviously destined for great things. In this memoir Hickam the raconteur takes us along on his adventures: college, a cannon, the army, Vietnam, underwater exploration, NASA engineer, and bestselling writer. It's a helluva journey, a triumph of the spirit. *Don't Blow Yourself Up* is destined to become a classic."

—Stephen Coonts, author of *Flight of the Intruder* and *Liberty's Last Stand*

"Just lovely. I cannot recall when I laughed out loud, and wanted to cry, and held my breath, and just thoroughly enjoyed the true story of a man's life. Homer Hickam by God lived some things, across the fields of a war, under the sea, and in the clouds. He even survived Richard Nixon. Top that."

—Rick Bragg, bestselling author, Professor of Writing, University of Alabama, Journalism Department

"If you've read his bestselling memoir *Rocket Boys* and think you know Homer Hickam, think again. Not only is Homer a man for all seasons and the true definition of a Renaissance man, but he is, without a doubt, one of the great storytellers of our time. In the pages of *Don't Blow Yourself Up*, you'll travel the world with Homer, all the while asking yourself, 'Is there anything this man can't do?' One thing is for certain—West Virginia's favorite son sure knows how to write a memoir that will keep you captivated from the first page to the last."

—Dreama Denver, award-winning author and wife of *Gilligan's Island* star, the late Bob Denver

"Homer Hickam brings us on a wonderful journey through his truly extraordinary life. Providing a beautiful account of his dreams, service, and adventure that led to contributions to the space program and the literary world, Homer takes us from rocket boy to rocket man to bestselling author. He writes about his experiences with an engineer's precision and a poet's emotion, not only sharing the details of the times in which he has lived, but also the deep inner feelings of his life's successes and disappointments in a most personal and incredibly honest way. This is more than a collection of stories from one man's life, it is an inspirational guide to how a person with an adventurous spirit and a good heart can live life to the fullest. Read this book and be inspired to reach for the stars."

—Mike Massimino, former NASA Astronaut

Don't Blow Yourself Up

The Further True Adventures and Travails
of the Rocket Boy of *October Sky*

HOMER HICKAM

A POST HILL PRESS BOOK
ISBN: 978-1-64293-824-1
ISBN (eBook): 978-1-64293-825-8

Don't Blow Yourself Up:
The Further True Adventures and Travails of the Rocket Boy of October Sky
© 2021 by Homer Hickam
All Rights Reserved

Post Hill Press
New York • Nashville
posthillpress.com

Published in the United States of America
1 2 3 4 5 6 7 8 9 10

To my brother (and hero) Jim Hickam who probably wondered what I was doing during all those years.

Don't blow yourself up.
　　　　　—Elsie Hickam, the author's mom

Didn't I tell you not to blow yourself up?
　　　　　—Elsie Hickam, still the author's mom

Contents

Introduction

If you're reading this, likely you've also read about my adventures as a young rocket builder in the little mining town of Coalwood, West Virginia. I wrote about that in a memoir called *Rocket Boys* (which was made into the marvelous movie *October Sky*) and then followed it with two sequels, *The Coalwood Way* and *Sky of Stone*, both set in my hometown.

But there was a bit more to my life than I wrote about in those books. After Coalwood, I went to a tough engineering military school where I famously built a cannon, and then I fought in a war, and then became a scuba instructor, dived on some deep shipwrecks, and unraveled the history of a giant battle along the American coasts. Along the way I worked for NASA, and then I wrote a famous book, had a movie made that was based on it, and did some other things. More importantly, I had a lot of great friends during all of it. And a few enemies, too. Such things happen in a long life.

After enough people asked me when I was going to do it, I decided to sit down and write about some of the things that happened in those years after I was a Rocket Boy in West Virginia. This memoir is the result. There isn't room to write it all down, but maybe I can hit some highlights up through the time *Rocket Boys* was written and *October Sky* was made, a stretch of nearly forty years. A lot has happened since, but endings are as important as beginnings. When I teach writing, I tell my aspiring writers, especially ones interested in writing memoirs, to think about where they're going before they go there. If you just write down everything that happened without running a thread through the piece that ties it up at the end, you may not ever figure out how to get there or when you're done. There's also a Bible proverb I've always admired that says, "It is the glory of God to hide a thing but the honor of kings to search it out." What I think that means is our Creator didn't just hand us all the answers but left it up to us to seek out what is true and real.

That's what this book is mostly about, stories about times in my life when I've learned truths about myself or other people or even the world that I think my readers might like to think about. Or, almost as important, those times that caused smiles or tears. I hope you enjoy my choices.

PART

1

Everybody's Favorite Cadet

To Go to College, You Actually Have to Apply

Once I started building rockets and got good at it, it looked to be pretty definite that I was going to leave Coalwood and go to college. The only problem was I forgot to apply. This, of course, was not my fault, because I was a teenage boy with a lot of things on my mind. This included building those rockets with some other boys while contending with life in a small coal camp and then going off to the National Science Fair and coming back with a gold medal. After that, to honor everybody who helped us, we had a day of launching rockets at our rocket range we called Cape Coalwood. I wrote about that glorious day in *Rocket Boys*, and it was also in the movie *October Sky*. It ended when my dad showed up to watch our last rocket that went miles into the sky and, for the first time in forever, acted like he was proud of me. That scene in both the book and the movie tends to make folks feel good and cry at the same time and, for that, I just say, "You're welcome."

What I didn't write about and what the movie people didn't show was when I got home after that final launch, the entire thing was over and done. Dad went back to work at the mine and Mom went back to painting Myrtle Beach on the kitchen wall and I put all the bent tubes and corroded nozzles and splintered nose cones in a basement corner and climbed the stairs to my room and, with the other boys off to wherever they went, found myself by myself. A very important part of my life was over. There was no need to build any more rockets and, since I'd graduated from high school, there was nothing to study or figure out, so there I was with a lot of success and not much to do with it. It was about then that I realized I hadn't applied for college, which, as mentioned earlier, was not my fault. Actually, it was the fault of the vice president of the United States because of a letter he'd written me that spring, a letter I'd picked up myself at the Coalwood Post Office without anybody else seeing it but me, and it was not a happy letter. In fact, it was soul crushing.

After a couple of days of playing with the dogs and reading novels taken from the stacks Mom and Dad kept around the house, I took a job at the gas station across the street to pump gas and change oil and fix flat tires. My parents didn't say a word one way or the other about my situation until it all just kind of welled up. According to my recollection, it was a hot day in July. After work, I came all sweaty and dirty into the kitchen and found Mom standing on a step ladder and serenely painting some puffy white clouds in her artistic rendering of a beach scene. At my entry, she looked over her shoulder. "What now, Sonny Boy? Wash your hands before you touch anything."

I washed my hands in the kitchen sink, petted Lucifer, our old black tom who was asleep next to the refrigerator, took a deep breath of paint fumes, and confessed everything. "Mom, I didn't apply for college and I don't know what to do."

After dabbing a little thoughtful gray onto one of the puffy clouds, she said, "I thought you were going to the Air Force Academy."

"They don't want me."

"Really? How's that?"

"Well, it's because of Vice President Nixon."

Mom put down her paintbrush, admired her work momentarily, and then climbed down from the ladder, pulled a chair out from under the kitchen table, and sat on it to face me. Acquiring a faint smile, she cocked her head. "Do tell."

At her prompt, I proceeded to tell my mother that for me to go to the Air Force Academy, Quentin, the genius who knew everything in our rocket group, told me I was supposed to get somebody from Congress to nominate me. When I asked Dad who our congressman was, he told me it didn't matter because the creature was a Democrat and therefore unworthy of my interest. When I explained why I wanted to know this information, Dad said I should apply to the vice president, one Richard Milhous Nixon, who was a good, honest Republican. This I had done with hopes high but, just before I'd gone off to the National Science Fair, the answer had come back from Mr. Nixon, which said pretty much how awful sorry he was but I just didn't quite fit the bill.

Mom gave me a look that clearly indicated she felt she'd wasted nine good months before my birth. "It wouldn't have mattered if you'd applied to God himself," she informed me, "because your eyes aren't good enough. I read the health requirements. Did you?"

Of course I hadn't and confessed as such. She allowed a deep sigh. "You want to be an engineer, you have to go to engineer school. Heard they got a good one at VPI."

VPI was the Virginia Polytechnic Institute, sometimes called Virginia Tech. I knew it fairly well because my brother Jim was going there on a football scholarship. He'd been offered to play football at a lot of colleges and had decided at first to go to West Virginia University to play for a famous coach he idolized named Art "Pappy" Lewis. But then Coach Lewis abruptly resigned and my brother, furious that he wouldn't get to play for him, switched over to Virginia Tech.

Mom went on. "I thought about sending you up to West Virginia University but it's so far away you have to overnight to drive up there. Why those politicians put that school nearly in Pennsylvania is beyond me, bless their hearts, but VPI's only about four hours from here driving slow so that's where you're going. I applied for you back in March and got you admitted. You show up first week in September. All the paperwork is on the dining room table."

After letting all that sink in, I asked, "How did you know I didn't get in the Air Force Academy?"

She didn't answer, just gave me that look that told me I had no secrets from her, not while she had access to my room and, now that I thought about it, knew very well the lady who put up the mail in the Coalwood Post Office.

And that was that. I could always count on my mother to do the right thing for me even when I didn't deserve it.

A Rat in Blacksburg

To get ready to go to college, I don't recall doing much. The literature about the school was on the dining room table, but I ignored it. I figured going to college wasn't all that complicated. Just like in every school I had ever attended, all I had to do was show up and be told what to do and when to do it. For their part, Mom and Dad, who surely were aware I hadn't read the letters and brochures since they remained unopened, never said a word. I guess they figured if I wanted to be ignorant, that was my right as a high school graduate.

With the money I'd saved from working at the gas station and previously accumulated with a newspaper route, I bought from the Sears, Roebuck catalog a motor scooter that I used to putt-putt around Coalwood all summer. I loved that motor scooter. It was a light blue color and had a lot of pep. I kept wishing I had Dorothy Plunk riding on the jump seat with her arms wrapped around me, but Dorothy was gone just like the rest of my high school buddies. Loneliness was my closest companion that summer, and I looked forward to getting away from Coalwood and making new friends and studying my heart out to be an engineer.

When the September date for me to leave rolled around, I armed myself with a small bag of clothes and some pens and pencils and started the scooter up. Dad was at the mine and Mom and our two dogs, Dandy and Poteet, were the only ones to see me off, and then there was just her since the dogs ran off to play. She opened the back gate so I could ride the scooter through it and onto the road. "Don't wreck and don't get run over," she said as I departed and, without looking back, off I went.

I have since imagined what Mom did after she closed the gate behind me. For a while, I think she probably watched the place where her little Sonny Boy had disappeared past the houses on Substation Row, and maybe she even shed a tear, I don't know, but then she went back inside the house and got busy with her art on the kitchen wall and that was that. She had done her duty. She had raised both her boys, even the young one who had tried several times over the years to blow himself up, stood by her husband even when she thought he was wrong to keep a job sure to kill him, and lived for nearly three decades in a place she didn't much like, and now she had other things to do. Before the year was out, she would start spending most of her time at a house she'd bought in Myrtle Beach, there to walk her beloved sandy strand, pick up shells and fossilized shark's teeth, and concentrate on her art.

Between Coalwood and Blacksburg were a hundred miles of steep, curvy mountain roads where there were plenty of opportunities to wreck and get run over, but heeding Mom, I avoided both. Dusk was starting to descend when I finally passed the small black-and-white road sign that announced I was entering the town limits of Blacksburg, Virginia. There were no other signs, no grand announcements that this was the home of VPI. I guess the people of Blacksburg figured if you didn't know that already, there was no reason to advertise it. My rump was worn out from the motor scooter and I was a bit tired, but I was too excited not to take a quick tour of the campus. When I saw a long mall, I guessed it was the entrance to the school so I turned into it. At the end, I saw some huge concrete pylons. To the right of them was a little hill with some multistoried brick buildings that I took rightfully as dormitories and to the left were more brick buildings, one of them announcing that it was the student union, and then a big stone building with a sign that proclaimed it to be the library.

Beyond the pylons there was a vast oval of grass. I would later discover the pylons were a war memorial with the names engraved on them of slain alumni during America's various wars. The grass beyond was called the Drillfield and around its circumference were some of the most beautiful buildings I had ever seen. Made of gray but yet somehow warm-looking stone blocks, they looked like fortresses and castles. The stone blocks, I would come to learn, were a local but unique and rare granite stone called Hokie Stone.

A magnificent building with soaring keeps towered over the others and as I admired it, a carillon inside began to play chimes followed by tones to mark the time. It was magical. Since the great buildings were casting long, dark shadows, I thought I'd best find my new home. Unfortunately, by the time Mom got me accepted to the college, all the dormitories were full so I had to live in town in a basement apartment. I sought it out and there I met another late applier and my roommate, a fellow from

California named Cecil C. Childress III. Since I was Homer H. Hickam Jr., at least in alliterative fashion, we had it covered.

"Where are your uniforms?" Cecil asked not too long after he'd welcomed me into our little dungeon.

"Uniforms?" I asked.

It turned out Cecil knew a lot more than I did about VPI. This was because his father had graduated from there. Cecil said he was in Blacksburg, mildly against his will, to repeat that experience. The uniforms I needed were for the military units we were both required to join. This was news to me. Jim, as far as I knew, didn't wear any kind of uniform except the one to play football.

Cecil took a moment to tell me about the Virginia Tech Corps of Cadets. It was, he explained, an organization where everyone was expected to live like they were in the military and wear uniforms and march around and salute. My brother was exempt because he played football. Since Jim had never mentioned any of this to me, I was astonished but, on the other hand, supposed it was sort of like the Air Force Academy so maybe it wouldn't be too bad.

Cecil took me under his wing, and the next morning we were off to the Cadet Corps tailor shop, there to purchase on credit two pairs of gray wool shirts, two pairs of gray wool pants with black stripes down their sides, one wool tie, one dark blue wool dress tunic with brass insignia, one white cross belt with a brass breastplate, one dark blue wool overcoat, one dark blue wool cap with a shiny leatherette brim and a black leather strap at the base of its crown, one black rubber raincoat so thick and heavy I could barely pick it up, two white cotton belts accompanied by a brass buckle, a black leather belt with the Cadet Corps crest on it, and a pair of black leather dress shoes. Black socks, fortunately, I already had.

10

The white belts, Cecil explained, were called rat belts. It was so that I could be identified as a freshman or, according to the Corps vernacular, a rat. A trip to the bookstore was next, there to buy a liquid brass polisher called Brasso, something called a Blitz cloth and a jeweler's cloth to complete the brass polishing process, a wire gizmo called a Spiffy, and black Kiwi brand shoe polish, the only one, so Cecil claimed, that truly worked to properly spit-shine shoes, which, he said, I would need to do every day. By then, I was essentially in full zombie mode, just doing what I was told. Everything seemed off-kilter somehow at this engineering school. When we would get to the engineering?

Once back at our basement with the purchases, Cecil looked over the unopened paperwork I'd brought with me to see what I should do next. He said, "You're in Squadron A over at Eggleston Hall, which is in the lower quad. They expected you last week." When I just looked perplexed, he added, "You better get over there and report in."

Cecil showed me how to spit-shine my shoes and how to tuck my shirt into my pants so that it was flat in the back without any bagging. He also showed me how to tie my tie and how to use the Spiffy to keep the tabs of the shirt collar straight and properly flat, how to wear the cap squared away with the brim no more than two fingers above my nose, and, lastly, how to walk or, as Cecil put it, to "drag right" and "square corners."

Every bit of this was truly mind-boggling stuff. To drag right meant to keep always to the right side of any sidewalk or hallway. To square corners meant to sharply execute a right or left turn anytime I wanted to change directions. Things just kept getting weirder and weirder and I was beginning to wonder if Cecil was making it all up.

After I got dressed up, my skin crawling beneath the itchy wool of the uniform, Cecil inspected me and said, "I guess it will have to do," and pointed me in the right direction, saying, "You either go now or eventually they'll come after you."

I went then. The lower quadrangle, where Squadron A was located, looked dark and forbidding like an old stone fortress. Passing under an arched sally port, I continued to the dormitory that was marked with a brass plaque that said EGGLESTON HALL. There was a heavy wooden double door that I opened and walked inside and up a few steps onto a linoleum-covered hallway that was so clean and polished I could see my reflection. The smell of wax and ammonia was almost overpowering. Everything—the walls, the brass doorknobs—just gleamed. When I spotted a fellow in a cadet uniform lounging beside a water fountain, I said to him, "Can you help me? I'm Sonny Hickam from Coalwood, West Virginia. Is this Squadron A?"

Which was the last thing I said for a good long while, mainly because for much of that good long while I had a bucket on my head and some cadets, all wearing black belts, were beating on it with brooms and mops and yelling at me about things I knew nothing about such as guard orders and the college motto and my general unworthiness to partake of the oxygen from the atmosphere.

Even through the noise and demands for answers to questions that seemed like nonsense, I managed to have at least one salient thought: *If this is college, I'm not certain I'm going to like it all that much.*

You Can't Go Home Again
Even When You Do

Note: The Virginia Tech of today and the Virginia Tech when I attended are much different. For those of us who arrived there in 1960 when there were only around five thousand students, the campus now seems crowded with nearly thirty thousand students and dozens of new classrooms, labs, and dorms. Student life is also much changed. In the early 1960s, only a hundred or so women students lived sequestered in an antebellum house called Hillcrest. Now, women make up nearly half of the students. Where there were only a few black, Asian, and international students when I went there, these students are now a significant percentage of both the undergraduate and graduate schools. The military system at Virginia Tech has also evolved. Today, the Corps still lives within a military environment but emphasizes above all else academics and leadership through a well-thought-out curriculum under the supervision of professional on-campus advisors. Women and all races are well represented in the Corps and in all leadership positions. Anything like the hazing we received as cadets is now strictly forbidden. Although our "old corps" turned out fine leaders in both military and civilian life, the quality of the leaders that now come out of the Virginia Tech Corps of Cadets is, in my opinion, vastly superior.

When a freshman in A Squadron quit and opened up a bunk, I left Cecil and moved into the full gale of rat life. There were always one or two upperclassmen just waiting to pounce and make me brace up, a position of exaggerated attention with chin well tucked, shoulders thrown back, stomach pulled in, and heels locked together. When it became generally known I was from West Virginia, I became even more of a fruitful target.

"What's a hillbilly doing in my school?"

"I don't know, sir."

"You don't know why you're here?"

"To go to engineer school, sir."

"Why did you say you didn't know?"

"I don't know, sir."

"You don't know much, do you?"

Miserably, I had to answer that, no, I didn't know much.

Somehow, I made it through that first academic quarter while dozens of my fellow freshmen flunked out or quit. Exam week came and went and I headed home for Christmas, fearful what my folks would say when they saw my report card since I had barely scraped by in chemistry and math. In Coalwood, I found my mom as she always was except a little more relaxed now that she had the Myrtle Beach house to escape to anytime she wanted. As per her usual, there was a giant thoroughly decorated pine tree with strings of tinsel and lights and baubles with an angel on top in the living room. Presents were stacked high beneath it, and Chipper, her beloved pet squirrel, was hidden within to ambush me or brother Jim or one of the twin Siamese cats who might be walking by. Chipper had to be the bravest squirrel there ever was in the entire history of the universe. Siamese cats are born hunters and not to be trifled with, but that didn't stop Chipper from jumping on their backs for a ride. He'd happily squawk while they ran and then he'd launch himself high atop a chair or the curtains just out of range of their claws and teeth. If you ever want a spirit animal with real spirit, let me urge upon you the West Virginia gray squirrel.

The first morning I was back in Coalwood, Mom sought me out at the kitchen table, where I was having a breakfast of Twinkies and hot chocolate just because I could. The food in the Virginia Tech mess hall was nutritious but bland. She looked at me with something approaching real concern that did not, as it turned out, have anything to do with my food choice. Finally, she said with some alarm, "You made your bed."

It took me a moment to discern her purpose for saying such a thing until I realized it was a statement of fact. She continued. "What have they done to you at that school?"

Making my bed had been entirely a reflex action. Now that I thought about it between bites of the Twinkie, I had even used hospital tucks on the sheets. I wondered if Mom had noticed until she said, "You even used hospital tucks on the sheets. How is it you know how to do that?"

"I'm in the Cadet Corps, Mom," I said. "We have to make up our beds every day."

"Where's your laundry?"

"I don't have any."

"Jimmie has two full bags."

"The laundry rat takes care of that," I explained.

"The laundry rat?"

"The executive officer makes up a list of freshmen to pick up everybody's laundry and then sees it's done. I've been the laundry rat more than just about anybody."

Her expression was one of astonishment. "So you make up your bed, take care of your own laundry, what else?"

I told her we also mopped and waxed our floors, folded our clothes, dusted and straightened our desks, scrubbed out our sinks, shined our shoes to a mirror finish, polished our brass until we could see our reflection in it, and generally stayed very tidy about our person, our room, and our barracks as dorms were called. We rats also got yelled at a lot and had to sit at a brace while eating, which I demonstrated.

"Good Lord," she breathed. "You do all that?"

"Yes, ma'am."

"I can't wait to tell your father."

The question just sprung out of me, a question tinged with hope. "Because he'll be proud of me?"

She looked at me as if I'd gone crazy. "No. Because he won't believe it!"

Since I had learned it was against the rules for a Virginia Tech freshman to have any kind of motorized vehicle on campus, I rode my scooter home at Christmas to leave it there. When I told Mom this sad fact, she said she knew a fellow who wanted to buy it and I told her to go ahead but to wait until I'd gone back to school so I could have it to putt-putt along Coalwood's streets one last time. When I rode it to the Big Store and went inside, I discovered Mr. Dubonnet at the soda fountain. John Dubonnet was Coalwood's union chief and also grew up with my parents in Gary, a coal camp twelve miles and three mountains away. He'd even taken my mom out in high school. After World War II, he'd come back to McDowell County and rose to lead the union in Coalwood and Caretta. Dad disliked him, but I thought Mom still had a soft place in her heart for her ancient beau.

Mr. Dubonnet waved me over to the drugstore counter and bought me a pop and asked how I was doing. Before I could answer, he said, "Heard you almost flunked chemistry."

Such unhappy information I knew must have come from Mom, so I didn't deny it. Instead, I provided an excuse. "We sit in this big room with our seats up high and I can hardly see the professor he's so far away. And I have to wear a wool uniform which is hot and itchy. And chemistry class is after lunch. Sometimes, I can't stay awake."

If I expected any sympathy from the union boss, I was instantly disappointed. "You'd best take advantage of college," he said. "Lots of boys in your high school class are working in the mine or are in the army." And then he asked, almost inevitably because it was information about the mine superintendent a union chief could use, "How's your dad?"

His question reminded me I didn't really know how my dad was because I hadn't seen much of him. He'd mostly been up at the mine. When I made that confession, Mr. Dubonnet frowned at me and said, "He isn't well, Sonny. That black spot on his lungs has gotten bigger. And there's a lot of turmoil at the mine.

Wildcat strikes, not enough money from the company for him to keep the mine safe. He's dealing with a lot."

"Can't you help him?" I asked.

"That's not my job," he said before adding, "but he's your dad. You should ask him how he's doing. He might like that."

After Mr. Dubonnet went off to shop in the grocery of the company store, I went back to my scooter to ride around and see anybody else I knew, but the streets of Coalwood were almost empty. Most of the mine operations had moved to our sister town of Caretta. No coal trains chuffed in and out, and no more long lines of miners marched to and from the mine. Coalwood seemed like a lonely fly caught in a web waiting for whatever fate had in store for it.

That night, I lay in bed and stared up at the ceiling and recalled those times when I was a boy listening to the crunch of hundreds of hard-toe boots as miners plodded by during shift changes. When I looked out my bedroom window, I saw only a few miners and a couple of pickup trucks going by. Where was the Coalwood I'd once known?

On Saturday evening, with Dad nowhere around, I asked Mom to let me borrow the Buick. She had no objection so I drove over to the town of War, the home of Big Creek High School. It was my intention to attend the Saturday night dance held in the place called the Dugout beneath the Owl's Nest Diner, but I found everything dark and locked up tight. I walked out on the bridge between the diner and the high school and recalled memories of a time and place in my life that was no more and would never be again. When I drove back through town, I saw some kids crossing the street to the old bus terminal. When I heard the thump of music, I realized the dance was there. Happy to find it, I parked the Buick and was thrilled to see Ed Johnson, who'd spun the platters at the Dugout, now holding court at the door to the terminal. After I'd surrendered a quarter, he asked, "Whatcha been doin', Sonny boy?" When I told him I was going to college, he asked, "Then what are you doin' here?"

It was a good question. I looked at the sparse crowd of dancers and didn't recognize any of them. I stuck around just in case anybody from my class showed up, but they didn't. When I decided to leave, Ed said, "Just so you know, I'm moving to Florida. This place is not what it used to be." I drove home listening to WLS in Chicago playing the latest in rock and roll. I didn't recognize any of the songs, and all the groups were changing.

A couple of days before I headed back to Blacksburg, I was surprised and happy to see Sherman Siers, one of the boys of the Big Creek Missile Agency, at our door. I'd been told Sherman was out of town but there he was. I wanted to hug him but, of course, we didn't do that kind of thing back then. We headed up to my room, where Sherman filled me in on how much fun he was having at the engineering school at West Virginia Tech in Montgomery and that he was making straight A's. He was just back from Kansas City, he said, where his college basketball team played in a tournament. When I sat there without much to say, he said, "Heard you had trouble in chemistry. And math."

Sherman wasn't trying to make me feel bad. It was just his way of being sympathetic. All I could tell him was I felt off balance at Virginia Tech. "If you don't like it, you should transfer," Sherman said.

"I don't know what to do," I answered miserably but happy I had somebody to talk to.

"You'll figure it out," Sherman said. Good old Sherman.

I made an attempt to change the subject by telling him about Ed Johnson and the demise of the Dugout dances. Sherman showed no surprise. "That's why I went to Kansas City," he answered. "Nothing's the same here."

My reply was wistful. "I miss the way things were."

"So do I," Sherman said. "We had some good times, didn't we?"

"I guess we did." I thought about that for a while and then said, "We didn't even realize they were good times. Isn't that strange?"

He laughed. "We sound like we're eighty years old, not eighteen."

He was right. We had our entire lives yet to go. It was time to look forward, not back, even if forward was kind of scary. I'd once told Jake Mosby, a Coalwood junior engineer, that I was afraid of the future. He'd laughed and clapped me on the back. "Old son," he said, "we're all afraid of *that*!"

It was my plan to hitchhike back to Blacksburg, but I was surprised when Dad volunteered to drive me there. We were mostly silent the entire time until we got to Eggleston Hall. When I put my hand on the door handle, Dad said, "Don't flunk out and don't quit."

"I won't, Dad," I quietly replied. When he said no more, just kept staring ahead with his jaw clenched, I got out and watched him drive the Buick away. It was only then, mindful of Mr. Dubonnet, I realized I still hadn't asked him how he was doing, not that he would have told me.

Flash, Everybody's Favorite Cadet

In 2014, during the fiftieth anniversary of my class at Virginia Tech, we were inducted into what was known as the "Old Guard" and so a lot of the fellows in my class showed up on campus. It was great to see them. While we were there, we boys of Squadron A were asked to accompany Colonel Patience Larkin, the alumni director of the Corps, to the attic of Eggleston Hall to see something there she thought we might enjoy. Puzzled, we followed, stairway by stairway, landing by landing, we old fellows with our bad backs and creaky knees, until at the very top, she unlocked a door and swung it open where was revealed not only an attic but our past. We stood there as old men while looking back at us was nothing less than ourselves of fifty years ago. Painted on the attic walls, forgotten for decades of war and peace and success and failure and happiness and tragedy, were all our names, usually with our class graduation date "64" written alongside. There were also handprints and messages. My name was prominent: "Sonny Flash Hickam EFC '64." It was like seeing the paleo cave paintings left by the Neanderthals. But why were these signatures and drawings there?

"Homer, what does EFC stand for?" Colonel Larkin asked.

It was if Cadet Private Sonny Hickam was beside me whispering the answer. "Everybody's Favorite Cadet," I confessed while Sonny grinned at me.

"I bet there's a story about that," she said, laughing, and she was right. There were stories behind all our graffiti, stories of perseverance and grit that had to do with the simple philosophy the Corps had in those days: *The best way to build up a man is to first break down the boy.* The graffiti on that attic ceiling was a testament that it hadn't quite worked out that way. We had bent but we never broke. When we were the rats of Squadron A, the attic was our refuge, the only place we could meet without the upperclassmen barging in on us. "Taps" was played every evening at 2200 hours, also known as 10:00 p.m., and all doors were supposed to be closed and lights out but, desperate to talk and share, we freshmen would wait a half hour or so and then sneak up to the attic. Maybe the upperclassmen knew about it and maybe they'd done the same when they'd been in our spit-shined shoes, but we never got caught.

Many people wonder why anyone in college would put up with a military system if they don't have to, and I understand their wonder. Without a doubt, I could've avoided it. All I ever had to do was ask my parents to let me transfer to another school and I'm sure they would've agreed. Also, after the first two years at Virginia Tech, I could have chosen to be a civilian student. Yet even though my fellow rats and I struggled under the system, most of us in my squadron would eventually choose to remain in the Corps all four years. The reason why was actually pretty simple—there is nothing like shared hardship to bring people together and weld them into a brotherhood, and that's exactly what we became. I wish I could list all their names and tell them how much I loved living, working, marching, and studying with them but they know who they are and that we are brothers forever. I will mention three of them in our squadron class, however, because Doug Murphey, Bob Edmunds, and Lynn Edney were the ones the Vietnam War took from us.

Lynn was among the first of us to adopt a strategy to get us through our rat year. Lynn had a sense of humor and was absolutely fearless. There were two sophomores I will call Cranky and Stanky who were busy flunking out of school and therefore had plenty of time to harass us rats. To get back at them, Lynn, who was not a smoker, took it up since it was well known Stanky smoked a particularly foul cigarette brand. One night after "Taps," Lynn tossed half-smoked Stanky butts in the urinals and around the building. When they were found, Stanky was made to police up every one of them while we rats snickered. As for Cranky, there was a big rat (a rodent, not a freshman) that kept being spotted in the halls. Lynn, a patient boy with a bow and arrow and a good aim, managed to kill the intruder one night and then toss it over the transom into Cranky's room while the boy lay asleep. The screams from Cranky at first call were delicious to those of us who knew what had happened.

Lynn showed the rest of us how to contend with the upperclassmen and that was to beat them at their own game. One of Cranky's favorite ploys was to make funny faces at us to make us laugh and then giving us demerits or extra duties for "inappropriate laughter." One afternoon, when I came in from class, he pulled this on me and, sure enough, I fell for it.

"What are you laughing at, Rat? Do you think I'm funny?"

"Yes, sir."

"Brace up, Rat Hickam! You better tell me I'm not funny!"

"You're not funny, sir!"

"Then why are you still laughing?"

"Because you're funny, sir."

"You will report to my room at 1900 hours and polish my brass and shine my shoes!"

This was an illegal order—I knew it, Cranky knew it—but he was so abysmally poor at shining his shoes and his brass that he came up with all kinds of excuses to force one of us to do it. At 1900 hours, I headed for Cranky's room with all my shoeshine rags and polish and Brasso but "accidentally" dropped it all outside the room of a "rat daddy" senior. A "rat daddy" was an upperclassman who didn't like abusing freshmen. This one was also a chemical engineering student and that meant he didn't like being disturbed while trying to study. At the clatter outside, and I may have dropped the stuff again while trying to pick it up, his door flew open. "What are you doing, Mr. Hickam?"

"Going to Cranky sir's room, sir. As ordered, sir!"

"Why are you carrying that Shinola and Brasso?"

"I cannot tell a lie, sir. To polish Cranky sir's brass, sir. And shine his shoes, sir. As he ordered me to do, sir!"

As anticipated, the senior turned to face down the hall where Cranky's room was located. "Cranky!"

Cranky's door opened. He stuck his head out, took one look at me with the senior, and quickly closed it.

"Go study, Mr. Hickam. I'll take care of this!"

The senior was still yelling at Cranky when I closed my door behind me. Cranky never bothered me again.

Although I was learning to fight back, I was still an easy target and the demerits started to pile up. In fact, by spring quarter, I had more demerits than any freshman in my entire class! This ultimately required me to visit none other than Major General John M. Devine, our renowned West Point–trained commandant who'd commanded an armored division in the thick of battle during World War II. He was a little fellow with a brush moustache and was rawhide tough. After I reported to his office with a smart salute, he allowed me to stay in a brace while he pondered me for what seemed a week before inquiring, with a resigned sigh, if I was ready to quit. When I assured him I wasn't, he tapped the record of my ineptitude with an index finger and said, "This demerits list shows you are not suited for this school."

"I'm not going to quit, sir. No way."

"Then why all these demerits?"

"I guess they're the way I learn, sir."

This made General Devine almost smile, don't ask me why, but then he reacquired his stern expression. "All right. I'm going to give you another chance but only one. You understand? You need to learn without getting demerits."

What I said next just popped into my head. "I'm going to become your favorite cadet, sir," I swore. "I'm going to be everybody's favorite cadet!"

General Devine laughed out loud at my declaration and shook his head. "Everybody's favorite cadet. I tend to doubt that." He waved his hand. "Get out, Hickam, and I better not see you in here again!"

I got out of his office, but my promise to be everybody's favorite cadet gave me a challenge. To reach this exalted status, I started wearing a clean rat belt, polishing my brass to a gleam that would knock out an upperclassman's eyes, spit-polishing my shoes until I could see myself in their reflection, tucking in my shirts so tight it nearly split their seams, and marching to perfection. I memorized every upperclassman's name and even their hometowns, which, along with everything else we rats had to know from the history of the college to the official guard orders, I could rattle off without error. Pretty soon, the upperclassmen started leaving me alone and went after easier targets. When my fellow rats were stunned by my sudden transformation, I laughingly told them it was because I was "Everybody's Favorite Cadet."

After my freshman year, I lived the adventure in the coal mines during the summer I wrote about in *Sky of Stone*, and then I was a sophomore. During that year, I applied to write a weekly column in the *Virginia Tech* newspaper. Although I was turned down, an editor there said I wrote with "flash," which I duly reported to my buddies in Squadron A. The next thing I knew I was being called "Flash," and so it was I became...

Flash Hickam, Everybody's Favorite Cadet, and that's why I wrote what I did on that attic wall.

Red and Pink Marked the
Corridors of Death

In an encounter I wrote about in *Rocket Boys*, it was in May 1960 that I met Senator John F. Kennedy. He wasn't so well known then and was struggling to win the West Virginia presidential primary against Senator Hubert H. Humphrey. Win he did, helped in part, I believe, by my question to him about going to the moon, which got him talking about getting the country moving again, and so it was by January 1961, now President John F. Kennedy swept into office under full sails. Maybe, karma being what it is, that was because his opponent, one Vice President Richard M. Nixon, had refused to nominate me to the Air Force Academy. I don't know but you never know. However it happened, President Kennedy sounded and looked good, and his big grin kind of lit up the room.

When I heard Kennedy's inaugural address on a radio in my room at Virginia Tech, I liked what he had to say when he promised we were going to fight tyranny, meaning the Communists in Russia and China. Since I was in school to be an engineer to help beat the Russians in the space race and also intended to become an officer in the military, I figured I was right in line with President Kennedy's speech.

Looking back on it, I don't recall any of the cadets I knew caring two cents about politics. As far as we were concerned, the USA had grown as it should since 1776 during war and peace, during which our country mostly did the right thing when it had to do it. Our history flowed from war to war including the one where we ended slavery in an awful bloodletting and then the country just kept getting better and more prosperous and that was all we needed to know except we were going to win out in the end, one way or the other. What we didn't know, while we were enjoying a crisp, beautiful Blacksburg autumn that year of 1962, was there was something strange going on in Cuba that was about to bring the entire world to the brink of destruction.

These days, a lot of people make fun of the 1950s and '60s when they see films of grade school kids hiding under their desks during drills for nuclear war. I mean, how could a desk stop an atomic bomb? Ha ha. Well, not so fast. As it was explained to us by our teachers, it actually made sense. We got under our desks to keep our little bodies from being pierced by flying glass from shattered windows. That might not work but wasn't it worth a try? These days, the fallout shelters that families built inside their homes back then are also thought of as pretty droll. Maybe so, but even if hiding out after the nukes dropped didn't work out, at least it showed parents cared enough about their children to prepare for the worst while hoping for the best. The point is most Americans thought back then that there was a real possibility that the Russians were going to hit us with atomic bombs and we'd hit them back. Many a young man got his first successful sexual encounter in those days by reminding his young lady friend that they might as well spoon because they were probably going to die awful deaths anyway. I mean, that happened. A lot. Trust me.

It was October 1962, my junior year at Virginia Tech, when I finally managed to get my own column in the *Virginia Tech*, our college newspaper. Simply put, I had this overwhelming need to write. Although I'd been turned down for a feature column titled "Corps in Column" the previous year, Jim Tankard, the new feature editor, agreed to give me a try in a column titled "Sound Off!" Patiently, the future professor emeritus at the University of Texas in Austin taught me how to open an article, get to the juice, and close out with some pizazz.

Though I did my best to be a good writer while still struggling through engineer school, there were other things going on in the world to worry about. One of them was when Premier Nikita Khrushchev of the Soviet Union noticed President Kennedy was busily installing American Jupiter missiles next door in Turkey. Khrushchev got it in his head that if that young upstart of an American president thought he was going to surround his country with nuclear weapons, he'd return the favor by putting missiles in Cuba. Cuba was only ninety miles from Florida, which meant our entire country east of the Mississippi was well within range. President Kennedy, getting wind of this, didn't take kindly to this plan and so the next thing I knew about it, I was with my cadet buddies huddled around our television set in the dayroom listening to the president tell us there was a very good chance that nukes were about to fly. Of course, he didn't say that directly, but from the steel in his voice and the phrases he used, it sounded a lot like an ultimatum, and anybody who knew anything about our military knew there were atomic and hydrogen bombs already in the air aboard B-52s, just waiting out there somewhere over the Arctic ice to head to Russia. Likely, Soviet bombers were also out there circling and ready to go. Toward the end of his speech, Kennedy gazed into the camera lens and with what I took as the utmost finality said:

"My fellow citizens, let no one doubt that this is a difficult and dangerous effort on which we have set out. No one can foresee precisely what course it will take or what costs or casualties will be incurred. Many months of sacrifice and self-discipline lie ahead—months in which both our patience and our will will be tested…"

"Months! Holy shit," somebody said. "We're going to war!"

"The Corps will be called up," somebody else said and nobody argued with that assessment, although privately I think there were more than a few of us who suspected we would be radioactive dust long before that happened.

When I heard a professor who was an expert on radiation was going to talk to the Corps, I gathered with a crowd in the Burruss Hall auditorium. It was packed, and I recall the sour smell of our sweat-damp wool uniforms. The man, an older gentleman with a kindly face like somebody's favorite uncle, was dressed in a tweed jacket and soon had us mesmerized by his calm, matter-of-fact analysis of the horror that was coming.

On a flip chart, he showed the likely targets for the Soviets and his assessment of the size of the bombs they'd use. Cities with a population of more than a million and the District of Columbia were probably going to be hit with ten- to twenty-megaton monsters. Smaller cities were going to get six to ten megatons. Military bases would be pounded by the more surgical five megatonners that would still leave craters miles in diameter. The closest military base to Blacksburg was Radford Arsenal, about twenty miles away. The good professor said Radford would probably only get hit by a small nuclear bomb. "Still," he went on, "we'll feel its effects here. If you're standing outside when it hits, you'll first see a flash that will permanently blind you. The heat will be close behind so, if you were lucky enough not to be blinded by the flash, I recommend you try to get behind something. The blast effect...well, it'll be like a hurricane. Buildings will come apart and debris will be flying everywhere with enough force to kill. Then will come the radiation, but not just from Radford. From everywhere."

He flipped his chart to show the normal winds of October in the United States with red and pink swaths marking the likely path of fallout and radiation from an attack on the East Coast. The only thing on his chart that I halfway liked was that Coalwood and, in fact, all of McDowell County did not fall within any of the radiation corridors. Maybe my folks would survive even if my brother and I didn't. But what kind of world would be left? The professor wasn't hopeful. "There will be massive casualties," he said. "There won't be many doctors or nurses left, and most of the hospitals will be rubble. It will be a nightmare where the living will envy the dead. Eventually, I suspect, most life in the northern hemisphere will die off. In the southern hemisphere, well..." He shrugged. "It depends on where the wind blows and the currents flow. Are there any questions?"

If there were any, I don't recall them. Mostly, everybody was shocked into silence. I slogged dismally back to the barracks and joined the Squadron A cadets in front of the television in the dayroom. No one said anything. We just watched the constant news, which really had nothing new to say. My textbooks were waiting in my room, but I saw no good reason to study, nor did I see any reason to work on my newspaper column.

On October 27, the news came that one of our U-2 reconnaissance planes over Cuba had been shot down and the pilot killed. "Those damn Russians! Kill 'em all!" I heard a cadet yell down the hall. Much of America echoed that sentiment. Shortly afterward, an American destroyer was reported to have depth-charged a Russian submarine. On our battered television set, we began to see film of fallout shelters being prepared and troops on the move in Florida toward Key West to jump off to Cuba. Civil Defense made announcements with advice on what to do if war came, which was mainly to listen for the sirens and get to a shelter if you could find one.

All that was left for the students at Virginia Tech to do was what we always did and that meant for the cadets to get up at 0600 in the morning and march in formation to breakfast and then spend the day in class or the library or in our rooms studying and then evening formation and dinner in the mess hall and back to our rooms for more studying or going down to the dayroom to watch the television. We just existed to see if we would continue to exist.

A week after Kennedy's speech, without any specifics, it was announced that the Russians had agreed to withdraw their missiles and the American blockade of Cuba was lifted. As the years passed, we would learn that we came very close to an exchange of nuclear weapons because of miscalculations on both sides. To this day, if you read most American historians, they will claim that it was Khrushchev who blinked and gave in. A deeper unpeeling of that historical onion shows very clearly that both Khrushchev and Kennedy blinked. The removal of the Soviet missiles from Cuba was celebrated by our big news media outlets while the removal of our Jupiter missiles from Turkey went mostly unreported.

Relieved that we weren't going to be called up and that we could continue our studies, the Virginia Tech Corps of Cadets went back to being ourselves. What we didn't know was that for many of us, in a place much farther away than Cuba, another crisis was brewing. When it boiled over, we would be tossed into its meat grinder, but for a while, at least, we slept the sleep of the saved.

The Skipper, Part 1

Once upon a time on a night when our windows were rattling with a fast-blowing, bitter wind and the snow was piling up outside in huge drifts, a situation otherwise known as Blacksburg during the winter, a fellow A Squadron cadet named Alton Benjamin "Butch" Harper turned up in my room and said he had decided I was just the fellow to help him do something very important.

At the time I was studying dynamics, which was getting the better of me, so I was happy to turn to him and ask, "What's that, Butch?"

His answer was simple and to the point. "We need to build a cannon."

Since I was a former Rocket Boy and therefore missed things that exploded, I perked right up and said, "Sounds good to me!"

This kind of instant agreement to an outlandish proposal has tended to get me in trouble over my life and this time was no exception, although it ultimately delivered up something unexpected and wonderful. Butch's cannon idea grew from the annual football game between VPI and our archrivals the Virginia Military Institute, also known as VMI. The contest, called the Military Classic of the South, was held every Thanksgiving Day in Roanoke's Victory Stadium and was filled with color and tradition and lots of pranks between the two student bodies. For the most part, the pranks were pretty bland, such as sneaking on opposing campuses and scattering leaflets and maybe painting statues in the opposing school's colors. Sometimes, however, things got a little out of hand.

In 1954, just before the big game, Virginia Tech cadets sneaked onto VMI's Lexington campus and kidnapped their mascot, which happened to be a kangaroo named Moe. In retaliation, VMI sneaked onto the Blacksburg campus and kidnapped a freshman cadet named Sam and demanded an exchange. After giving it some thought, the VPI kidnappers decided they'd just keep Moe. It was only after much consternation from the administrators of both schools that the 'roo nappers gave in. When they did, VMI got the last laugh by binding Sam's legs and making him hop to freedom across the football field during the exchange. These days, of course, the perpetrators on both sides would have been kicked out of school and maybe even served jail time while people on social media wrung their hands and cried and said it was proof young people had gone terribly weird. Our sense of humor as a nation has surely changed, which I think is kind of sad. On the other hand, I don't hold much with kidnapping kangaroos or even freshmen.

Every Thanksgiving morning for many decades saw our Corps at the Blacksburg train station where we piled onto some old passenger cars pulled by a steam locomotive along a spur to Roanoke called the Huckleberry. It was called that, or so it was said, because the train went so slow along the seldom-used track that it was possible to get off and pick huckleberries along the way. In Roanoke, excited crowds gathered along the street as we poured off the train and formed up to march to the stadium. We were always led by our band with blasts of trumpets and rolling drums and our drum major excitedly thrusting the ceremonial baton skyward as if punching holes in the sky. We were quite the stirring sight.

The band that led us was over 120 strong and was called the Highty-Tighties. Like many stories about the Corps, the story on how our regimental band got its nickname had a couple of versions. The version the band liked was that once during a parade in Richmond, the drum major tossed up his baton, missed it when it came down, but caught it on the first bounce. Somebody, probably in a bowler hat with a beer bottle in his hand, shouted out "Hoity-Toity," meaning "show-off," and the name just naturally caught on.

The other story, the one that seems to me to be the most likely, was that during the raucous, roaring 1920s, the band members lived in a section of their barracks called Division E and gave itself the nickname by making up a cheer that went like this:

> *Highty Tighty, Christ Almighty*
> *Who the hell are we?*
> *Riff ram, goddamn, we're from Division E.*

Either way, the name stuck and the band was proud of it. They were an accomplished bunch and could really play stirring music that got the blood going. My unit, Squadron A, always followed the band, which was our alphabetical right. Crowds cheered us as we young, smartly dressed cadets marched past as if we were soldiers going off to war.

Once inside the stadium, we formed up by air force squadron and army company and made our traditional cheer:

Hokie, Hokie, Hokie High!
Tech, tech, VPI!
Sola Rex, Sola Rah,
Polytech, Virginia,
Ray Rah VPI,
Team, team, team!

Unhappily for those of you who don't care and happily for those of you who do, I will now sort of explain where the "Hokie" thing came from. In an 1896 contest for a new cheer, a student invented it but later, under pressure to explain, swore it didn't mean anything. However, if that was so, why did it stick? My hunch is "Hokie" had a hidden meaning, lost over time, that meant something to a bunch of Virginia farm boys with a tendency toward barnyard humor. In other words, it's probably dirty but nobody knows for sure. And there you have it.

After our cheer, we cadets climbed into our reserved seats to watch the VMI Keydets march in and go through the same process. The crowd never stopped cheering throughout. They were dressed in their finest, women in big hats and fur coats with corsages in school colors, men in suits, neckties, and fedoras. There was the smell of popcorn in the air. Alcohol was forbidden, but there were many flasks lifted from coat pockets and surreptitiously inclined to the lips. Boys, shouting in excitement, hawked programs. Flags fluttered in the autumnal breeze. There was a sense of joy and grandeur about the whole thing.

After both cadet corps got seated, ours a big rectangle of blue and gray, theirs a square of entirely gray, we began taking turns at chanting at each other. *"We're going home! We're going home!"* was one of our chants because we knew the gray-clad boys across from us had to go back to Lexington before being released while we were free the instant the game was over.

Their favorite chant coincided with the rolling out of their "Little John," a cannon—actually more like a small mortar—that they fired with a roar, sending a perfect smoke ring aloft to drift across the field. *"Where's your cannon? Where's your cannon?"* came the VMI chant. We had no reply and no matter how the football game came out, we knew they had the better of us and there was nothing we could do about it.

Or was there? Butch Harper was in my room that winter of 1963 to tell me we should build our own cannon and stop VMI's irritating chant forever.

"How do we get permission?" I asked.

"We don't," Butch replied, "because I already tried."

1963 was a year of change for Virginia Tech. Longtime president Walter Newman retired and a feisty new president named Dr. T. Marshall Hahn took over. Dr. Hahn was not a fan of the Corps—he saw it as an impediment to expand the student population. As if in confirmation that the Corps was in trouble, General Devine retired as our commandant. He was replaced by Brigadier General M. W. Schewe (pronounced "Shay-we").

Butch said he'd gone to see General Schewe about buying a cannon but the new commandant told him to forget it. There were no funds or purpose for it. When Butch asked for permission to see Dr. Hahn, the general replied he wouldn't stop him but he was wasting his time. That proved to be true since he never made it past T. Marshall Hahn's secretary, who said the new president was much too busy to see him that day or approx-imately forever.

"How much money would a cannon like Little John cost?" I wondered.

"It doesn't matter," Butch said. "We're not going to buy some popgun. We're going to build a real cannon."

"How are we going to do that?"

"Didn't you tell me you used to build rockets? Like that."

Like that, I reflected, was complicated. Building our rockets in Coalwood went through a lot of ups and downs and ins and outs over a three-year period. On the other hand, we'd built our rockets because we wanted to, not because anybody said we should or even that we could. We just did it. So maybe that was the way to build a cannon. Just do it.

My first decision was that our cannon should probably look historical like a Civil War cannon. In the college library, I learned that Civil War cannons were made out of brass, iron, or steel. Brass, I suspected, was the easiest to work with and would also look the best. I could just imagine it gleaming in the sun at Victory Stadium or on the Drillfield. When I told Butch my opinion, he agreed brass was just the thing. "We throw away scratched-up brass around here all the time," he said. "We'll just collect up what we need." Soon, he was going from unit to unit with a cloth sack in hand to beg for old brass.

My next step, although I had no idea how, was to design the barrel. When George Fox, another classmate in Squadron A, heard about it, he showed me a classified ad in the back of *Popular Mechanics* magazine. Its headline read:

PLANS FOR A REAL CIVIL WAR CANNON $1.50

Within an hour, I had a dollar bill borrowed from George and two quarters of my own in an envelope with a three-cent stamp on it and on its way. A couple of weeks later, I had in my hands the drawings of a real honest-to-gosh Civil War cannon but without any information at all on how to build it. But since I was, after all, in engineering school, I figured somebody on campus had to know how to build a cannon! The one place I was pretty sure didn't know how was the department I was in, the Aerospace Engineering Department. Reflecting on a class I'd taken in materials science in the Industrial Engineering Department, I recalled how much I'd felt at home. How to operate a lathe, a drill press, and a milling machine were skills I'd learned as a West Virginia rocket builder. The perfume of oil and hot metal was nostalgic. If there was anywhere that knew how to build a cannon, I suspected this was the place to go.

With my cannon plan rolled up in a cardboard tube, I startled Professor Herb Manning, the IE Department head, by arriving unannounced at his office. This simply was not done at a regimented place like VPI, but there I was. "Professor Manning, can you tell me how to build this cannon?" I asked and proceeded without invitation to unfurl the plan on his desk. It was a cheeky move that could have gone terribly wrong.

Frowning, Manning studied me over his half-glasses. "Why do you want to build a cannon, son?"

I gave him the story about the VMI chant and how frustrated it made us feel. Manning pondered that and then stood and leaned over for a look at the plan. "Where'd you get this?"

"*Popular Mechanics*, sir, the classified section."

Manning's frown went deeper. "It's actually a fairly accurate drawing, but it would be enormously expensive to produce."

"We're collecting brass from our spare belt buckles, buttons, and breastplates," I apprised.

He shook his head. "This drawing is for an iron cannon. Brass is a softer material, which means you'd have to modify the design. How do you plan on firing it?"

"I don't know," I confessed.

"I'm not surprised," Manning said. He sat down and looked thoughtful. "You know, I've always wanted to build a cannon. I'm kind of a Civil War buff."

"So you'll help us?"

He rolled up the plan and held out his hand for the cardboard tube to stuff it back inside. "Let me think on it."

"Yes, sir! Take all the time you need." I turned to leave.

"Mr. Hickam?"

"Yes, sir?"

"You ever barge uninvited into my office again, you'll be given a mop and a bucket and made to swab out this entire building. You understand?"

I grinned all the way back to our new barracks, Brodie Hall.

Come spring break, I hitchhiked to Coalwood to see my parents, Chipper the squirrel, our Siamese cats Tiki and Tech, and our little dog Poteet, still with us after so many years. Poteet had even been there the night in 1957 when the Big Creek Missile Agency launched its first rocket, which actually performed more like a bomb. As I like to tell it, it wasn't our rocket that streaked into the sky that night but my mom's rose garden fence.

We were at the kitchen table when I gave my news about the cannon. Five years before, I'd told my folks and my brother Jim

I was going to build a rocket and Mom's response was, "Well, don't blow yourself up." This time, her fork halfway between her plate and her mouth, her eyes widened and she said, with firm conviction, "You're going to blow yourself up!"

Mom cast a glance at Dad, who was pretending not to hear anything. She turned back to me. "You were supposed to be our backup boy in case we lost Jim for some reason. Instead, you've been nothing but trouble, always trying to kill yourself one way or the other."

Later that evening, when I was in the yard playing with Poteet, Dad ventured outside for a word. "What are you going to use to build your cannon?"

"Brass."

He frowned. "It would be better out of iron or steel."

"It's still going to be brass," I said. "We can get it for free because we're collecting it. Belt buckles, that kind of stuff."

Dad cocked his head in that way he did when he doubted something he'd just heard, which was, admittedly, pretty often around me. "How much does a belt buckle weigh?" he asked.

I allowed as how I didn't know, which didn't seem to surprise him. He said, "Quick calculation in my head for a full-sized cannon says you'll need at least three, maybe four hundred pounds. You got that many spare belt buckles around?"

Since I didn't like being made fun of, I made an excuse and stalked away. What, after all, did Dad know about cannons and brass or anything?

When I got back to Blacksburg, I checked in with Butch. Things were going slow on the brass collecting, he confessed. He shook a sack, which looked pretty light. My next stop was Professor Manning's office, where I contritely asked his secretary for an audience. To my surprise, I was sent immediately in.

Professor Manning looked up from his desk and then pointed to a table on which rested what appeared to be a cannon barrel. I couldn't believe it! But it turned out it wasn't a barrel at all.

"That's the form," he said. "A grad student and I turned it on a lathe over spring break. You can see it's in two halves. We'll use it in green sand to make the mold. What do you think?"

"Prodigious!" I exclaimed. "Thank you, sir!"

"We'll make the mold this week. Free of charge. I'll just chalk it up to lab work."

I had a sudden inspiration. "After you make the mold, can I borrow the form?"

"What for?"

"To show it to the other cadets. It'll help us collect more brass."

Manning gave my idea some thought before saying, "You are not to let anybody know the Industrial Engineering Department has anything whatsoever to do with this fool project. Understand?"

"I do, sir."

"Where did you get this form?"

"It was donated, sir."

"By whom?"

"By someone who wishes to be anonymous."

Manning smiled a rather grim smile. "All right, Mr. Hickam. I'll let you know when the mold is done. By the way, I have a question for you. When are you going to switch to IE?"

At his question, I realized it's what I'd wanted all along. "Is now OK?" I asked.

"It is," he said. "Another question. Which foundry is going to pour the cast?"

On that question I had no idea. When I reported in to Butch about the form, he was thrilled. When I asked about a foundry, he shrugged. "We'll figure that out," he said and waved me away.

A few days later Professor Manning sent word the form was ready for pickup, preferably at night. I recruited a rat and we went inside the IE Department after "Taps" and sneaked the form back to our barracks. Over the next week, Butch carried the form around to all the companies and squadrons to show them what our cannon would look like. Pretty soon, his sack of brass grew heavier. The addition of spent rifle shells from the ROTC firing range added to the amount. Once more, I reminded Butch we needed to find a foundry and figure out how to pay for the casting. Between us, we had about fifty dollars.

"We'll get to that," Butch said, "but first I've got to get myself promoted."

We were nearing the end of our junior year when announcements were made as to our ranks the senior year. As freshmen, we were all privates with no chance of promotion. As sophomores, private first class was as far as we could go. Corporal was the highest rank as a junior but for seniors, the stripes fell on us like spaghetti out of an overturned bowl. The most exalted positions were on the regimental staff, and that was why Butch presented himself at the new commandant's office.

General Schewe wasn't nearly as gruff as General Devine, but he still had stars on his epaulets and was quite prepared to take action against a cadet he didn't think lived up to the Corps code of behavior. To demonstrate this, he had recently drummed out a cadet in the middle of the night where the drummers lined up and thrummed a low moan while we all did an about-face as the poor boy was marched past us and was sent on his way. Actually, the boy was in my class. Actually, he was in our squadron. Actually, he was a good friend. But actually, I couldn't argue with the general's decision. Drunk and disorderly and showing one's buttocks in the infamous "moon" position before startled pink faces in the dining room of the women's dormitory of another college wasn't exactly to the highest standards of the Virginia Tech Corps of Cadets. Still, I missed him. He told the best jokes and always made me laugh.

"What do you want, Cadet Harper?" the general demanded in his gravelly voice after Butch walked up two paces from his desk and smartly saluted.

"Sir, I want to be the S-2 on the regimental staff next year. In fact, I insist on it."

"Insist?" His face coloring, the commandant leaned forward. "And how is it you insist on such a thing?"

"Because we need me to be there."

"Who's we?"

"Virginia Tech, sir."

"Is this about that damn cannon? The administration has not approved it."

"Nor have they disapproved it, sir."

"How far along are you?"

"Sir, I suspect that's something you're better off not knowing."

The general's eyes narrowed. "In my entire career," he growled with menace, "I have never had someone demand to be promoted. You're way out of line, Cadet Harper! You are hereby dismissed. Get out of my sight!"

Butch saluted and marched out of the commandant's office. When the announcements were made for our senior year, Alton B. "Butch" Harper was promoted to S-2 Intelligence and Public Information Officer on the regimental staff.

The Skipper, Part 2

When school let out in early June 1963, I went home to Coalwood. Mom was away at the house in Myrtle Beach, Dad was taking his meals at the company Club House, and I stayed at our house and looked after Poteet and the Siamese cats. Although I had summer school starting in mid-July, I asked Dad if I could work at the mine and the next thing I knew, I was a junior engineer for the Olga Coal Company. This meant a large portion of my time was spent at a drawing table, but I also went inside the mine to gather information for the mining engineers. While I was on my uncle Robert Lavender's section to measure drainage pipes that needed replacement, an unsupported coal rib collapsed on top of me. Fortunately, somebody noticed and Uncle Robert and his miners dug me out before I suffocated. A couple of weeks later, O'Dell Carroll, former Rocket Boy and now in the air force, showed up at the office where I was working on some blueprints. Without so much as a howdy-do, he walked up to me and said, "Damn it, Hickam! You coulda died! You got to stay out of that mine!"

The bright, shiny face I had known in high school had matured, but it was still O'Dell. "It's just summer work, O'Dell."

"It better be!"

Later that day, O'Dell and I drove down to old Cape Coalwood. We walked its length looking for artifacts of our rocket-building days. Locating the occasional twisted aluminum or steel shard, we were able to instantly identify the rocket and what had happened to it and how we'd fixed the problem that had caused it to blow up. "Good days," O'Dell said wistfully.

"The best," I answered.

"Did I hear you're writing a column in the VPI newspaper? You should write about what we did here at Cape Coalwood."

Since I was sure nobody in Blacksburg or anywhere else would care two cents about that, I changed the subject. "How's the air force?"

He provided a glum shrug. "Got orders to Germany."

"Don't let the Russians get you." When he didn't reply, I clapped him on the shoulder. "You'll make it to college, O'Dell."

My prediction was correct, but that was to be a few years later. I had supper with the Carrolls that eve and the next day, O'Dell went back to the air force. In mid-July, I arrived back on campus at Virginia Tech for summer school and then stayed on to train the entering freshmen. In his new regimental staff quarters, Butch called me in to talk about the cannon. He had a confession to make. "All I've got is about fifty pounds of brass," he said. "And no foundry and no carriage."

I added to his list of problems, "Even if it gets built, we have no idea how to fire it."

"You take that one," Butch said, "and I'll figure out the rest. We also need to come up with a name, something catchy."

The last thing I was worried about was a name for a cannon that didn't exist and, seeing how far behind we were, had a very good chance of never being made. Putting aside the naming and the foundry and the carriage, I put on my thinking cap on how to fire the blame thing. Recalling the movies that showed old-fashioned cannon crews, I knew a little about what they had to do. From a barrel of black powder, a portion was measured and then rammed down the barrel, followed by cloth wadding and then, if it was to be lethal, a cannonball. A fuse from a touchhole on the back section detonated the powder. After that, the barrel was swabbed out with a kind of wet mop and the loading commenced again. It was a complicated process that I was certain we could not do. This was for a couple of reasons, one being none of us were trained to do it and the other was I doubted we'd ever be allowed to show up at a football game or anywhere else with barrels of black powder. Firing our cannon had to be somehow simplified.

My pondering took me back to that time in the yard when we boys had reduced my mom's rose garden fence to splinters. How had we done it? I recalled we'd first emptied the powder out of cherry bombs left over from the Fourth of July and then we'd packed it inside an old flashlight, punctured the bottom of the flashlight with a nail, inserted one of the cherry bomb fuses, and glued it inside a de-winged model airplane. It might have looked like a rocket but it was decidedly a bomb.

As it turned out, my location for recollecting the rose garden detonation was at a hamburger joint in Blacksburg and, for some reason, my eyes strayed to the plastic squeeze bottles on the table that held ketchup and mustard. I picked one of them up. The walls were thin, the plastic soft, the tip a perfect receptacle for a fuse. Instantly, I knew I could make it into a bomb! But what explosive to use? Cherry bombs were expensive, and making black powder was a tedious exercise requiring potassium nitrate (also known as saltpeter), sulfur, and charcoal ground to a fine powder. But then I remembered George Fox owned an old musket. He'd know how to get black powder!

It turned out George had several cans of DuPont gunpowder, which was, he said, better than black powder. The cans were in his closet in Roanoke, so that weekend he hitched a ride home to get them. My job was to procure some mustard or ketchup bottles of the appropriate design. Since they were also used in the cadet cafeteria, I went inside and boldly walked into the kitchen. Nobody was there, but I poked around and, before long, found a box of empty red ketchup squeeze bottles. Honor code being what it was, I couldn't just take them so when a cook walked in, I told him what I needed and why. He shrugged. "Take them. I don't care."

He didn't need to tell me twice. When George showed up Sunday evening, he not only had the gunpowder but also some fuses he plucked out of leftover fireworks. Right there in my room, we began assembling our first cannon bomblet. "Where do you think we should test it?" I wondered.

It was past midnight. George suggested we test it on the Drillfield, but it occurred to me that maybe there might be a grad student crossing it from the labs whom we might not see, so I proposed instead the unlit hill that sloped down from Brodie Hall to the road at the mall. George agreed and we slipped outside into the cold, clear night. There were only a few windows in Brodie that were aglow with lights—probably chemical engineering students still studying. After choosing a spot in the darkness, we placed the gunpowder-filled squeeze bottle on the grass, put a lighter to the fuse, and took off. A few seconds later, there was a big, bright, and loud explosion with echoes that rolled back and forth amongst the buildings of the quadrangle along with a great spout of smoke. Within moments, nearly all the windows of the upper quadrangle lit up, and George and I realized we had not planned our escape. Without consultation, we darted behind the bushes beside the entrance steps to Brodie Hall. Before long, cadets came pouring outside to see what was to be seen, and George and I surreptitiously slipped in amongst them. When nothing else happened and the smoke drifted away, most of the cadets decided it was just a big firecracker set off by a prankster and went back to their rooms. We guilty bomb builders mixed in with them.

The next morning, the Corps was assembled for breakfast and held at attention while Cadet Colonel Bob Russell, our commander, read a demand from General Schewe that whoever had blown up the big firecracker outside Brodie Hall was to let himself immediately be known. George didn't move and neither did I. Before long, somebody started to snicker and then laughter rippled through the Corps. Bob gave it up and sent us marching off to breakfast, where George and I chose a table by ourselves. Before long, Butch came over and sat down. He looked at me and then at George. "Well done," he said. "Well done."

"How much brass have you collected?" I asked.

"Not enough, but I'm working on it."

"A foundry? A carriage?"

Butch just shook his head.

The next night, a rare event occurred. The phone rat called down the hall, "Phone for Hickam, sir! Phone for Hickam, sir!"

Mystified on who might be calling me, I left my desk and its stack of homework and made my way along the hall to the phone booth. The telephone rat stood at a brace, but I told him to stand at ease and sat down and took up the dangling receiver. When I answered, I heard my mom. "Hello, Sonny Boy," she said and immediately got down to cases. "What's wrong with you?"

There were so many things wrong with me I couldn't think of any one of them in particular so I blurted out, "We're short of brass!" and then explained in probably too much detail our unhappy cannon situation.

Mom had no solution except to say, "I knew there was something." She followed by giving me a litany of her most recent events, including how things were in Coalwood. "It gets worse every day," she said in a voice quiet enough that I knew Dad was probably within earshot. "There's wildcat strikes nearly every week about this or that. Your dad can't run any good coal."

"How is he?" I asked.

"I just told you he can't run any good coal."

"I mean...*how is he*?"

I could feel her shrug. "He's fine," she said, and I knew he really wasn't. The sure implication was that Dad's black spot on his lungs was not getting any smaller and his beloved mine was failing.

Mom told me that Tiki and Tech were being good cats and Poteet was about the same and then said she had some TV program she wanted to watch and hung up. I held the receiver in my hand for a long time. The phone rat finally got up enough courage to peek inside. "Sir, are you done?"

"Sorry," I said and hung up the receiver and went back to my room and gave Mom's call a little thought. She'd maybe called me three times since I'd started college. What had precipitated this call?

A couple of days later, I was standing in dinner formation when a guard rat sought me out. "Hickam sir, there's a man who wants to see you. He said he'd be in his car down on the mall."

I asked permission from Captain Bill May to leave the formation, got it, and walked down to the street in front of Brodie Hall. Astonished, I saw Dad's big blue Buick Electra with its swept-back tail fins and beside it my father in his work clothes. Fearful that maybe something awful must have happened to bring him all the way to Blacksburg straight from the mine, I hurried down the steps. After spotting me, he walked behind the Buick, unlocked the trunk, and lifted open the big hatch. Inside, I saw the gleam of brass. It took me a moment to realize it was filled to the brim with brass scrap. He opened the back door and I saw more brass on the floor. "Will this help?" he asked. "I figure there's about two hundred and fifty pounds there. Gears, bar stock, what have you. The Buick was a little tail heavy." When I just looked dumfounded, he said, "I told you we had scrap brass at the mine. Why didn't you ask me for it?" When I just stood there in shock, he shook his head. "You want to help me unload it?"

Together, we lifted the scrap out of the Buick and piled it all up on the grass between the road and the sidewalk. "Dad, do you want to eat at the mess hall?" I asked. "Or maybe see my room?" Dad had never expressed any interest in seeing how I lived as a cadet, so I was hopeful.

"Got to get back," he said.

"To run your coal," I said with an edge of bitterness I couldn't quite conceal.

If he noticed my unhappiness, he made no sign of it. "See you, Sonny Boy," he said and drove away. I watched the Buick's taillights until they disappeared and then walked to the mess hall, where I interrupted some A Squadron rats and told them what I wanted them to do. Butch Harper returned to his room after supper. In front of his door was a gift from Coalwood, West Virginia. It was, he would later say, the most beautiful pile of scrap he'd ever seen.

The Skipper, Part 3

Now that we had enough brass, things started happening. Butch went to the yellow pages, spotted an ad for a foundry in Roanoke, called it, and got on the line with a fellow named Paul Huffman who, as it turned out, was a Virginia Tech graduate. When he heard what Butch had in mind, Mr. Huffman told him he'd do the casting for free. Then Butch heard that the Lorton Reformatory had a workshop where prisoners built Civil War cannon carriages for state and national parks and that, yes, indeed, they had an extra one he could buy. With the money saved by the free casting, Butch had just enough. "This is meant to be," he told me, and I was starting to believe he was right.

By then, it was October and time was very tight for us to pull everything together by Thanksgiving. The barrel needed to be cast and the carriage picked up. Since the two had been designed and built completely separately, there was no guarantee they would fit together, so we needed at least a little time for modifications. And we still had to make sure the cannon bomblets worked when tossed down the barrel, and there was also the question of a name for the cannon, one that Butch insisted we just had to have.

"Can't we just call it the Virginia Tech Corps of Cadets cannon?" I asked.

Butch rolled his eyes. "Sonny, you don't know a thing about public relations." This advisory was so true, I had no answer except to allow he was correct.

We delivered the mold and the collected brass to Mr. Huffman, who got right to the casting. He even paid his employees overtime to work through the night and into the next day to get the job done. Later, we would discover that when the brass shells from the firing range were poured into the molten vat, some of them were still live and his men had to dive for cover as they ricocheted around his shop. We were forgiven even that.

After inspecting the melt, Mr. Huffman was uncertain as to its quality and, without asking us, substituted a portion of it with his own stock of gunmetal-quality brass. The resulting mix was a strikingly beautiful barrel. We brought it back and hid it beneath a canvas tarp in the dayroom of Brodie Hall with a note stating that anyone touching it would be in violation of a number of cadet regulations, all of which we made up. One of them I recall was "Complete and Utter Contempt for Corps Property."

The next thing that happened was Butch rented a van and took off for the reformatory. With so much time spent on the cannon, I didn't want to cut any more classes so I stayed behind. At Lorton, the prisoners loaded aboard the carriage, which was absolutely beautiful. Triumphant, Butch turned the van for home with a car of cadets following as protection in case VMI had sniffed the project out and might try something. Before long, hearing the horn of the car behind, Butch pulled over. One of the cadets got out and told him some terrible news.

Back at the barracks after returning from classes, I was talking to George Fox in the hall when a freshman cadet, looking ashen-faced, dragged up to us and gave us the same news Butch had just received. "Sirs," he said, "President Kennedy has been shot."

The national nightmare caused by the assassination of John F. Kennedy began. My recollection is of morose cadets in our dayroom glued to the same small black-and-white television we'd watched during the Cuban Missile Crisis. It was all ghastly as we saw the reporters interviewing Kennedy family members and other politicians and officials about the awful event in Dallas. Two days after the assassination, we saw Lee Harvey Oswald being shot by Jack Ruby. And then we saw the funeral procession and Jackie looking so miserable and little John-John saluting and Caroline so sad and the prancing horse with the boots backward in its stirrups. We saw French president Charles de Gaulle and the leaders of the world as they followed on foot our president's casket being drawn by a team of horses. We saw the quickly assembled eternal flame on the grave. We saw our new president, one Lyndon Baines Johnson, who most of us knew very little about except he was from Texas. We saw it all, and it was all stupefyingly simply awful.

The only distraction I had was Butch coming to get the box of bomblets to test the cannon. The cannon was the last thing I had on my mind, so I gave them to him and went back to the television. That night, he and some other cadets placed the barrel on the carriage and it fit perfectly. Afterward, they put the full assembly in the van and drove it to the college golf course, waited until it was dark, and then Butch lit one of the bomblets and tossed it down the barrel. The report he gave back to me was it wasn't loud enough. When he came into my room, he looked kind of odd and I noticed his head was shaved on one side. "What happened?" I asked.

"The first time I tested one of your bombs," he said with a shrug, "it went off. Set my hair on fire."

His report sent me off to ponder the two problems he'd raised: the fuses weren't long enough and the cannon wasn't loud enough. I'd already ordered some long coils of green fireworks fuses from an Edmund Scientific catalog that was expected to arrive any day, so that part was solved. As for making it louder, I decided to double up on the powder, which I figured ought to do it. All that was left on our long list was to figure out a name. The next night, I went over to Butch's room for that purpose.

"How about the Major Williams cannon?" he proposed.

Major Williams was an alumnus who was a World War I hero. "No," I said. "We already have a barracks named after him."

"Big John?"

"That's like naming it after the VMI cannon. No."

"The Hokie?"

"Don't think so."

"The Gobbler?"

I sighed. "Uh-uh."

"Maybe we should name it after President Kennedy."

An idea suddenly flew into my head. "How about Skipper? Kennedy was the skipper of a PT boat. And it's a name we already use in the Corps."

It was true. Skipper was what we called a senior cadet who had no stripes. Such a fellow, usually a rebel against authority, was almost always interesting and colorful just like we wanted our cannon to be.

Butch's face lit up. "Sonny, that's perfect!"

I shut up. Sometimes, when lightning strikes, you just enjoy the ozone in the air. To this day, I don't know how that name popped into my head.

But it was perfect and Butch, who knew something about public relations, was smart enough to know it.

And now we knew what our cannon was going to be called.

But would there be a game where we could show it off?

The Skipper, Part 4

Whether the Thanksgiving game would be played was in doubt until after the president's funeral. I thought it unlikely, but in the end it was decided to go ahead and have it, probably because there was too much already planned and Roanoke would lose a lot of money without the game. There was also a sense that after days of grieving, something normal was needed. Whatever the reason, we were told to prepare to go to Roanoke on Thanksgiving.

I took the assignment as the Skipper's first "commander," which meant I was in charge of all the loading and firing on game day. George was dispatched home to gather up more gunpowder and build us some more bomblets. To smuggle them into the stadium, he asked his father, a medical doctor, to put them in a doctor's black bag and walk in with it. Dr. Fox, also a Tech grad and up for a good prank, was happy to do it.

Once everyone was seated in the stadium, an announcement over the loudspeakers asked for a minute of silence in honor of our dead young president. A hush fell over the thousands of people in the stands. It was so quiet I could hear the clanking of the chains on the flagpole at the far end of the stadium. Afterward, the national anthem was played and people rose and sang their hearts out. The teams ran onto the field to warm up and then, as if God had declared it time to stop mourning and get on with life, the Military Classic of the South roared back to life. The women in their furs and corsages smiled, the men in their fedoras raised their flasks to their lips, and the chants between the two corps began.

We went through the usual litany and waited until, sure enough, Little John was brought out by the VMI cheerleaders and a charge prepared. After it went off with a bang and its usual perfect smoke ring was sent aloft, we heard the dreaded chant come across the field. *"Where's your cannon? Where's your cannon?"*

I had two helpers for the Skipper, and we waited on the sidelines. Beside me was the black bag with its bomblets. Butch, ever the showman, organized what happened next. At his signal, the Highty-Tighties struck up a rendition of "The Parade of the Charioteers" from the movie *Ben-Hur*. As the triumphal music played, a team of freshmen, using thick ropes, came pulling our cannon down the track and up next to me and my team. Fans on our side of the stadium burst into cheers and applause. As the march wound down, I directed the freshmen to turn the barrel to face the VMI stands, but then Little John roared forth again and the subsequent chant revealed Butch's theatrical entrance had gone largely unnoticed on the other side of the field. *"Where's your cannon? Where's your cannon?"*

Butch came running up to me. "Fire it now!" he cried. "Now, Sonny! And make it really loud!"

Although I had doubled the amount of powder in the standard bomblets, I also had one that was even more powerful. At a Blacksburg hardware store, I'd found plastic tubes that held screws and bolts and bought a dozen of them, emptied them of their hardware, and packed them full of powder from cherry bombs and torpedoes I'd bought from a fireworks stand just outside of town. Along with a standard bomblet, I wrapped this conglomeration up in duct tape and stuck a fuse in one of the tubes. When Butch kept insisting that I hurry up and respond to that awful chant, I lit my monster and tossed it down the barrel. That was when I saw, to my horror, some VMI football players run over to get a closer look at us.

"Where's your cannon? Where's your cannon?"

The Skipper erupted with a huge high-pitched bark like the maddest junkyard dog in the universe and reared back, its wheels coming completely off the ground. A huge spout of smoke erupted across the field like a gray-black fist. A shock wave rippled through the VMI Corps and continued on to the press box, where it cracked the glass in front of startled announcers and reporters. As the huge cloud of smoke rose from that powerful charge, I saw with vast relief no bodies lying on the field. Later I would learn as soon as they saw me throw my hideous spewing monstrosity down the barrel, the Keydet players had very intelligently run like rabbits.

Butch came racing up and said something, but I couldn't hear him because my ears were ringing. Gleeful tears were streaming down his cheeks as he pointed toward our Corps. Gradually, I began to discern their chant.

"Here's our cannon! Here's our cannon!"

It wasn't long before policemen arrived. "Point that thing toward the end zone," one of them said, and we did before they stalked off.

It was a very high-scoring game, Virginia Tech winning easily, and I used up all the remaining bomblets but only after I'd emptied each of them of half their powder. I deduced Butch's test on the open golf course did not take into account that an enclosed stadium would concentrate the sound. That combined with my contraption had caused Skipper's official introduction to the world to be an ear-shattering success, although I will confess I felt no triumph. I was too busy tossing up my thanks to the good Lord for saving me from blowing up myself and everybody around me.

After the game, Dad came down from the stands. I knew he and Mom were attending, mainly because Jim was playing in the game. Dad looked so proud, an expression I knew was not for what I had accomplished ever in the entire history of my life but for my brother's prowess on the football field.

Dad looked the Skipper over. "Some of my coal mine is in it," he said to the other cadets while looking inordinately pleased.

What I said back to him came from a place inside me I had no idea was there and I regret to this day. "There's nothing from your mine in it," I snapped. "Your brass was too cheap. They put in their own brass at the foundry." That was not true but there it was. Said and done.

Dad took off his fedora, squinted up at the sky, and took his time to look around the stadium and the scoreboard and the people moving toward the exits. I felt paralyzed, as if I couldn't breathe. Everything just seemed to disappear until it was just me and my father. He put his hat back on and then put his hand on the Skipper's barrel and the world coalesced around us. He looked at me and said, "Maybe there isn't any Coalwood brass in this cannon, Sonny, but I guess there's still some Coalwood in it because, whether you like it or not, there's always going to be some Coalwood in you."

And with that, Dad walked away. I thought about calling out to him to tell him what I'd said wasn't so, but the words stuck in my throat. When he joined Mom on the sidelines, he said something to her and she turned and raised her hand to me in greeting and in goodbye. She looked like she was about to cry. Dad took her arm and led her away while I turned to the suddenly dreary task of carrying Skipper home.

Note: Although Butch, George, and I had our minds primarily on one-upping the VMI Keydets for at least one annual Thanksgiving Day football game, the result was something we did not expect, and that was our cannon was embraced by subsequent decades of students and administrations. The Skipper is now considered an icon of Virginia Tech and an important part of the school's heritage. Although sometimes we of that class who built the cannon like to brag about what we did as if we were something special, the truth is it was the students and faculty who followed us that made the Skipper into the marvelous symbol of determination and explosive spirit it is today.

PART

2

American Soldier

Fort Lost in the Woods

After Virginia Tech, I was pretty much handed a lemon but I didn't make lemonade out of it. Instead, I just bit into it and swallowed the whole thing. That's why when I was in Officer Candidate School (OCS) and an upperclassman was beating me with a mop handle and others were lining up to batter me as close to senseless as they could without—and I know how crazy this sounds—bruising my face, it occurred to me that maybe, just maybe, it was conceivably possible that it was my fault I was in that situation. After all, I had been given every opportunity to be hanging out at the Officer's Club with a gin and tonic in my hand rather than getting whacked on by future officers and gentlemen of our armed forces.

Here's what happened and, yes, it was all my fault. The first two years in the Virginia Tech Corps of Cadets, I took Air Force Reserve officer training with the expectation I'd end up in that service as an officer, but as I closed out my sophomore year, one of the uniformed professors of the United States Air Force

Reserve Officer Training Corps (ROTC) called me to his office and told me I was being cut from the program. He went straight to the heart of it. "Your grades put you in the lower half of your class and your eyesight means you can't be a pilot. We already have a surplus of non-pilot officers so something has to give. You are part of what's giving. Why don't you talk to the army?" He pointed. "Next building." And that was that.

Since I knew it was pointless to argue, I didn't. As for walking next door to talk to the US Army ROTC, I should have done it but I didn't. Whether they would have offered me a slot, I will never know. I just walked by their headquarters and went back to Brodie Hall because I didn't want to transfer out of my beloved A Squadron to one of the army companies. Since there were other ways to get a commission, I figured I'd manage it after graduation one way or the other.

And so it was that after I graduated, I immediately sent off applications for a commission to the air force, the navy, and the army. While waiting for an answer, I took a temporary job as an engineer with a small coal mine in Logan, West Virginia, where I was supposed to study one of their crews and see if I could come up with a way to reduce its size or maybe even get rid of it. Although the miners on the crew knew exactly what I was up to, they were still friendly and, after a couple of weeks, simply adopted me as an extra man. Under their tutelage, I put up roof bolts, shoveled gob, drove the shuttle cars, and filled in anywhere I could. They even taught me how to pack in powder, place the blasting cap, yell "Fire in the hole!" and twist the firing handle to blast across the coal face.

One day, I got two envelopes in the mail. One was my draft notice, the other a contract from the United States Army for something called the College Option Program to earn an officer's commission. All I had to do was complete eight weeks of basic training followed by eight weeks of advanced training and then twenty-three weeks in Officer Candidate School, a total of nearly ten months. With little choice, I signed the army contract, notified the draft board, and set forth into the unknown of the federal military training system.

My orders came for basic training at Fort Leonard Wood, Missouri. I said goodbye to my Logan crew, packed a few things in a small VPI duffel bag, and asked Dad to come pick me up in the Buick and take me to Bluefield to catch a plane. Along the way, we talked about this and that. He liked all the things I'd learned in the Logan mine. "There's still a lot of coal in West Virginia," he said. "You already know a lot about mining. You can make a good living here."

"Let me get the army out of the way first," I told him.

"Try not to get yourself killed," he said. "Your mother would be upset."

"I'll do my best," I promised.

Dad leaned over the steering wheel and craned his head to look up into the surrounding mountains and trees. "There's no country like this anywhere, Sonny."

"I know that, Dad," I said.

"You're not coming back, are you?"

"Probably not, sir."

When we reached the airport, Dad, his expression a neutral mask, didn't get out of the car. "Tell Mom I'll write," I said as I retrieved my duffel and then watched as he drove away. It was only then that I realized I had yet again lost an opportunity to ask him how he was and tell him his brass was in the Skipper cannon.

The first plane took me to St. Louis, where I reported to the army liaison office in the airport. The sergeant at the counter directed me, along with some much younger recruits, to an old DC-3 owned by an airline I'd never heard of. It might have been End of the Line Airlines, I shouldn't wonder. Within minutes of us taking off, one of the ancient plane's two engines caught on fire. It wasn't a little fire, it was a big one, and pretty soon we were streaming along like a fiery meteor. Some of the boys started to cry, but I just stared out of the little window and reflected that nothing I could do was going to help. Anyway, being on an airplane that was on fire seemed to be just about what I should have expected at that juncture in my life.

We circled for a while, flames spurting and smoke billowing and the engine coughing, until we suddenly made a dive that was breathtakingly steep. At the bottom of it, the plane suddenly leveled out and then plunked down on a small dirt runway. The engine was still smoking as we taxied along until a fellow ran out with a handheld fire extinguisher and put out the blaze. Some of the recruits got out of their seats but the steward, an old fellow who was wearing a pair of work coveralls, told them to sit back down. "I'm going to talk to the pilot," he said and disappeared into the cockpit.

After some tinkering by the same fellow who'd put out the blaze, the engine somehow miraculously restarted and, without a word from the pilot or the attendant who were still inside the cockpit with the door closed, we rolled up on the dirt runway and took off again. Flying very low all the way, so low I could see people below gaping up at us and not a few of them ducking, we finally put down at the airport in Waynesville, Missouri. It was a hard landing, and I wouldn't have been the least bit surprised if the landing gear collapsed, but we trundled along until, suddenly, the defective engine made a big poofing sound and caught on fire again, the wind pushing the smoke toward the fuselage. Within seconds, the interior filled up with acrid smoke. The cockpit door was flung open and the steward, his expression one of only mildly suppressed panic, clawed at the main hatch. That was when one of the recruits ran down the aisle, pushed the steward aside, somehow got the door open, and jumped out. The steward yelled for the rest of us to stay put. The pilot, his face ashen and his cap askew, suddenly emerged from the cockpit, brushed past the steward, and also jumped out. There was, I noted, no copilot.

Fortunately, before anybody else could join this impromptu jump school, steps were rolled up and we all ran down them and sprinted away from the plane while men with fire extinguishers ran past us to spray the engine until it finally calmed down. When I looked around, I saw the boy who'd jumped was being tended to by the pilot. "Broke a leg," I heard the steward say just as a bus painted olive drab rumbled up and a soldier in fatigues and a ball cap got off, took one look at the general chaos, and yelled, "Anybody who's for Fort Wood, get aboard!" We couldn't get on fast enough.

An hour or so later, we shaken survivors of what was essentially a plane crash passed through the gate of a military post that was dressed in a winter-drab coat of ice, snow, and mud. Fort Leonard Wood, forty-thousand-plus acres of woodland sprawling across the Ozark Mountains of Missouri, was called "Little Korea" because its stark training ranges and mud-soaked hills and vast piney forests resembled that of the small peninsular country that was the site of the nasty war fought from 1950 to 1953. Its other nickname was "Fort Lost in the Woods" and suited it well.

We pulled up to a brick barracks building amid blowing sleet and a howling wind. A drill sergeant in a Smokey the Bear hat climbed aboard. "All right, ladies," he said, "get off the bus. It's going to be a busy day."

We piled off the bus into the bitter cold while more drill sergeants appeared and, without yelling, pulled and pushed us into some semblance of formation. To my surprise, we were treated with patience and even something akin to care and concern. While we shivered, few of us dressed for the cold, we were told that we were going to get our haircuts and then our vaccinations. On the bus to the barbershop, I listened to the others talking among themselves and learned we were a mix of reservists, regular army, and a sprinkling of college grads who, like me, were in the "College Op" program.

With the vocal encouragement of the DIs, we lined up for our haircuts. Mine didn't need much since I still had my VPI crew cut, but other boys suffered as their long locks dropped to the barbershop floor. It was all quick and impersonal, the barbers having little to say. As soon as the shaving was done, we were sent back to the overly warm bus, which put most of us to sleep, and I woke to a bunch of bobbing bare heads as we trundled past gray piles of snow. With more quiet direction, the DIs herded us out of the warm bus through the frigid air into an overheated medical facility. The smell of Clorox and alcohol was nearly overwhelming. While waiting to get our shots from a high-pressure device, several boys passed out in the line, one of them in front of me who I caught in my arms. A DI came over and helped me drag the shaken boy to a chair. "Son," the DI said to the fainter, "take a breath. This ain't gonna kill you."

The boy sobbed. "I want to go home."

"So do I," the DI said, "but I can't until you get your damn shots." He leveled me with a stare. "Take care of him," he said.

"Yes, sir," I answered.

"Yes, Sergeant," he corrected. "You one of those College Op types?"

"Yes, Sergeant."

He studied me. "I'll salute you when you make it, but right now, I'd appreciate it if you'll help this boy get his shots."

When the medics pointed at us to come on up, I helped the boy stand and took him by his elbow. "This is not going to hurt," I told him. "Watch me get mine. There's nothing to it."

The pressure guns were on both sides of the line. The medics holding them probably heard my bravado and, maybe for fun, jabbed me on both shoulders at the same time, which made me jump from the shock of the twin assault. I might have even yelled "Ouch!" Behind me, I heard a soft thump as the boy passed out again. The medics ordered me to move on. To this day, I'm not sure what happened to that poor lad but, wherever he is, I regret I didn't set a good example. But those damn shots hurt!

My best move in Basic, I figured, was to keep my head down and just be another trainee. The first few days were a blur, but I recall we hustled all over the post to pick up uniforms and field gear and take written tests. The week that followed was essentially drill and marching stuff, which I knew cold from VPI. Still, I didn't do any kind of smart moves but only exactly what I was told. Perhaps it was that instant compliance that tipped the DIs off that they had something of a ringer in their midst. Every so often, I noticed Sergeant Lepard, the senior DI, watching me. He had three platoon sergeants named Kitchens, Brockman, and Morales. Kitchens was a black noncommissioned officer with a head-up posture, smart uniform, and confident air. Brockman was a young NCO who always spoke softly. Sergeant Morales always looked like he was worried. Considering the raw youths he and the other sergeants had to turn into soldiers, I thought he had just cause. Even as I watched them, the DIs watched all of us, probably trying to figure out who we were and how they could keep us motivated. The four sergeants kept looking over in my direction, but I did my best to avoid eye contact. I wanted no trouble.

Since it was so cold outside, we wore our field jackets and the funny-looking caps called pile caps with the front brim turned up and side flaps tied on top. We looked like the photographs I'd seen of soldiers in the Korean War, which was, after all, appropriate for our "Little Korea" training post. We were issued M14 rifles that weighed and handled about the same as the M1s we had at VPI, so I had no problem with them during drill.

One evening, after we'd returned from the mess hall, Sergeant Lepard gave us the order to fall out and go inside, but Sergeant Brockman told me to wait. It was freezing cold and our breaths were spouts of smoke as he took me aside. He hemmed and hawed a bit before asking, "Look, son, where'd you go to college?"

When I told him, he broke out a pack of cigarettes and offered me one but since I'd never smoked and saw no reason to start, I turned him down. He lit up and eyed me. "You seen some of the other boys," he said. "They ain't gonna make it lest they get some help. Me and the other DIs ain't here at night. Just wondering if you'd take 'em under your wing. Talk to 'em, you know? You willing to do that?"

Without waiting for me to agree, Sergeant Brockman named the four recruits he wanted me to mentor. One of them, an overweight hulk, was in my bunkroom. His name was Iggy, and he had the letters "BORN TO" tattooed on the back of one hand and "LOSE" on the other. A judge back home, I'd heard Iggy say, had ordered him to enlist or go to prison. The other three boys Brockman named were also there compliments of the penal system.

"I'll do what I can," I said while wondering privately if there was really anything to be done. Iggy had a huge chip on his shoulder. How was I supposed to get through to him when for eighteen years, no one else had?

The opportunity came one night when Iggy got into a fight. It was actually more of a shoving match and his opponent was only about half his size and it looked like the battle wouldn't last long, but since I had been appointed their squad leader, I told them both to knock it off, which brought Iggy into my face. He raised his fists, boxer-style. "We goin' around," he threatened.

"Didn't that hurt?" I asked.

He lowered his fists. "Huh?"

"The tattoos. *Born to lose*. Didn't that hurt?"

He took on a smug expression. "Yeah. I got it done in jail."

If he expected me to be impressed, I disappointed him by simply asking, "Why?"

Iggy's expression was one of puzzlement. "'Cause I wanted to."

"No, I mean why would you want to tell the world you were born to lose? That's the last thing in the world I'd want to let on even if it was true."

"You're College Op, ain't cha? Always had it easy."

Around us was a cold cinderblock room painted a puke-green color with olive drab cots and footlockers laid out end to end and the other boys cleaning their gear. Looking around, I pointed out the obvious. "We're all in the same boat."

"No, we're not. You and me, we're nothing the same."

"I grew up in a coal camp, Iggy. My people were all coal miners. I think we might have more in common than you think."

He waved me off. "College boy!"

Despite an unpromising first encounter, I'd made an opening, one that, to my surprise, Iggy decided to enter. Over the next few days, while we were cleaning our gear, he began to tell me something about himself. He had no father that he knew, his mother was a drunk, and he hated school and his teachers. He also saw himself as stupid. My approach was to praise Iggy when he did anything right. When I made a point of doing the same with the other three, they began to ask me questions about how to do things better. I explained the need for dry, clean socks, which led to talking about general hygiene, which was, at first, simply why it was good not to stink. A shower should be taken every day. Teeth needed to be brushed. I was astonished they didn't know these things. I didn't try to force anything on them, but before long I realized I'd become sort of an older brother to the four boys who were not quite men. They soaked up my attention.

One of the standouts in my recollection of Basic was the meticulous instruction we received on the M14 rifle. The firing ranges were sophisticated and included automated targets that fell when hit and rang up a score. Our instructors were excellent and patient, but Iggy, no matter how much they tried to show him what to do, couldn't hit the broad side of a barn. "Help him out, Hickam," Sergeant Lepard told me.

Between his time on the firing line, I went over the instructions with Iggy how to correctly hold the rifle, how to aim with one eye lining up the sights, and how not to jerk the trigger but to squeeze it while momentarily holding his breath. Then something occurred to me.

Standing in front of him, I said, "Close your left eye."

"Why?"

"Just do it."

Rather than close his left eye, Iggy instead closed both eyes. I told him to close his right eye and the same thing happened. "I can't," he said. "They don't work one at a time."

This was a revelation. Iggy had never mastered his own body. This explained why so many times in formation, he stepped off on the incorrect foot. It wasn't that he was stupid and didn't know his left from his right. It was just that he never had to think about it before. There was a disconnect between his conscious brain and his body. I took a few minutes to work with Iggy until he was able to close one eye at a time. After that, with the ability to line up the sights of his rifle, he started to at least occasionally hit the target.

For my own part, I surprised myself at being a good shot. For a West Virginia boy, I'd never been interested in hunting or guns. Brother Jim owned a .22 rifle and let me shoot at tin cans from time to time, but that was about it. Now, in the frozen wilderness of Missouri, I pleased myself by earning an Expert Badge in rifle qualification. Maybe it was genetic. A West Virginia thing! But I still didn't care anything about shooting a deer.

Training eventually had us get our hands on real live hand grenades. These were the M26 variation, and they were nasty little things with a serrated coil under tension inside that, once exploded, sent out tiny steel shards that were nearly impossible for a surgeon to remove. Our training cadre, I was fairly certain, was nervous about their bunch of nincompoops tossing them.

We were bused to a distant range where a number of positions were set up with barriers that were designed to limit the number of casualties should our grenades go awry. A sergeant came forth and harangued us for a minute or two on how dangerous the M26 was and how it was absolutely necessary we did exactly what we were told when we were told to do it. After that, we were sent by squads to the instructors, who started us out with unarmed practice grenades. After working in the coal mines, my arm was strong and I had no trouble arcing the inert "lemons," as the M26s were called, over the barrier. Iggy, however, bounced his back off the barrier. Sergeant Brockman sought me out and told me to help Iggy before he "kills every goddamn one of us!"

Taking a thoroughly shaken Iggy aside, I walked him back to the road and we talked it over. "I can't do it," Iggy said as we heard the first of the live grenades go off.

"They're not going to let you graduate if you don't."

"Then I quit." There were loud booms as more grenades went off, followed by cheers.

"They're not going to let you quit. They'll just make you start over. You know that."

It was true. The news from Vietnam wasn't good, and the Russians were forever rattling their sabers. The army needed soldiers. Once in, getting out usually wasn't an option. Iggy's lips quivered. The shock wave of more detonations hit us. "I'm going to die!" he cried.

I picked up a small rock. "Look, Iggy, let's practice with this. I'll watch."

Iggy tried and the first thing I noticed was he was throwing sidearm rather than overhand. I demonstrated proper form and kept finding rocks for him to toss, encouraging him until one of the trainees was sent down to fetch us. The entire platoon was waiting. There were jibes sent in our direction. "Come on, Sonny, put it out there! Iggy, you gonna blow yourself up!"

The cadre made everybody calm down, I took up position, and the range sergeant handed me a real live honest to gosh it's gonna kill you if you don't get it far enough away grenade. I took a breath, pulled the pin, let the lever flip off, counted one thousand as instructed, and threw the blame thing with everything I had and then knelt behind the barrier. The grenade went off, I earned some light cheers, and it was now Iggy's turn.

"Just get it over the barrier," I told Iggy as he shuffled past with his head down while he wiped at his nose with the back of his sleeve.

From our platoon, I watched and might have even prayed. As soon as Iggy pulled the pin and the lever flipped off, I cringed because I could tell he was going back to the sidearm throw. Sure enough, Iggy slung the grenade sideways but with enough loft that it got over the barrier but not by much. While Iggy dropped and curled up in a ball, the grenade went off and everybody ducked. When I looked up, Iggy was on his feet, still alive. When he looked back at us with a big grin, I started a cheer. "Yay, Iggy! Way to go, Iggy!"

Even though his throw was less than stellar, they didn't make Iggy throw another grenade, probably because the DIs felt they'd pushed their luck far enough. No doubt, they would hoist a number of beers in the NCO Club that evening. If I could have, I would have joined them.

At the end of Basic, we had a parade and everybody graduated, including Iggy and the other boys sent to us by the criminal courts. It was a good day and everybody scattered with orders for either technical or combat arms training. To my surprise, Iggy was sent to cook's school. Apparently, the infantry didn't need any side-armed grenade throwers. What followed for me was eight weeks more at Fort Leonard Wood for some intense combat engineer training. We learned how to build bridges, roads, airfields, and field fortifications, handle explosives and land mines, and operate a variety of crew-served weapons. At the end of my sixteen weeks at Little Korea, it was my strong belief that I had been thoroughly and well trained for World War II and the Korean War, but that thing happening over in Vietnam? I wasn't so sure.

Per my College Op contract, I was next promoted to sergeant E-5 and assigned to the United States Army Engineering Officer Candidate Regiment (USAEOCR, pronounced "U-socker") at Fort Belvoir, Virginia. There, my fellow College Op candidates thought we would learn how to be officers and gentlemen and, most important, how to supervise combat engineers. We had no way of knowing that instead we were about to go into a kind of hell and, coming out of it, I would not much like myself for a long time.

The Beatings Will Continue
Until Morale Improves

We were starving even while sitting at a table loaded with hot, nutritious, and presumably delicious food. Most of us hadn't eaten for days and yet we'd been run ragged all over Fort Belvoir, harassed every step by tac officers (short for Training, Advising, and Counseling) and upperclassmen of the Engineer Officer Candidate Regiment. After a day of classes followed by brutal physical training, we were marched into the mess hall and ordered to sit with upperclassmen at each table while civilian waiters, depending on the meal, brought out plates of sizzling steaks, fried chicken, mashed potatoes, corn, vegetable salads, macaroni and cheese, fresh baked bread, mounds of soft butter, eggs, bacon, and sausage. While the upperclassmen dug in, we were not allowed to eat. Instead, we were peppered constantly with questions that, considering our exhaustion, we were almost certain to screw up one way or the other.

"Chain of command, Smack. Get it right and the table can take three bites. Go!"

"Smack" was from the acronym SMEAC, which stood for Situation, Mission, Execution, Administration, and Communications, the five steps army leaders were required to consider before a mission. At OCS, they had changed it from a memory aid to an epithet. There was nothing lower than a Smack.

"Sir, the chain of command is—"

"Not fast enough, Smack. Nobody eats!"

Sometimes, they'd let us eat a few forkfuls of food before being ordered to lay our forks down again. The civilian waiters silently removed our plates and dishes and bowls and most of the food while we were rousted up and out back to the barracks at double time.

It was not hyperbole to say the lack of nutrition, the constant harassment, and the lack of sleep left most us failing physically and mentally. Every morning, we got up hours before the tac officers arrived and desperately prepared the barracks for inspection so that we might get at least a small amount of approval and perhaps be allowed to eat. Every bunk and footlocker, every toilet and urinal, every sink and mirror, every square inch of the floor, all had to be immaculate or our lead tac officer, a short stub of a first lieutenant, went completely berserk. He tore off mattresses, turned over footlockers, and strewed the contents while screaming red-faced at the top of his lungs. In stunned silence, we stood at attention and waited for his fury to end. When he left, he was replaced by upperclassmen who ordered us to go into the front leaning rest position followed by ten, twenty, fifty, a hundred push-ups, whatever number they could come up with to keep us busy. When the lead tac officer came back in and saw the mess he'd caused was still there, he would go crazy all over again. He once brought a bucket of sand and threw it across our polished floor, then skated on it in his boots, deeply scratching the linoleum to where it was almost impossible to bring it back up to a shine.

After the first month of OCS, most of us were reeling. We were into a type of dangerous psychosis. Hunger filled our every thought when we could think at all from the lack of sleep or our aching bodies. We ran double time to classrooms, where we were supposed to learn how to be engineer officers, but we weren't learning anything except how to bite the inside of our cheeks in a desperate attempt to stay awake. Classrooms were not air-conditioned but hot and sweaty, as might be expected in a fort built on an old swamp. Anyone caught sleeping or even with droopy eyelids was ordered outside for push-ups and sit-ups or jumping jacks or squats while being screamed at for being worthless.

Once while in a morning formation before class, an upperclassman casually tossed a biscuit down in the dirt and I watched in wonder as two of my fellow candidates, both college graduates, fell on it, wrestling with each other for its dirty crumbs. When the tac officer cried out for sick call and anybody stepped forward, they were ordered back into formation. While we were all on our hands and knees going around the barracks with orders to pick up every loose piece of anything that wasn't grass, one of my classmates managed to get up on the roof of our barracks and jump off. I heard somebody yell out just in time to see him hit the ground. The tac officer began to scream at him to get up, but it was clear by the twist of his leg that it was broken. He never cried out; he just lay there with dull eyes. When he was hauled off, the tac officers and upperclassmen descended on us screaming in fury for letting the "accident" happen. Of course, it was no accident. The man was getting out any way he could.

After some of my fellow candidates, weak from starvation, passed out while marching in formation only to be rousted up and pushed ahead as if they were prisoners of war, I decided the situation was desperate and ridiculous enough to do something equally desperate and ridiculous. Our barracks of old World War II wooden construction were lined up beside other barracks inhabited by enlisted troops training on various combat engineering military occupational specialty (MOS) tracks. When I caught the whiff of pizza one night, I sneaked outside and stood in the darkness and watched a civilian go by with a stack of pizza boxes. It was hard not to attack him and take those pizzas away. Instead, I made a plan.

Every evening, we were made to double-time down to a big, open field where a training sergeant waited to put us through various exercises or make us do laps. Usually, the tac officers and upperclassmen were elsewhere. On one of the laps, when I noticed nobody was paying attention, I simply kept going, ran back into the barracks area, and slipped amongst the enlistees until I found two of them sitting on the stoop taking a smoke break. "Hey, fellows," I said, "I wonder if you could help me."

By the stripes and decals on my helmet, they knew I was an officer candidate, which naturally made them cautious, but before long I'd made a deal. For a hundred dollars, they would order ten pizzas that night and stow them underneath their barracks. We agreed where they would put the pizzas and where I would leave them five twenties, just about every cent I had to my name. There was no way of knowing if they would do what they said, but at that point I was willing to be reckless.

After dark, without saying a word to anyone, I sneaked outside. By slipping amongst the shadows, I found the pizzas, left the money under a rock, and carried five pizzas into the washroom and then went back for the other five. When, by their noses, my fellow candidates realized what was in the washroom, they descended on it like ravenous dogs. Afterward, with not a crumb left, the problem was what to do with the boxes. To keep anyone else from being blamed, I chose to sneak outside with them and toss them into the dumpster behind the enlisted barracks. On my last run, I was seen by an upperclassman on guard duty. He shined a flashlight on me but then turned it out and, foolishly, I thought maybe he was going to show me some pity.

They came for me the next night, probably after debating what to do and perhaps consulting with the tac officers. I heard them when they threw open the door and could sense each and every fellow member of my company go quiet beneath their thin blankets, afraid to do anything that might draw attention to themselves.

But it wasn't anyone else they wanted.

Just me.

They stomped up to my bunk and tore the covers from me. "Get up, Smack! Now!"

I tumbled onto the floor and stood at attention in my skivvies and bare feet. A foul breath hit me in the face. "Get going, Smack!"

I felt a hand brush my leg. It was my bunkmate below. Willie Merkerson. A tough Green Beret master sergeant prior to OCS, Willie could have climbed out of his bunk and easily destroyed the men who had come for me.

But I knew he wasn't going to do that. Willie, a black man who had risen through the ranks, wanted his commission as much as I did, as much as every one of us. We'd gone too far to give up. He and I had become instant friends in OCS. He encouraged me and I followed his lead. He picked me up and carried me when I fell during a run, totally exhausted. He pulled me out of the river when I tried to carry too many sandbags and fell off a timber trestle bridge. He was always encouraging me. Now, about to be taken by the upperclassmen to an uncertain fate, he was silently telling me to take whatever was going to happen. There was really little doubt about what that was going to be. They were going to beat me up.

I was marched barefoot down between the row of bunks where my company cohorts still lay unmoving and silent. "Double-time, Smack. Our barracks. Go!"

I ran down the wooden stairs and onto the gravel path to the dirt road and then to the barracks where the upperclassmen lived. The door was flung open and I marched inside and stood at attention while a crowd of angry faces circled me. "Drop! Give me fifty!"

Maybe, I thought, they were just going to make me do a bunch of push-ups and sit-ups, so I was glad to do it. I dropped and started but when I reached twenty push-ups, somebody suddenly threw himself on top of me. My arms buckled and my face smashed into the floor. "Don't hurt his face, moron!" one of them yelled.

Rough hands rolled me over. "Get up, Smack! Get up! Naw, his nose ain't broke. Not even bleeding. Smack, you organize a pizza run last night?" I remained silent. One of their faces pushed into mine. It was twisted with hate and fury. "Did you?"

"Yes, Candidate."

"You broke the honor code!"

"No, Candidate. I—"

Something sharp slammed me in the back that caused my knees to buckle. Involuntarily, I gasped at the shock as much as the pain. It was the end of a mop handle, and it had made a dent.

Men with shaved heads in fatigue pants and boots and olive drab T-shirts moved in. The steamy air was suffused with a palpable hate. "You're ruined, Smack. You're going to be kicked out! You broke the honor code."

"No, sir!"

A boot kicked me hard in the shins while the mop handle was stuck hard in my back again, this time catching a kidney. Thunder and lightning burst in my head, and I put up my hands just in time to deflect a boot aimed at my stomach. "Put your hands down! I said put your hands down!"

I lowered my hands and this time my stomach got the boot and I crumpled. "Get up! I said get up!" I got up. "What's the honor code, Smack?"

I gritted my teeth for a moment and refused to answer, but when I sensed the mop handle was about to be plunged into my back again, I gasped, "A candidate will neither lie, cheat, steal, or tolerate any candidate who does."

"Did you organize a pizza run last night?"

"Yeah, yeah, I did."

"You cheated! You're done, Smack. Gonna get kicked out of OCS. Straight to the 'Nam. Who was in it with you?"

"Nobody. Just me." That was the truth.

The point of a pocketknife blade flitted around one of my eyes within millimeters of touching my cornea. "Tell us who helped you or lose an eye."

"Nobody."

After a moment of hesitation, the knife was withdrawn and, with a silent signal, one of the upperclassmen who was built like a wrestler came at me and started swinging. His fists pounded on my arms, my back, my chest. "Not his face, not his face!" one of them kept saying. "Not his face!"

When I got knocked down, I got right back up and took the pounding. "Stay down, Sonny!" I heard one of them say. It was one of the upperclassmen who was a Virginia Tech graduate and had been caught up in the same nightmare as I had except a class ahead. We had a moment of eye contact before he turned away and a fist caught me in the ribs. I went down but got back up. I couldn't let them win. I was also hoping they'd slip up and hit me in the face. If they broke my nose or gave me a black eye, I'd have to be allowed to go on sick call, where a doctor might ask me how it happened and I would tell the truth.

"For God's sake, stop it!" somebody finally yelled. There was a stunned silence, a lot of nervous glances, and then somebody grabbed me and pushed me toward the door. It was the Virginia Tech grad. "Get out of here! Run!"

I ran, disappearing into the rows of barracks and then doubling back to my own. After slipping inside and making my way through the darkness past inert forms on the bunks, I climbed into the sack.

"You OK?" Willie asked.

"Fine. I'm fine."

"Those bastards. I'd like to kill every one of them."

I felt the same way, but I knew that opportunity wasn't going to come. All any of us could do was grit our teeth and get through this nightmare any way we could. For me, that meant I needed to change, to become hard, to be tough, to outthink and outlast my tormentors. I had a girlfriend, a sweet young woman who was a nursing student in Roanoke. All through Basic and advanced training and during OCS, she had written me loving letters of support. When I received a normal and nice letter from her a day after the beating, I felt a cold fury that she didn't understand what I was enduring and never would, which led me to write an angry letter back, telling her we were done, that I had changed, that nothing was more important than what I was doing.

And it was the truth. I had changed. Getting a commission in the United States Army had become the most important thing to me in the world. My mind was filled with nothing else except an arrogance that I couldn't yet identify but did not fear, although I should have.

One day, the harassment stopped. The tac officers disappeared, the upperclassmen sat silent in the mess hall, and we were allowed to eat. We marched to classes by ourselves. We slept undisturbed. That weekend, we were completely left alone. We even had time to read and study ahead. The following Monday a few tac officers returned, but not all of them, and the ones who did were subdued. The upperclassmen's ranks got smaller. Nothing was explained.

Life was still hard, we were still harangued, classes on top of classes, field exercises on top of field exercises, but something had happened to cause a change. Only later, after graduation, would I learn that the army inspector general had gotten wind of how the OCS at Fort Belvoir was being run and demanded a review. Officers were relieved, candidates cited for cruelty were booted out. It was, we were to learn, the fellow who'd flung himself off our roof. He'd gone first to the medics and then his congressman and busted it all wide open.

Once my class was into upperclassmen status, we left the lower classes mostly alone. We had no interest in repeating the torture we'd endured but focused instead, as we should have from the beginning, on learning what we could on combat engineering field operations. Released on the weekends, a few of us rented an apartment in Georgetown to crash and get away from the military for a little while. For me, that included visiting Big Creek High School graduates who'd settled in the area to work for the federal government.

The commissioning ceremony was held in October 1966, and I finally got my almighty butter bar. My mother attended but, when the time came, I didn't invite her out on the field to pin the bar on me. Instead, I turned and asked Willie Merkerson's wife to do it with the idea it would honor him for getting me through OCS. When I walked over to where Mom stood, I could tell I'd hurt her feelings. After I thanked her for coming, she gave me a look that turned my blood to ice and then silently turned and walked away.

From There to Nowhere

My first duty assignment as a US Army officer was to Dugway Proving Ground in Utah, the Beehive State, also known as Zion. It was the home of the Latter-day Saints, also known as the Mormons. All I knew of them was the Mormon Tabernacle Choir, and even them I didn't know much about except to hear them sing "God Bless America" on the radio from time to time. One of their future members, however, was waiting for me. She didn't know it, and neither did I.

Before I could get myself to Zion, I went home to Coalwood, there to present myself to my mother and see if I could somehow make up for how I had treated her during the commissioning ceremony. Before going into the army, I'd bought a red Volkswagen Beetle that I called Grindl. After paying a fellow to drive it from West Virginia to Fort Belvoir a week before I graduated, Grindl was a welcome sight. I drove her to Aberdeen Proving Ground for some short training and then headed home. On the way, I decided to go through Blacksburg just to see the old campus.

It was midnight when I got there, and I knew I needed to sleep before traveling that last hundred miles. I headed for Brodie Hall and went inside. Everything was quiet. I looked on the doors to see if any of them lacked a name tag and when I found one, I eased it open and saw that the room was empty. After locking the door behind me, I went to sleep on the bare mattress of the lower bunk until I was awoken by the familiar rumble of cadets heading to breakfast formation. After going back to sleep for another hour or so, I got up and went down the stairs, got in my car, and headed for Coalwood. It was surreal, that one last night in Brodie Hall with all my classmates long gone, some of them already fighting overseas.

The house was dark when I parked in the back alley behind it. With only an army duffel bag that contained my uniforms and a few pieces of civilian clothes, it was easy to carry everything I owned. I wasn't used to knocking on the door so I didn't, entering through the kitchen. All was quiet. After looking in every room, I realized nobody was in the house except Tiki, Tech, and Chipper. Poteet had died while I was in OCS. I petted the twin Siamese cats, made sure Chipper had some food, and then deposited my bag in my old room. I contemplated picking up the black mine phone and dialing Dad's office number to see if he was there but decided to wait.

He came in after dark. He looked tired and drawn. "Hello, Sonny," he said. "Your mom will be home in the morning."

"I fed the cats," I told him. "And Chipper."

He thanked me and, carrying the *Welch Daily News*, went into the living room. He shook the newspaper open and sat down and started reading. Following, I picked up a magazine off the coffee table and sat down on the couch beside him. His eyes still riveted on the paper, he said, "You upset your mother."

"I know," I answered. "I didn't mean to."

He rattled the paper. "Where you headed?"

"Dugway Proving Ground. It's in Utah. They test chemical weapons there."

"What do you know about that?"

The truth was I knew absolutely nothing, but I didn't want to tell him that. At the end of OCS, I'd been told I couldn't be a combat engineer officer even though I'd finished near the top of my class. It was because of my eyes. I was considered too nearsighted to be in a combat arms unit. They'd transferred me to the Ordnance Corps, which I knew nothing about but figured I could learn.

Mom, as promised, showed up the next day from Myrtle Beach in the little Karmann Ghia she loved. Rebel, the big German shepherd that my brother had given her, was in the back seat. As soon as she parked, Rebel bounded out of the open window and into the yard to run around it a few times while barking at imaginary intruders.

Dressed in pedal pushers, a pink blouse, and a yellow sunhat, she said, "Hello, Sonny Boy," as I came outside to help her carry in her bags.

"How was Myrtle Beach?" I asked.

"What do you care?" she replied, which meant I was still in trouble.

After I carried her things to her room, I came back to the kitchen, where she had a pot of coffee brewing. When she poured herself a cup, I sat down at the kitchen table with her. "Mom, I know I hurt your feelings at the commissioning ceremony and I'm sorry."

She waved my apology away. "It doesn't matter." She looked at me. "This place is falling apart. People are moving away and leaving the houses empty. Trees are growing up through them. There's a fire in the mine they can't get hold of. And they're going to close the Coalwood Post Office."

"Mom, on the commissioning ceremony…"

"I said it doesn't matter."

"Yes, it does. What can I do to make up for it?"

It was a question that gave Mom a delicious opportunity to come up with a mischievous punishment. In past times, I could count on her to smile and let me know what I needed to do—wash the windows or shovel coal into the furnace or some such—but now she had nothing to say. That meant I was still in the doghouse. I remained there all that day and evening. She went to her room and stayed there. Dad, who was still taking his meals at the Club House, came home and read the paper and went to bed.

The next morning, I carried my duffel bag down to Grindl. Dad had risen before sunrise and gone to the mine. Mom's bedroom door remained closed. Clearly, I wasn't just in the doghouse; I was in the doghouse basement. For a good long while I sat in the kitchen, hoping she would come down. When she didn't and I couldn't wait any longer, I visited the Siamese cats, who were sleeping curled up together on the living room couch, and then sought out Chipper, who rewarded me by giving me a few chirps. "So long, little buddy," I said. He was already so old, I doubted I would see him again and, as things turned out, my suspicion was true. He would pass in my mom's arms a year later.

After seeking out Rebel and finding him in the basement, I petted him, contemplated the table where I'd once built my rockets, and then walked out into the yard and gave Coalwood a last look around. There was nothing and nobody moving. Coalwood was asleep, and it was doubtful it would ever wake up.

Nobody saw me off, and Grindl and I headed for Welch and beyond. After consulting the map, I had decided to drive through Fort Collins, Colorado, to visit with O'Dell, who had completed his air force service, married a lovely young woman, and was busily attending Colorado State University. How long it would take to get there I wasn't sure, but I had written him a letter that identified at least the week I hoped to arrive.

It was February and before I got far, it started to snow. By the time I started across Kentucky, it was snowing so hard that Grindl's wipers weren't strong enough to push the snow off the windshield. To keep from burning up the wiper motor, I opened the window and used my hand to wipe the snow off until I had a small hole to look through. Doggedly, I kept going but finally, somewhere outside of Louisville, I could go no farther and pulled over to the side of the road behind a big tanker truck to wait the snowstorm out. I leaned the seat back as far as it would go and tried to sleep, but that was impossible because it was too cold. Eventually I pulled my fatigues out of my duffel bag and used them as blankets. Mostly, my feet were cold. Every once in a while, I'd start Grindl up, take in some heat, and then turn her off. This went on through the night.

After the sun came up, a truck went by spreading ashes on the road and the tanker roared awake and pulled in behind it. Following its lead, I did, too. Before long, the road turned to slush and, after finding a grocery store on the west side of Louisville, I bought a loaf of bread and a jar of peanut butter and kept going, crossing the fabled Mississippi River in St. Louis and headed for Kansas City. There, I treated myself to a steak dinner at a roadside restaurant and then slept in its parking lot.

The next day, I drove across Kansas that was "flat as a flitter," as my Grandmother Lavender would say, the terrain on both sides of the road vast farmland. It wasn't long before I saw for my first time a real honest-to-goodness tumbleweed. And then another and then hundreds. Grindl and I zipped along across Kansas while dodging them, some as big as the little car. As the sun went down, I found myself in the small town of Hays and decided to park beneath its water tower for the night. Protected from the winds by a small tree-lined fence, I slept soundly. Waking fresh and happy, I kept going. On the western horizon, I saw a mountain like a white spear tip that seemed close but was in fact almost four hundred miles away. It was Pikes Peak! The mountain was like a beacon, and I imagined the wagon trains coming across Kansas that used it to guide them day after day and probably for weeks as they worked their way westward to their promised land.

Before I got to Pikes Peak, I turned north and worked my way across Denver and on to Fort Collins, where O'Dell and his wife, Jeanne, greeted me with unreserved love at their tiny apartment. As Jeanne, a Coalwood girl, settled down on an easy chair to listen, I told my stories about being in the army. When I was done, O'Dell asked me about our hometown. "It's dying," I told him. "You can just feel it."

"I know," he said quietly. "But Daddy will stay. He'll raise his flowers and tend to his bees." He studied me. "Why didn't you let your mom pin on your bar?"

"Because, O'Dell," I said, "there are a lot of stupid people in this world, and I am one of the most stupid."

He studied me some more. "Maybe you ought to give yourself a break," he said and changed the subject. "Will they send you to Vietnam?"

I had no idea and said so. Actually, I hadn't thought about it. First, I needed to get to Dugway and figure out what they wanted me to do there.

"I love it out here," O'Dell said as Jeanne nodded her agreement. "The mountains, the rivers, the air. It's like a different world."

We went out on their little deck and looked up at the sky as the stars came out so amazingly bright that we allowed ourselves to get lost in them. They reminded me of who I used to be, a boy full of hope who imagined building the rockets to take people up there. When I left the next morning, Jeanne gave me a quilt from Coalwood as a gift. She started to cry and I couldn't hold back the tears either. I hugged her and then shook O'Dell's hand and drove quickly away. It would be many years before I would see either of them again.

Snow, different from what I had known in the East, began to fall as I headed north. It was light and fluffy, powder as it was called, but it had the same effect on the road, which quickly iced over. In Medicine Bow, Wyoming, I found myself in a near whiteout. When I saw a gas station ahead, its lights dim within a ghostly swirl, I pulled over and ran Grindl right into a deep ditch, invisible beneath the powdery drifts. Unable to open the door, I rolled down the window and crawled out into the snow, swam through it onto the road, and then, wet and shivering, trudged to the gas station.

The attendant within, a friendly young man in a cowboy hat, told me not to worry, that he had a tow truck and would have me out in no time. While I dried off beside a wood-fired potbelly stove, he and a mechanic from the garage next door soon had Grindl out and parked beside the gas pumps. They refused to take any money, wished me well in the army, and I went on my way, although not far until I found a wide spot in the road, got out the quilt Jeanne gave me, and bedded down in Grindl.

The next day, I figured I'd fiddled around enough and was ready to get where I was going. Rather than follow the main road to Salt Lake City, I instead plunged south on a road that looked fine on the map but soon turned into a dirt road that crossed into steep mountains covered with patches of snow. Herds of sheep appeared that were using the road to move along. Beeping Grindl's horn, I eased carefully through them while they watched me with a mixture of concern and curiosity. The road got narrower until at last it was a single lane. At a washed-out bridge, I considered turning around but, trusting it wasn't too deep, drove across the shallow creek. Eventually, I emerged on a paved road somewhere near Vernal, Utah, and turned westward.

That afternoon, I made it to Salt Lake and was astonished at its beauty. Set in the Uinta Mountains, the city was the cleanest and freshest-looking I'd ever seen. After finding a side street to park, I bedded down for the night and the next morning set out to find Dugway. It was at what seemed the ends of the Earth, far out into the Great Salt Lake Desert. For miles there was nothing, and then there was a sign and a guard post and a gate.

WELCOME. DUGWAY PROVING GROUND. UNITED STATES CHEMICAL CORPS.

I stopped at the gate, presented my orders, and was waved through into a there that was deliberately nowhere.

Way Down West in
the Land of Zion

Dugway Proving Ground proved to be an interesting assignment, but I can't say much about what went on there in terms of my duties. In fact, I'm not going to say anything at all except it was a lonely place for a single young army officer. Although there were civilians that worked there, including a few women, they were almost all married and left the post at the end of the day. There were some army nurses who worked in the post hospital, but they were mostly older. The closest big town was Provo, home of Brigham Young University, so I signed up for night classes just to be around people near my own age. Twice a week, I made the four-hour round-trip drive from Dugway to BYU to take creative writing classes. BYU had a beautiful campus, set in the high mountains, and I found the students and faculty friendly and relaxed. Although I was aware the college was owned and operated by the Church of Jesus Christ of Latter-day Saints (Mormons), nobody ever mentioned religion in the classes. When I saw a dance notice on a bulletin board, I drove over on the weekend and attended. Everybody seemed to be having fun. In later years, I would say that after VPI, I thought BYU was a party school.

Although I didn't know anybody, I decided to ask some of the girls to dance. They were willing and it was astonishing to actually feel a woman's hand in mine and smell their perfume—heady stuff. One of the girls I asked was a gorgeous brunette who I noticed had a slight limp. She had a bright smile and after the dance didn't run off but stayed. "Who are you?" she asked straightaway. "You're older than most of the boys here."

I explained who I was and she introduced herself. Her name was Sherry, and she was a music major from California. She said right up front that she had polio when she was a little girl and that explained the limp. I told her about Sherman Siers, one of the Rocket Boys, and his limp from polio and that it never slowed him down. That earned me a smile that lit up the dark dance floor. A slow dance started and she slid into my arms and showed no particular wish to leave them. Before the evening was out, we scheduled a date for the next Saturday.

The long drive back to Dugway flew by. Although Sherry hadn't quite signed up for it exactly, it already felt to me like maybe I had a beautiful California Mormon girlfriend! I counted the days, hours, and minutes until Saturday rolled around. Dressed in a cute outfit with a short skirt, she was waiting for me outside her dorm and off we went in Grindl to Salt Lake City to see a movie. It was a Sandra Dee comedy but it didn't matter since we didn't pay much attention to it. Mostly, we made out in the back of the theater.

Afterward, we walked to the temple grounds, where she told me a surprising thing. "I've applied to audition to be in the choir after I graduate," she said. "My parents are all for it. The only thing is I'll have to move here. That's required." She spun around in front of the monument to the seagulls that had saved the Mormon pioneers after a locust infestation. "I love Salt Lake and I can get a teacher's job. Grade school music teacher, I hope." She stopped and looked at me. "How about you?" she asked. "What's next for Sonny Hickam?"

It was a question for which I had no answer so I said I didn't know, but as she stood there looking a little disappointed at my nonanswer, it occurred to me that maybe she'd like to hear about what it was like growing up in Coalwood. I even tagged on a few lines about building rockets.

"Is that why you're taking creative writing? To tell stories about where you grew up?"

That idea had never occurred to me. I mean, who would care what happened in Coalwood? "I like to write," I told her, "but I'm an engineer and I guess I'll work at that. Or maybe I'll stay in the army. I just don't know." Her big brown eyes made me want to fall into them. "I like it here," I heard myself say. "It's been a long time since I've liked it anywhere."

"You're damaged goods, Sonny," she replied with a smile and slid her hand into mine. "Some girl's hurt you." She looked at me closely and cocked her head as if reading my mind. "Whoever it was had to be pretty stupid."

"It wasn't like that," I answered.

"Oh, I'm sure it was," she said with the authority only a woman can manage. She reminded me of my mom in that regard.

I started to tell Sherry about OCS and what a jerk I'd been during all that and how I'd forced the breakup with a sweet girl, but I decided not to tell it since I didn't want her to be afraid I might treat her the same. So, wisely or unwisely, I just shut up and continued to bask in her obvious affection.

Nearly every weekend I could get away from Dugway, Sherry and I went out, but it didn't take long for me to understand she was also seeing someone else. When I thought I had to work one weekend but the test range was closed because of high winds, I called and asked her out on a Saturday date. She hemmed and hawed around a little before admitting she already had one. Sherry's dad was an attorney in Los Angeles, and she was going out with the son of a law school friend of his. My feelings were hurt, but I did my best to cover it up by lapsing into gibberish how it was my fault for waiting so late to ask and then launching into some lame conversation about a movie that was being filmed at Camp Williams, a nearby National Guard training site. The movie was called *The Devil's Brigade*. "They're asking for extras," I told her. "Maybe I'll go over there on Saturday and see about it."

She wasn't fooled by my misdirection. "It's just a friendly date," she said, but I knew better. He was undoubtedly a member of the LDS church and if Sherry was going to be in the choir, she would need to live in Salt Lake. It was my guess that after she told her parents she was seeing me, they had picked him deliberately to meet her.

The following weekend there was work I couldn't avoid, and the weekend after that Sherry graduated from BYU. She didn't invite me to attend. When we got together again, it was at the apartment her parents had rented for her in Salt Lake. Her affection in my direction had not diminished, but I still felt obligated to ask about her date. "I told you it wasn't really a date," she answered. "We just had dinner and talked. My parents think the world of him."

"What do you think?"

"I think you should attend my audition. It's on Wednesday night. Will you come?"

She had misdirected my question and we both knew it. "I'll be there," I swore.

She smiled a wan smile and looked around the sparsely decorated apartment. "I wish I had a cat," she said. "I've always had a cat."

I chuckled. "I wish I had a cat, too," and an idea, not a particularly bright one, formed in my agitated brain.

On Wednesday, I appeared at her door with a gift that wasn't actually a gift but a loan: two Siamese kittens. I'd seen an ad in the *Salt Lake Tribune* for one and instantly fallen in love with the little boy kitten and his sister, too. The idea I had was to forge a deeper relationship with Sherry by asking her to take care of "my" kittens since I wasn't allowed to have a pet at Dugway. She was delighted with the idea. "I'll be glad to keep them! What's their names?" She sat on the floor to cuddle them.

"I haven't named them," I said. "What do you think?"

"Nephi," she said. She touched the nose of the boy kitten, who looked back at her with puzzlement. "We'll call you Nephi."

Nephi was a respected character in the Book of Mormon. "Nephi it is," I said.

The female kitten was more rambunctious. She was already on top of the couch eyeing the window drapes. When she lunged for them and grabbed hold and started climbing, we both laughed. "How about Amelia?" Sherry asked. "She's like Amelia Earhart, a natural-born flyer!"

"Agreed," I said, and so it was.

Being allowed within the historic, hallowed Mormon Tabernacle during Sherry's audition was an honor I knew wasn't given to everyone and certainly not a "Gentile" like me. She introduced me to others in the choir and the members of the permanent staff who were conducting the audition. They were exceedingly warm to me, thanking me for being in the army while so many other young men were trying to avoid service. Members of the choir were there not to sing but to do chores around the tabernacle, including, to my surprise, sweeping the floor and even cleaning the toilets. They were intrigued by me and why I was there. While we sat between auditions, the men especially liked to tell me of their own military service and their various pilgrimages as young men going around the world on missions. Some of the stories were surprisingly bawdy, although always delivered with a sly wink.

When it came Sherry's turn, she delivered what I took to be a perfect performance, although afterward, while we played with Nephi and Amelia, she thought she had done poorly. "They'll never pick me," she said. "Anyway, there's a worry about who I am."

"What do you mean?"

She allowed a shrug. "I'm a single woman from California who lives in a temporary apartment in Salt Lake City. I have no job. I'm not considered permanent. They don't like to invest time and money in someone who's just going to leave."

Sherry needed an anchor in the Salt Lake City area that the choir directors would respect. Somehow, I suspected, no matter how nice everyone was to me, they didn't see a second lieutenant in the United States Army who wasn't a member of their religion and wasn't from Utah as any kind of potential anchor for her. It began to sink into my heart that I wasn't doing her any favors by sticking around.

Yet every time I tried to draw away, she would call and say she wanted to see me and, anyway, the kittens, especially Nephi, missed me. And every time I felt as if she had lost interest in our relationship, I would summon up my courage and call her and, not always but most of the time, she'd say please come to Salt Lake and visit Nephi, who needed so much to see me, and Amelia, too.

On one of our dates, just for the fun of it, I took her to an MG dealer in Salt Lake. I'd always admired the little sports cars and thought, even though I couldn't afford it and liked Grindl just fine, it would be fun to take a test-drive. While a salesman and I pondered an MGB, I looked around and discovered Sherry sitting in a sleek Porsche. The dealership also included that iconic brand. When I joined her, she folded down the sunshade on the passenger side and flipped open a mirror built into it. "I love this," she said at what was then an unusual feature. She leaned back into the leather bucket seat. "Dad has a Porsche, but he never lets me ride in it. He said it was the one thing in the world that belonged to him and only him." She looked as sad as I ever saw her look. "He can be selfish."

I got out and asked the salesman if he would take Sherry for a test-drive in the Porsche, but he shook his head. "Sorry, sir. It's been sold and, anyway, we don't allow our Porsches out on test-drives. Just our policy I'm afraid, sir."

Over the next few weeks I was busy every weekend with work, and my calls with Sherry became more infrequent. Finally, she called and I could tell she had been crying. "I've been wanting to talk to my friend about something," she said. "But it's my friend I think I might hurt if I do."

The lawyer had asked her to marry him. There was a lot of pressure on her to accept, presumably from her parents and maybe the choir directors, too. "What are you going to do?" I asked while choking up.

"I don't know."

"Can I see you?"

"Oh, please. Nephi and Amelia miss you. Especially Nephi. I can tell the way he cries when you're not here."

We set a date for noon the next day, and I took leave and left Dugway very early to do something I knew was completely, utterly wrongheaded but I was determined to do it anyway. At her apartment, I asked her to follow me to the street. There sat a brand-new silver Porsche 912 with bright red bucket seats. "I bought it."

Pure delight crossed her pretty face. "Oh, Sonny! Can you afford it?"

"I've saved up," I answered, which wasn't true. The monthly payment would take almost two-thirds of my monthly pay. And I'd traded away my beloved Grindl, too.

Sherry sat in the bucket seat and flipped down the mirror and laughed. "Did you buy this so I'd have a mirror?"

"No," I said, "I bought it so you could take a ride in a Porsche. At least this one time."

Her smile faded. "This one time?"

I settled in behind the wheel and started the Porsche up. Its engine made a majestic sound. "How about we cross the Great Salt Lake Desert? Together."

She looked at me. "Yes, please."

It was one of those days you put down in your life's book as perfect. We flew across the desert, not in a metal car built by men, but on a steed fashioned by the gods. If we touched Earth in our winged Pegasus, I do not recall it. When we crossed into Nevada, we stopped and bought a loaf of French bread and, to my surprise and her insistence, a bottle of wine. I had transferred the quilt O'Dell and Jeanne gave me from Grindl to the Porsche.

Sherry spotted a road that led across into some hills and suggested we go there for a picnic. When we found a big cottonwood tree, we spread the quilt beneath it and ate the bread and drank the wine and…drank the wine.

At her apartment, when it was time for me to go, she asked, "Can I keep Nephi and Amelia?"

"Let me have Nephi," I said and she put him in my arms and turned away.

Nephi was quiet as we drove the long, lonely road back to Dugway. After sneaking him into my bachelor quarters for a few days, I asked one of the army nurses to keep him for me at her house and she agreed. I began to visit him every evening I had free. A woman of Mexican-American heritage, the nurse didn't care for the name Nephi and called him Gato, which I learned meant "cat" in Spanish. To avoid confusion, I started to call him that, too.

The nurse was just back from Vietnam and talked about some awful and bloody things she'd seen there. As she told her stories, it made me think that I was trained at Virginia Tech and in the army to defend my country and maybe I wasn't doing that to the best of my ability at Dugway. When I made a phone call to the Pentagon to talk to an officer in personnel, he assured me I had nothing to worry about. The army's plan was to leave me at Dugway for the duration of my service agreement. I told him that wasn't what I wanted.

I heard one last time from Sherry. She called to say she thought maybe I would like to hear that Amelia had missed Nephi for a while but now seemed to have accepted that he was gone. The cat slept on her bed every night and still liked to swing on her curtains. "How's Nephi?" she asked.

"He's fine," I said and left it at that.

"Are you still taking creative writing at BYU?"

"Not this semester. Why?"

She was quiet for a while. "You should write about us. People like to read sad stories."

When I got my new orders, the nurse agreed to keep Gato until I got back. The Porsche went into storage. When I called my parents to tell them, nobody was home. That was all right. The path I'd chosen was all mine.

You Don't Belong Here

The US Army contracted with commercial airlines to fly its troops back and forth across the Pacific Ocean during the Vietnam War, so a big, shiny new Northwest Orient Boeing 707 got the job to carry me and a bunch of rowdy soldiers across the Pacific from McChord Air Force Base near Seattle to Cam Ranh Bay with a stopover in Anchorage and Japan. Aboard with us, whether they liked it or not, were a few harried stewardesses who, after trying to keep order, finally surrendered and strapped themselves in their jump seats or disappeared into the cockpit. Bottles of smuggled booze appeared and a kind of madness began to run up and down the aisles. A few fights broke out, but mostly there was just a steady roar of jokes, dirty songs, and manic laughter. For my part, I just watched and stayed out of the tempest.

My seatmate was a lieutenant in the artillery by the name of Rick Terrell, a graduate of Texas A&M, which, like VPI, was designated a military college with a similar cadet corps. Right off, we had that in common. He also had a bottle of Scotch whiskey that he offered up. Although I had never tasted the stuff, I agreed. It was a long flight and I figured it might help pass the time. After we'd had a few drinks, Rick asked, "Do you know how to call in artillery?"

The answer was I didn't. It hadn't been covered anywhere in my training. "I will teach you," Rick said and proceeded to do so. He was a great teacher. He pulled a map from his pack and taught me grid coordinates. "No matter where you go," he said, "get the push for the forward observer and if you get in a jam, call him up, tell him the situation, where you are by grid coordinates just like I showed you, and tell him to fire for effect. Back off if you can. There might be short rounds. By the way, where you headed?"

"First Cavalry Division," I said.

"Your MOS?"

"Mechanical Maintenance Officer, but I graduated from Engineer OCS and at my last duty station, I was sort of in the Chemical Corps so I'm not sure what my job will be."

Rick laughed. "Well, good luck, Sonny. We'll see if a Hokie knows what to do in a combat zone."

"Like an Aggie does?"

He raised his paper cup. "An Aggie just taught you to call in artillery and to drink Scotch and don't you forget it!"

I never did.

When we landed at Cam Ranh Bay, Rick told me to look out the window as we taxied and when I did, the first thing I saw in Vietnam was a truck loaded with coffins. No flags covered them. Our running calls in Basic and OCS came to mind:

> *If I die in a combat zone,*
> *Box me up and send me home.*

Pin my medals 'cross my chest,
Tell my mama I done my best.

I wondered what the mothers across the wide, wide Pacific Ocean would think about their boys singing that cadence before they shipped out to Vietnam. The click of seat belts being unbuckled and soldiers standing up to look through the windows on that side were an indication that they had also seen the coffins. The stewardesses yelled at everyone to sit down but when they were ignored, the poor women, their Northwest caps askew, gave up. "Jesus Christ" seemed to be the most prevalent phrase being used as the trucks went by with their cargo of death. "Jesus Christ, Jesus Christ!"

"Sit down, all of you!" a colonel emerging from first class bellowed, but he was immediately shouted down.

A master sergeant stood up in the aisle and gripped the seats on both sides. "You men sit down!" he bellowed. "What did you think you'd see here? You're in a goddamned combat zone!" He grabbed one miscreant by the collar of his khakis and pushed him into a seat. "I said *sit down!*"

With these evident truths clearly enunciated, everyone sat, the plane trundled on and stopped, and the engines whined down. The stewardesses opened the door and stood back as the plane emptied of rowdies. We were directed to buses with metal screens welded over the windows that took us first to temporary enlisted quarters and then, with just a few of us left on the bus, to temporary bachelor officer quarters. As we filed into a wooden barracks with a tin roof, an administrative NCO took a copy of our orders at the door. After a glance at mine, he stopped me. "First Cav Division? This can't be right." He flipped through some papers on his clipboard. "First Cav's got no requisition for your MOS. And I don't see your name here either. Grab a bunk. I'll see if I can sort it out."

When I told Rick, he thought it was funny. "Maybe they'll put you on a plane and send you home," he cracked.

We grabbed adjoining bunks and, jet-lagged, proceeded to follow the time-honored tradition of soldiers that if you can sit, sit. If you can lie down, lie down. And if you can sleep, sleep. We slept.

Two days later, I was still waiting for the sergeant to come back with my orders. Rick was headed for the Fourth Infantry Division up in the Central Highlands, but there were no flights going there so he was told to stay in place. To pass the time, we roamed Cam Ranh Bay, although the beach that we heard was beautiful was off limits, reserved for troops on in-country rest and recreation leave known as R&R. At night, we found a barracks with a television and watched whatever they had on, usually situation comedies like *I Love Lucy* or *I Dream of Jeannie*. It was hot, damp, and boring. Mosquitoes bit us everywhere we went despite the spewing clouds of insect spray that roaming trucks left behind. We attended a couple of lectures where we were told that the two most dangerous things about Vietnam were malaria and loose women. Both could put us in hospitals for the rest of our short, miserable lives. "Maybe we're making war on the wrong enemy," Rick said. "Bugs and broads!"

On the third morning, a runner found me and sent me to admin and, after sitting for a couple of hours, a clerk handed over my new orders. My orders to the First Cav were cancelled and I was reassigned to the 704th Maintenance Battalion of the Fourth Infantry Division at Camp Enari near Pleiku. When I told Rick I was going to the same place he was, he said he'd been told that if we waited around for orders to get a flight, we'd be around for at least another week. What we should do, he said, was to go on out to the airfield and, with the orders we already had, try to hook a ride to Pleiku. That sounded good to me—I was tired of hanging around with nothing to do but slap mosquitoes that were everywhere and avoid loose women who were nowhere—so we picked up our duffel bags and hitched a ride to the landing strip and waited until we found a Caribou transport going to Pleiku Air Base.

We grabbed two seats in a plane filled mostly with grunts just freshly arrived in-country. When we landed at Pleiku and the ramp was dropped, we looked out on red earth and green hills and Rick cracked, "So I said to myself, 'Self, what are you doing here?'" This got a laugh from the grunts, and we all walked out with our duffel bags on our shoulders and stood around until finally we were chased off by an air force sergeant who told us to get off the tarmac and go wait for a bus to Camp Enari. He pointed to a road and we trudged over to it and, like forlorn orphans, stood in a clump to wait for a bus nobody was sure would come.

Finally, an empty deuce and a half stopped, the driver yelled at us to hop aboard if we were going to Enari, and most of us did. Once off the base, the truck wandered through miles of ramshackle huts and shops built with what looked like leftover plywood, flattened tin cans, and landing strip planks. Some of them had signs that spelled out WASHING CLEANLY, HANDING EXACTLY They were laundries, a spec five said, who explained he'd been in-country for seven months and was coming back from an R&R at Nha Trang. When we passed a conglomerate of pink stucco buildings surrounded by a chain-link fence and topped with concertina wire, the spec five announced that we were passing by Sin City, the officially recognized by the United

States Army houses of ill repute that the South Vietnamese Army operated. We naturally all craned our necks to see the girls, but all we saw was a guardhouse with a Vietnamese military policeman at the gate.

When we crested a hill, we got our first view of Camp Enari, the base camp of the Fourth Infantry Division. It was huge. Several thousand men lived in rows of wooden barracks and offices networked by boardwalks in the shadow of a saddleback mountain. The mountain, we learned from the spec five, was named Dragon Mountain, but most everybody called it Titty Mountain. Stripped of forest and slick with grass, it was easy to see why, although, if so, they were the breasts of a huge green female alien. "Enjoy the view, boys," the spec five said to the grunts. "Sin City mamasans don't got much in the way of titties. All they got is the clap."

"I'll take whatever they got, buddy," one of the newbies said and the others hooted approval. The lecture on sex and disease at Cam Ranh Bay apparently hadn't made much of a dent, and Sin City was obviously already on their young minds.

Once through the Camp Enari gate, the truck trundled on and let us all off at the big PX building that was somewhat in the center of the camp. The grunts wandered off with the spec five leading them. Rick, after asking directions, headed to his artillery unit, and I did the same to find the 704th.

The sun beat down as I made my way across the boardwalks and paths. Not a single tree was standing to provide shade. Numerous metal tubes buried in the ground for urination stunk of stale piss as I walked by. The few soldiers outside were involved in mundane chores. Some were leaning over and slowly walking while picking up cigarette butts and other trash, some were burning diesel fuel in barrels dragged out from beneath outdoor privies, and some were painting rocks that marked the paths to the various units. They were all moving slowly like convicts forced into hard labor. A garbage truck trundled by with two soldiers standing on the back. One of them yelled "Short!" at everyone he saw, the word meaning he was close to the end of his tour. No one paid any attention to him. The slightest breeze caused a cloud of nasty red dust to rise up and float across the base along with the stink of urine and burning diesel mixed with shit. Camp Enari, from what I'd already seen of it, was just about the most depressing place I'd ever been.

Eventually, I found a collection of tin-roof, wood-framed hootches with a big one designated as the HQ of the 704th Maintenance Battalion. Inside, I found a clerk and handed over my orders. He frowned at them and then disappeared inside an office. After some muffled talk within, he came out and said, "Major Looter will see you, Lieutenant. Good luck."

Why I needed good luck to see an army major I wasn't quite certain, but I supposed I did after meeting the man. With a bullet head, piercing slate-blue eyes, and fatigues as crisp, starched, and pressed as I'd ever seen stateside, he glared at me from behind a huge desk as I entered and reported with a salute. He didn't salute back. Instead, he said, "I told those idiots I didn't need any more 4815s! What the hell am I supposed to do with you?"

I was sure I didn't know, and probably my expression suggested that. "You look like you've got an attitude, Lieutenant. Do you have an attitude?"

"No, sir."

He shook his head. "Last thing I need is some damn butter bar lieutenant with a freakin' attitude. I'll bust that out of you, don't think I won't! Now go do your job!"

"What's my job, sir?" I asked.

"How the hell should I know? You don't belong here! Your orders are completely screwed up. What are you, really? Chemical Corps? Wait, are you IG? You can't fool me, Mr. Inspector General Office, if that's who you are."

It was dawning on me that maybe Major Looter was not perfectly all right in some important mental categories. "I went to combat engineer OCS," I explained, "but because of my eyes, they put me in the Ordnance Corps, but then I worked for the Chemical Corps. I'm not with the IG." When his only response was to continue to stare at me with a thoroughly disgusted expression, I added, "I went to Virginia Tech. Engineering school. And I was in the Cadet Corps."

He shook his head in despair. "Jesus H. Christ. Specialist Matterhorn! Get your butt in here!"

The clerk appeared so fast that I was certain he must have been loitering just outside. Looter handed him my orders. "Do something with him," he said. He gave me an angry look. "You better change your attitude, Lieutenant!"

"Yes, sir," I said and meekly followed the spec four back to his cubbyhole.

"Look, sir," Specialist Matterhorn said with a sigh as he sat down, "I can do a couple of things for you. You can stay here and sit at a desk all day"—he looked around and shook his head—"or I can send you somewhere out in the field."

"Field," I said immediately.

"Officially, you need to go to the replacement depot first," he advised. "You know, the reppo-deppo. That's where they tell you stuff you probably already know like don't catch malaria and hang out with boom-boom girls." He pondered inwardly, looked around the warren of offices, and then said, "Nah, sir. I got a hunch about you. Your best bet is to get off Enari."

He wrote something on a scrap of paper and handed it over. "Go there. We've got a direct contact team with the First Brigade. Spec Five Cooper is in charge. He could use your help." He tapped a stack of documents in a piled-up in-box. His out-box, I couldn't help but notice, was empty. "I'll figure out your orders and get them squared away." He looked around furtively before saying, "Now, get out of here." When I didn't move, he asked, "What?"

"I don't have a helmet or a rifle."

He gave that some thought and then picked up a helmet off the concrete floor. "Here, you can have mine." He went to a locker, unlocked it, and handed me an M16 rifle from several. He wrote down the serial number. "Take it," he said. "These are extra. I'll do the paperwork later."

"Extra?"

"Don't ask."

"Ammunition? Magazines?"

"We're out. You can get some when you get there. Now, sir, honest to God, if you don't get out of here, one of these battalion field-grade shitheads is going to grab you and make you do his job and you'll never get off this base camp and believe me, you want to get off this base camp." He lowered his voice. "Everybody's crazy here."

Taking him at his word, I got out of there and, once outside, I saw the name he'd written down. It said Dak To. Not knowing what else to do, I walked to the Enari airstrip and went inside the office, which was a trailer with a wooden porch and a ramp. Inside, a spec four was using a grease pencil to write on a board with the headings "Aircraft," "Destination," and "Time." When he turned around, his grease pencil still poised, I said, "I need to go to"—I read it off the paper—"Dak To."

He lowered the grease pencil. "Say what, sir? Are you sure?"

"I think so. Why not?"

"They're gearing up to have a hell of a battle up there. Might be the biggest in the war. You just in-country?"

"Afraid so."

He shrugged. "I can get you up there," he said. "Not so sure about getting you back."

He directed me to a bench, where I watched the comings and goings of helicopters and some small fixed-wing aircraft before I was directed to a UH-1 helicopter, a Huey Slick as such was called, and climbed aboard with my duffel bag, which held everything I'd brought to Vietnam. Aboard the Slick was what I took to be four infantrymen loaded down with ammunition, rifles, and grenade launchers. They gave me the once-over. "Where you going, Lieutenant?" the spec four across from me asked. Although I guessed he was only nineteen or twenty years old, he had old eyes, maybe war-weary.

"Dak To," I answered.

"Which outfit?"

"I'm not exactly sure."

"Welcome to Vietnam, sir." He studied my M16, which I gripped with its butt on the floor. "You got any ammo?"

"Not a single bullet. Nor a magazine."

"Hey guys," he called out. "Lieutenant needs some pregnant 22s for his piece. And some magazines, too."

Before long, I had a bandolier of magazines, fully loaded with .223 (also known as 5.56 millimeter) ammo, and several boxes of the shiny little bullets. "Now, you're ready to go to war, sir!" the spec four said with a laugh. The others joined in with jollity at my expense just as the chopper lifted off, nose down, and rushed over the runway before lifting suddenly across the inward slope of Dragon Mountain. In a blur, the metal skin of a bleached fixed-winged airplane wreck of some type swept past.

The spec four saw where I was looking. "French," he said. "This war's been going on a long time before we got here."

"Any advice?" I asked.

"Stay low and don't try to be a hero, sir. That's about all I can tell you."

The helicopter kept rising and then leveled out while the door gunner swiveled his M60 machine gun snout downward at the canopied forest passing below. Before long, the infantrymen had their heads hung down, either asleep or feigning it, while holding their helmets over their groin. They were all sitting on their flak vests. After about a half hour, my stomach protested when the Slick suddenly dipped its nose and the ground leapt up to meet it. The grunts woke at once and plopped their helmets on and pulled on their flak vests. We settled into some tall grass and they bailed out while I sat there and waited for us to lift off. The copilot turned in his seat and yelled something at me.

I couldn't hear him above the deafening whop-whop of the blades and the turbine engines, so I clambered over to him and yelled into his ear, "I'm supposed to go to Dak To!"

"This is Dak To! Get off!"

Puzzled and pretty sure I wasn't where I was supposed to be but knowing when I wasn't wanted, I picked up my duffel bag with my spare jungle fatigues and boots and socks and underwear and T-shirts and my shaving kit and got off and ducked my head beneath the whirling blades. When it took off, the downdraft of the Slick hit me harder than I expected and I ate some dirt and grass.

After the noise of the helicopter receded, strong arms lifted me to my feet. "Damn, Lieutenant," the spec four who'd sat across from me said. "What the hell are you doing?"

"I was supposed to go to Dak To," I said. "The pilots said this was it."

He laughed while his buddies had some good guffaws, too. "This is the valley, sir. You want to go to Brigade. It's like ten clicks that way."

When I looked toward where he was pointing, all I saw was forest and hills. When the spec four and the others walked off, I slung my duffel on my shoulder and hurried after them.

Sweat streamed into my eyes and soon my fatigues were a soaking mess. My shoulders ached as I kept switching the duffel from one to the other and my rifle, too, and the bandoliers. Finally, we entered a clearing that held shelter half tents and a couple of field tents. Grubby and tired-looking grunts were sitting around with no shirts on. They seemed to all be either cleaning their M16s or eating C-rations. The spec four who I was starting to think of as my spec four pointed at one of the field tents. "You need to see the captain, sir," he said and then walked away to sit with his buddies. I dragged myself and my gear to the tent where I found a captain sitting at a field table with a radio on it and a couple of notebooks. He looked up as I lurched to his table. "Who the hell are you?"

"Lieutenant Hickam, sir. Ordnance Corps."

"MOS?"

"4815."

"No need for you here. Where are you supposed to be?"

"Brigade."

"Ten clicks that way."

"Yes, sir."

He studied me. "You're lost, aren't you."

"Yes, sir. Completely."

He chuckled and as he did, I thought to myself it was clear now why I was in Vietnam. To cheer up the infantry! "An APC will go into Brigade tomorrow. You can spend the night here."

An APC was an armored personnel carrier, sometimes called an M113. There were a couple of the boxy tracks set along the perimeter, their fifty calibers pointing outward into the bush. "Where do you want me?" I asked.

He swept his open hand around the camp. "Just find a spot."

The unmistakable thunder of artillery rumbled in the distance. "H&I fire on that hill there," the captain said, nodding toward a nearby peak. "They keep saying we're going to have to take it. I'm hoping they're wrong."

H&I meant harassment and interdiction, which I knew meant was more or less firing blindly where the artillery hoped the enemy was. My stomach growled and I realized I hadn't eaten all day. When I mentioned that, the captain pointed to a large tent. "Mess tent. Get some C-rats and water. Make yourself at home."

After eating some cold C-rations probably left over from World War II, I bedded down in the mess tent with my extra fatigues used as a blanket. When I asked about shaving, the mess sarge said there wasn't enough water for that so it could wait. The temperature dropped steadily through the night. My fatigues were still damp from sweat, which added to the chill, so mostly I shivered and tossed and turned until I heard the camp stirring just before sunrise. When I heard an APC start up, I trudged over to the crew and asked them if they were going to Brigade. When they said they were, I ran and got my gear and climbed the ramp and sat down inside. After a while, abused by the constant noise and rattling ride and not being able to see anything except aluminum walls, I asked the driver if I could come up on top, and he shrugged so up I went.

We were on a muddy track through some tall trees that had skinny trunks but thick foliage, enough that the sun only occasionally winked through. The gunner was on full alert. About two hours later, we reached a tent city that was chaotically filled with clattering APCs and roaring M48A3 Patton tanks and rumbling trucks going here and there on makeshift roads. Overhead, helicopters, both Slicks and gunships and the occasional transport heavy-lift Chinook chopper, flew with whop-whop spinning blades. Besides all the vehicular noise was the continuous rattle of generators set up all over the camp in a sea of wires snaking along the ground.

When the APC stopped, I thanked the driver and grabbed my duffel and rifle and bandoleers. "Here you go, Lieutenant," he said and tossed me down a flak vest. I touched my fingers to my helmet in thanks. While looking for my unit, I happened upon a small dirt patch between tents where bodies had been left, each wrapped in shelter halves or camouflage covers. Almost all of them had their boots sticking out from beneath their covering. Helmets and big rocks were lying on the corpses, I presumed to keep the downdraft of the helicopters from blowing off the covers. They were in a perfect line as if in military formation. Everyone walking around seemed to avoid looking at them.

Eventually, I found a scrappy-looking Quonset hut open on both ends with a plywood sign outside it that had 704th MT crudely painted on it. Inside the Quonset were tool chests spaced around its interior and two men, no hats or shirts, working diligently on an engine. "Looking for Spec Five Cooper," I called out.

One of the men who was holding a spanner wrench turned. He was painfully skinny with a mop of blond hair. "You found him."

"Headquarters sent me to help out."

Cooper scrutinized me. "Help out how?"

"They didn't say. I just got in-country."

"Was it Spec Four Matterhorn sent you?" When I didn't answer, Cooper shrugged a bony shoulder. "Well, you're here. My name's Coop."

"Lieutenant Hickam. How can I help?"

"You know anything about engines and transmissions?"

"Not really."

The other mechanic, a sad-eyed, grease-covered, sunken-chest fellow who needed a haircut and a shave, eyed me suspiciously and, after a good groin scratch, went back to work. This was all amidst an overwhelming amount of noise from trucks, APCs, and tanks, the pounding of helicopters, and the endless clatter of generators.

Coop pointed to a corner of the hut where sat a field table with shelves and cubbyholes. "Sir, if you don't mind, take a look at our paperwork. We got so many work requests, I've just piled them up."

"I can do that," I said before adding, "Look, I used to work in a coal mine and I'm an engineering school graduate. I know my way around tools. Tell me what to do and I'll do it."

"Do you know your way around an M88?" he asked.

As it turned out, I did. Dugway had one, and I had learned how to drive the massive trapezoidal-shaped armored vehicle and use its winches and lifters. It was officially known as a Vehicle, Tracked, Recovery, or VTR.

123

"We have to go out and get tracks or trucks broke down or blown up. The 88 driver's around here somewhere. When he goes out, how about you go with him and help rig the tow?"

"You're the boss, Coop," I said and rolled up my sleeves and got to work in the midst of the chaos of a battle joined but not yet fought.

Past the Tea Plantation

The battle of Dak To was, like most battles during the Vietnam War, controversial. Among its many variables, it was one of the first set-piece fights between main force North Vietnamese Army (NVA) units and "straight leg" (meaning non-paratroop or other special training) infantry. US Army grunts right out of basic training were sent up against an army of tough, hardened, well-equipped veterans who were well dug in. Our soldiers had the advantage of enormous firepower behind them, but in the end it all turned into a slugfest that required them to go up steep, corrugated, heavily forested mountains to rout out an enemy equipped with heavy and light machine guns, mortars, and rockets. Ultimately, it was a big, bloody, muddy mess.

My observation of it came within the cocoon of ceaseless noise that went on every hour and minute and second of every day. After I sorted through Spec Five Cooper's grease-stained stack of work requests and signed off on all of them to make them legal, I set up a filing system and made an inventory of his repair parts and replacement engines and transmissions, then put in high-priority "red ball" requests to Camp Enari for more supplies. After I'd done that, I picked up a wrench and went to work under Coop's direct supervision. When calls came in that a vehicle somewhere needed retrieval, I joined the spec four driver, a fellow named Tucker, to ride the M88.

On our first run, Tucker suggested I man the fifty caliber mounted atop the giant track and, though I'd not been trained on it, I took my station and, while being tossed around by the lurching vehicle beneath me, did my best to figure out how to operate it without actually pushing down on its V-shaped trigger. Once out in the woods, I asked for a demonstration and after turning the ammunition belt around the right way and clearing out the mess I'd made of it, Tucker pulled back the charging handle and told me to give it a go. Gripping its handles, I used the thumb trigger and was shocked at how loud and clearly lethal it was as a stand of trees simply melted from the onslaught of the heavy bullets. "Don't waste ammo, sir," the driver said. "We've only got this one can."

Clear coordinates were forbidden over the radio, so we searched for the damaged vehicle while swarms of gunships roared across the sky toward a series of mountains, folds in a green napkin of forests, with layers of clouds that seemed to be snagged on their ridges. Deuce-and-a-half trucks raced by us loaded with troops, and other trucks raced in the other direction. Medevac choppers, their dull red crosses against olive drab glowing in the hot sun, stuttered back and forth. Artillery behind us boomed and, when we stopped and turned off our engine, we heard the breathless whisper of shells passing overhead. We usually stayed on our radio push but when I got on the wrong frequency, it was filled with someone shouting for artillery support. "Right on top of us!" was part of the request, and then the frequency went dead.

The entire experience was grim. For three weeks, I stayed with the little team while, entirely without any information on what exactly was happening, a huge battle occurred only a few miles from us. Since the only water we had came from what we could scrounge from the units around us, we did not bathe, although I did once when I spotted some troops in the river beneath a concrete bridge and convinced Tucker to stop long enough to let me get a wash. After stripping down to my skivvies, I waded in and got some of the grime out of my hair and off my skin. What I thought was a suntan on my arms washed off. I also took the time to soak my jungle fatigues and, when up to my waist, take off my skivvies and wash them as best I could. There were Vietnamese women with their laundry on the riverbank and amidst all the chaos and noise, they still laughed and pointed at the naked Americans in the river even while they beat their clothes on the rocks and wetted them and wrung them out. The sheer strength and determination of these women to do their chores was lost on me at the time but, upon reflection, I cannot but help admire them for doing what they thought needed to be done for their families even inside all that madness.

Although I did not know it at the time, the battle joined by the Fourth Infantry grunts was also joined by elements of the First Cavalry Division, 173rd Airborne Brigade, and other American units. The South Vietnamese Army, or Arvin as we called them, a play off the abbreviation for Army of Vietnam (ARVN), was also brought in to the fight. When I saw a number of grunts waiting for trucks to take them wherever they were going, I asked them what was going on. Although they didn't much want to talk, I gradually learned that they'd been ordered to storm the hills through a tangled mess of battered forest splintered from artillery and gunship attacks and air force bombs. To go up those hills was essentially suicide and to order such an attack did not make any sense to the men ordered to go, but when the truck arrived, go they did.

A medic tent was erected near us, and "dust-off" choppers endlessly came and went to drop off the dead and wounded. One day, a truck full of tangled bodies piled on top of each other backed up to the tent but then, to my astonishment, one by one they got up and slid off the truck and wandered away except for a few who limped in to see the medics. They were infantry, worn out and dirty and half dead from no sleep and seeing their buddies killed and maimed. I would never forget the blank stares they gave me through their hollow zombie eyes.

The airfield, which was about a half mile away, came under rocket attack nearly every night. While trying to get some sleep, we heard the thuds as the 122 mm Russian missiles landed and exploded. Invariably, there was the sound of gunships aloft and sometimes the buzz of their miniguns as they sought out the enemy somewhere in the vast cloak of darkness that covered everything outside our hastily erected perimeter. One night, we became aware of a volume of noise like we'd never heard before. When we looked toward the airfield, we saw what appeared to be little suns that shuddered and died and then grew bright again. We would learn later they were C-130 cargo planes being hit by rockets.

Coop woke me one morning to tell me we were about to be joined by the rest of his company. The next day they arrived, and the company commander, a captain, caught sight of me. "Who are you?" he asked.

"Lieutenant Hickam," I said.

"Why are you here?"

"Battalion sent me."

"Are you assigned to my company?"

"I honestly don't know," I confessed.

"I'd better call Major Looter," he said.

"Let me do that, sir," I said, knowing full well any word to Major Looter was going to set him off in directions that I probably wasn't going to like. Fortunately, with the need to get his equipment and men arranged, the captain shrugged and off I went to consider what to do.

Coop sought me out while I was busy with a tank we'd just brought in with the M88. It wouldn't start, so I had its engine lid off and was contemplating it without a single clue what to do. Coop took one look and said, "It's burned up, sir. Can't be fixed. We'll have to swap its engine out. Probably its transmission, too." He went on. "I talked to Tommy about you, and he said Charlie Company out at the Oasis has an empty lieutenant's slot you can fill."

"Tommy?"

"Spec Four Matterhorn."

When I just stood there, Coop added, "If you go back to Headquarters, somebody there will grab you. You'll be pushing papers and never leave base camp."

"Where's the Oasis?"

"West of Camp Enari. Past the tea plantation. Go to the airfield, tell them where you want to go, and get the hell out of here." He hesitated. "That's my advice, Lieutenant."

Good advice is hard to come by and I thought Coop was giving me some very good advice, so I took him up on it, packed my grungy clothes in my duffel, pulled on my flak vest, plopped on my helmet, picked up my M16 and its bandoleers of ammo, and slipped out of camp. Whether the company commander ever missed me I don't know, but I doubt it.

It took an overnight huddled in the thrown-together shack beside the Dak To airfield that passed as the passenger terminal, but I at last hooked a ride on a Slick heading out to the Oasis with a quick stop at Camp Enari. When we landed in the shadow of Dragon Mountain, I didn't get off the helicopter lest I be spotted, and I rode out to the firebase hard by the Cambodian border with six bags of mail and some other supplies dumped on top of me.

The chopper pilots put us down near a large sandbagged field fortification I would learn was the Brigade Tactical Operations Center, or BTOC. Some men, ignoring me completely, grabbed the mailbags and disappeared within the dusty camp of sand-bagged tents. I picked up my pathetic kit and started looking for Charlie Company. I found them on the far west perimeter where some sweaty men without shirts or helmets were working on a tank engine. When I asked them where their commander was, they pointed to a small tent. "Who's commanding?" I asked them.

"Captain Orsenico" came the reply.

Before I reached the captain's tent, I was hailed from behind and turned to meet a friendly-faced bespectacled young man in an olive drab T-shirt and filthy pants unbloused at the boots. He stuck out his hand. "Nick Jarrett," he said. "I'm the XO. We've been expecting you. Do you have your orders?"

I shook Nick's hand and gave him a quick rundown of all that I'd been up to since arrival in the highlands. He looked puzzled. "Don't think you're who we were expecting, but I'm sure they'll get it all sorted out at Battalion. I need a supply officer." He gestured toward two vans with an improvised wooden shack between them. "It's a mess. We don't know what we have or what we need. Could you take a crack at it?"

"Sure," I said.

This easy response obviously pleased Nick, and he led me to the captain's tent. "Huey," he called. "We got us a supply officer."

There was stirring within the tent and then the flap was thrown back and a man emerged who had the face and squint of an unhappy eagle. "This our louie?" he demanded.

"I don't think so," Nick answered.

"Specialist Matterhorn at Battalion sent me here," I volunteered.

"That rascal?" Orsenico was amused. "Name?"

"Lieutenant Hickam, sir. Sonny Hickam."

"Sonny?"

"Yes, sir."

"What's your real name?"

"Homer."

He frowned. "I ain't gonna call you Sonny like some kid. You're Homer from now on. I'm Huey unless in front of the boys. Now, to cases. If you can get the supply shed in good order, I'll be forever grateful."

"Yes, sir, that's fine," I replied. "But I don't want to stay a supply officer. I like the repair work."

He studied me. "Let's see what you do with supply. Then we'll talk."

Nick steered me to a small tent that was built on a plywood platform. A sandbag revetment was built around it except for the entry. "We get mortared now and again," Nick said. "Usually, they aim at the BTOC. I roll out of the bunk and hit the floor when I hear the first boom. About all that can be done."

There was a steel cot with a thin mattress on one side of the tent and another on the other side. "Pick the side you want. If that other louie gets here, he'll go in with you if that suits."

It suited me just fine. The tent interior looked like a five-star hotel compared to what I'd lived in up at Dak To. Gratefully, I placed my duffel and rifle and ammunition and flak vest on the bunk that had actual sheets and an olive drab cover.

"That all you have?" Nick asked. "If you need more fatigues, let me know and I'll call Head and Head and get them sent out. How about a camouflage cover? They make great extra blankets. It gets cold out here at night."

And so it happened that I began my temporary duties as supply officer for Charlie Company, 704th Maintenance Battalion, Fourth Infantry Division, II Corps, Central Highlands area, in the Republic of Vietnam, a small country fighting for its life against its big brother to the north. Toward that end, South Vietnam had about a half-million American troops to help out, including me, even though, it appeared, I was still somewhat if not entirely unofficial. It was about then I started to wonder how or if I would get paid. After all, back in Utah, I still had a Porsche to pay for.

The Oasis

One day, Nick came into the dusty confines of the makeshift supply shack. "Huey's got something for you," he said.

The captain's tent contained a single bunk and a field table and two chairs. We found him there pondering a mimeographed legal-sized document. He looked up when Nick and I entered. "Homer," he said, "I have news for you."

He handed over the document, which appeared to be official and it was. Spec Four Matterhorn had obviously been busy. It was orders that assigned me to C Company as a Mechanical Maintenance Officer. Naturally, I checked to see if my name was spelled correctly—Hickam so often misspelled—but it was correct. Hickam, Jr. Homer H. 1LT.

"It's good to be official," I said.

Huey said, "Look again."

I looked again and this time the 1LT popped out. "I've been promoted!"

"So it seems," Huey said and stuck out his hand, and then Nick offered his. I was now First Lieutenant Homer H. Hickam Jr. with all the rank and privileges that position implied in the United States Army, thanks probably to Spec Four Tommy Matterhorn. "Get back to work," Huey said and, with my new exalted silver bar at least indicated on that scrap of paper, I turned to.

Life for me on the Oasis was fine. As the supply officer, I was at least useful. Actually, there was no way I could make the situation worse than it was. The shelves and bins and crates that held the parts for everything from tanks to field radios was a complete mess. Mechanics and other repairmen spent hour upon wasted hour sorting through the piles of parts until they found what they were looking for while making even more of a mess in the process. A Spec Four Alvarez was given to me to help, and we began sorting through it all by separating the parts into major categories such as M48A3 tank, M113A1 armored personnel carrier, M88 recovery vehicle, M151A1 jeep, deuce-and-a-half truck, five-ton truck, field radios of various types, and so forth. To keep the repair crews from swiping parts while we were sorting them, I had Alvarez bring his cot into the shack and sleep there. When he was on guard duty on the perimeter, I dragged in a sleeping bag and bedded down on flattened cardboard boxes for the night.

While Alvarez and I accomplished our tedious duties, which included setting up an inventory and issuing system, the sounds and sensations of the war rarely stopped. Gunships and Slicks pounded the air, and occasionally a dust-off named *Stringbean* came whirling in from the boonies with wounded soldiers. When that happened, our mechanics dropped what they were doing and manned the stretchers. When I could, I also carried the litters. An artillery unit equipped with 105 mm and 155 mm howitzers was on the other side of our area and blasted out fire missions all day and into the night, which shook the supply shack, sometimes causing the shelves to collapse. Eventually, I strengthened them with what I decided was abandoned lumber stacked neatly beside the BTOC. As I recall, it was around midnight when I made that decision and nobody was looking.

Every evening, Charlie Company occupied four of the bunkers set along a perimeter of concertina wire that surrounded the firebase. I took it upon myself every few days to pull a watch with the enlisted guys, each four hours long. The first time I showed up, I realized our men had set up their claymore mines wrong, mainly by not inserting the detonator or hooking up the wires to the charger. It turned out they were afraid of the deadly little things, which were curved plates on little legs with one side inscribed FRONT TOWARD ENEMY. Inside them was a layer of C-4 plastique explosive and steel ball bearings. No one had ever shown our mechanics how to detonate them, so they had simply and probably wisely decided to leave them alone. To take that fear away, I demonstrated to each set of guards how to properly test the charger without blowing themselves up, insert the detonator, and then place the mine far enough away so it wouldn't blow back on them and also not blow a hole in the concertina wire of the perimeter, which would give the enemy a nice little hole to surge through. War is complicated.

Eventually, the lieutenant whom I had been mistaken for arrived, a first lieutenant who had actually been trained as a mechanical maintenance officer, a Cornell graduate, and a great guy named Frank Stepanik. Frank and Nick became a solid team and kept the brigade's wheeled and tracked vehicles operational. Frank also bunked with me, and I found him intelligent, competent, and cheerful, always a good combination. We had lots of interesting conversations about not only the peculiar war we were participating in but also life in general.

As supply officer, I was also able to go anywhere I chose on quick trips to Camp Enari, always staying out of sight of Battalion, of course, and pretty soon managed to come up with multiple boxes of C-rations for snacks plus a block of C-4 that, if detonated, would have destroyed everything within a quarter mile but I used for cooking. Frank was a bit dubious of this, but I fashioned a little stove from some filter covers, sliced off C-4 slivers as fuel, and heated up our spaghetti and meatballs or whatever can of C-rats we had, and, before long, he accepted my technique.

One night, while we were eating our plastique-heated snacks washed down by water in tin cups, a bullet whipped through our tent from the direction of the perimeter. It was the first of a half dozen. While the dust fell on top of us from the zinging rounds tearing through the tent canvas, we heard a nearby bunker open up for a mad minute and then everything settled down. While Frank and I contemplated the holes in our tent and wondered how to fix them to keep out the rain, he also wondered aloud what would have happened if the bullets had hit my block of C-4. "C-4 won't explode without a detonator," I told him and then explained that it was a stable chemical compound called a secondary explosive and therefore difficult to detonate. To cause it to explode, I went on in my authoritative fashion, a primary explosive was required, the kind found in a detonator also known as a blasting cap. Frank pondered my explanation and then wondered how I knew about that kind of thing, so I got to go through my Rocket Boys story and then the Skipper cannon at VPI and then blowing up the face in the Logan coal mine and then what I'd learned about explosives in advanced training at Fort Leonard Wood and OCS at Fort Belvoir.

All this Frank thought was interesting experience for a fellow who hadn't, after all, gone to Cornell. "I trust you not to blow us up," he concluded, a trust, perhaps somewhat misplaced, that explains why we got along so well.

Nick Jarrett, Frank, and I became close friends. Nick had grown up on a farm in Mexico and knew how to take nearly any machine apart and put it back together again. We also had a warrant officer named Willy Williams who was a Marine grunt during the Korean War. His team was responsible for all the electronic gear used in the brigade as well as looking after all the small arms. Willy had access to any weapon anybody might want and before long I had managed to gain an M79 grenade launcher, which looked like a small one-tube shotgun but shot a 40 mm grenade. I also picked up an M2 carbine, and a .38-caliber six-shot revolver. I also acquired a pet from the artillery unit, a banana cat I named BC. It was a raccoon-like animal of some type with a fluffy ringed tail that I dearly loved. BC ate bananas and canned pineapple and any other kind of fruit I could get. He slept with me, curled up in my armpit or on my pillow, and never showed the slightest inclination to leave even though he was free to go. Frank, to his credit, never complained even when BC left little brown gifts on his bunk.

Charlie Company also had two dogs, Smokey and Shortround, yellow dogs with curly tails, who loved us but disliked the Vietnamese and anyone over the rank of captain. Eventually, the mechanized unit beside us begged for Smokey because they needed a reliable pet, and Huey decided to let him go. Sadly, we would later learn Shortround's brother was killed along with the crew who took care of him when the APC he was riding on was ambushed. Shortround stayed on to become our beloved guard dog. To my surprise, he liked BC. Sometimes, I would return to my tent to find them, dog and banana cat, curled up on my bunk. Somehow, I came up with some flea powder and dusted my blanket from time to time. Fleas were a small price to pay for the friendship of Shorty and BC.

By mid-December I had the supply shack inventoried and a system for ordering and issuing parts. That was when Captain Orsenico came inside the supply shack to look around. Before he left, he hemmed and hawed a bit before saying, "You want to go to Blackhawk Firebase? They've asked for a direct support team. It's out by the Mang Yang. I can give you Flynn, McCormick, Phillips, and Loomis. You'll be supporting the Second of the First Cavalry Regiment. They're called the Blackhawks. They guard Highway 19 from Pleiku to the top of the pass, which means they wear out a lot of engines and transmissions. They've got some good mechanics but they can't change out the big stuff. I'll give you an M88, too. How about it?"

That was the longest speech I'd ever heard out of our usually taciturn company commander, but it was both welcome and un-welcome news since I'd kind of settled in at the Oasis, liked my fellow officers Nick and Frank and Willy and Huey, too, liked the men I worked with, and, of course, had BC to worry about. Still, I agreed to go and, as part of my decision-making process, asked a medic next door who often came over and fed BC if he would take him. The delight of the corpsman was evident, and so it was that I gave BC up and packed my pathetic duffel bag once again with my pathetic belongings and made up a little crate to hold all my weapons and my block of C-4 and a few boxes of C-rats and prepared to leave. The four mechanics in my team packed their tools and personal gear aboard the M88 while I went to Huey with a request. "Can I have a jeep?"

"If I had one to give you, but I don't."

"There's one behind the supply shack that I've never seen move."

"It belongs to Battalion. When Major Looter comes out here, he likes to drive it around."

"When's the last time he came out here?"

Huey pondered my question. "Been a while."

"Come on, Captain."

"Do you even know how to drive a jeep?"

"It's not that complicated. Hand over the keys."

"It doesn't have keys."

He sat there looking at me, and after a few moments I got the drift, thanked him, said I'd let him know how things were going at Blackhawk, left his tent, tossed my duffel bag and my crate of small arms in back of what was officially a Truck, Utility, Four by Four, M151A1, checked the oil, checked the radio in back, and studied the ignition until I figured out how to start the blame thing, which consisted of flipping a switch, pulling out the choke, and then pressing a starter button on the floor. After it roared to life, I checked the gas and started to pull out but was stopped by a wall of mechanics headed up by a fellow I knew as Sergeant Hadley.

"Sir, where you going with that jeep?" Sergeant Hadley demanded.

"Blackhawk Firebase," I said.

Hadley signaled me to remain where I was, and he and a couple of mechanics soon returned with a stack of sandbags. After taking my stuff out, they packed eight sandbags into the back of the jeep and then put my gear on top of them. "These

M151s'll flip on you if you don't have a lot of weight in the rear," Sergeant Hadley explained.

Adding those sandbags was Sergeant Hadley's way of telling me he and the guys liked me. There wasn't much to say except thank you, which I said and then drove out of the Oasis to dodge between barreling convoy trucks and roaring rumbling tanks and APCs. When I finally burst free of the dust they threw up, I rolled past the tea plantation, where workers in the fields with their conical straw hats were toiling away, and thence past Dragon Mountain and Camp Enari and across the potholed streets of the city of Pleiku. After spotting a truck that had 2/1 Cav on its bumper, I followed it to Blackhawk Firebase along Highway 19 East, where I would soon encounter more death and destruction along with a threat of court-martial and maybe even a firing squad.

Blackhawk Firebase

Blackhawk Firebase was situated where it was to protect a portion of Highway 19 between An Khe, the home of the First Cavalry Division, and Pleiku. The highway was important because it started over on the coast at Qui Nhon, a port city and an American logistical center. It was vital to keep the road open. Between Pleiku and An Khe was a fabled pass called the Mang Yang that was the site of a major battle in 1954 between French forces and the Viet Minh, the precursor to the NVA. It occurred after the battle known as Dien Bien Phu that many historians mark as the end of the First Indochina War, but it was the running battle along the Mang Yang that truly broke the French. A fully equipped regiment known as Mobile Group 100 was trying to get to Pleiku across the pass when the Viet Minh fell upon them. Before it was over five days later, nearly fifteen hundred Frenchmen and auxiliaries lay dead along Highway 19. In his book *Street Without Joy*, Bernard Fall dedicated a chapter to the battle that finally persuaded the French to give up in Southeast

Asia. Although the title of his book referred to another road near Saigon, there was little joy to be had by the French on Highway 19, nor, for that matter, by we Americans. Every mile of it was ambush city.

Blackhawk Firebase was much smaller than the Oasis and tidier, too. The Blackhawks were a tough, disciplined outfit, and their commander let me know right off I was expected to be just as tough and disciplined even though, theoretically, I didn't belong to him. His name was Lieutenant Colonel Joe Gay and when I met him, he was winding up his year in Vietnam after bringing his unit over from the States. Upon hearing of my arrival, Colonel Gay called me in, told me to get myself squared away, and handed me over to one of his lieutenants, who took me to the western perimeter, paced off where I was to set up, and walked away. My mechanics looked at me with expressions that begged the question on what to do next. I didn't really know except to unload the M88 and then see if the Cav would feed us and also look for some temporary shelter. Flynn and the others turned to unloading their gear while I walked into the interior of the firebase, found the mess tent, and let the cooks know they'd have a few extra mouths to feed. They shrugged. "Send 'em on, sir."

"Can I eat here, too?" I asked.

"No, sir. Officers gots their own mess."

The Cav officers' mess was in a neat little hootch, and I went inside its screen door, looked around at its clean interior with real tables and real chairs and real stoves and real cooks and the smell of real food, and asked the mess sergeant if he minded me eating there. He said there was a monthly charge, so I paid up. On the way back, I spotted the Cav's maintenance tent, went over and introduced myself to a master sergeant who was in charge, and asked him if my boys could sleep in his tent while we pulled together our own shelter. I was met with indifference. We could sleep anywhere we liked.

I chose the M88 to sleep in and the next day, stiff from a night on steel plates, called into Battalion and requested two tank and two APC engines and transmissions to build up our inventory. As it turned out, Captain Orsenico had already thought of that and, before long, some 704th trucks showed up and we soon had engines and transmissions in shipping containers on the ground. After walking to the Cav maintenance tent and letting the NCO there know that we were more or less open for business, I sought out the supply people and asked how to get sandbags and lumber and some pierced steel planking and concrete since I had in mind to build a house bunker. The friendly sergeant explained how it might be done but it required me to go to Camp Enari, where I still was afraid I might yet be caught by Major Looter or some other officer in the 704th Maintenance who'd want to put me behind a desk. With no choice if I was to build the shelter I had in mind, I drove to Enari and sneaked around until I found where construction materials were stored. It turned out I could get everything I wanted if I got a request from Battalion, which meant, no matter what, I was going to have to take a chance of being captured. After waiting outside his office until I saw Major Looter leave, I sneaked in, found Spec Four Matterhorn, and told him what I needed.

"You're a sly dog, sir," he admired. "But sure, I'll fill out the request and sign it for the major." Within a couple of minutes, he handed over the form and I darted from building to tent to hootch to stay hidden until I reached the fenced-off area with lumber and concrete and everything I needed. The soldier at a little guard shack took the form and told me to come back tomorrow with a truck big enough to carry it all.

To get a truck meant calling Captain Orsenico on the long line, which was always an exercise in frustration. I always imagined the switchboard in Camp Enari consisted of one bored troop with two lines to be plugged in that he enjoyed pulling out the moment I was about to say why I'd called whoever it was. Once connected, you had to keep saying the magic words "working, working" if there was the slightest pause in the conversation or he'd pull the plug. Anyway, I got my truck and sneaked in to Enari to make sure it got loaded.

My boys and I jumped right on it and within a week, we had our house bunker built. It was a most amazing home and safe, too, since I built it like a timber trestle bridge on a concrete pad. Around the top we placed screens to keep out the bugs but allow in air and light, and we built up sandbag revetments eight feet high around it except where I put in front and back doors. The roof was made of high-grade steel planks meant for runways and covered with several layers of sandbags. Inside were two rooms, one at the entry for my desk and my bunk and a larger one in the back for everybody else. Specialist Loomis procured from somewhere a 5 kw generator and hooked up electric lights inside. When the Cav officers came over for a look, they couldn't believe how fancy we were. We also built a shower with a black rubber water bag that the sun kept hot, a two-seater toilet with sawn-off oil drums to catch the offal, which we burned with diesel fuel, everybody taking a turn, including me, and a pee tube. While making ourselves comfortable, we also rolled up our sleeves and got to work. Just as at Dak To, I worked as a mechanic when Flynn needed an extra one.

Before long, Captain Orsenico sent over a van with a shop and an electronics specialist to look after the Cav radios. Whenever we needed anything special, I'd jump in my jeep and drive over to Pleiku Air Base, Camp Holloway, or Camp Enari and scrounge. After a while, a newly assigned mechanic named Leslie "Red" Arthur became my driver and we became professional scroungers.

One day, after we'd scrounged up a stack of deuce-and-a-half clutch plates that were still usable from the can yard at the air base, Red was driving us back to Blackhawk when we encountered a convoy of trucks coming from the east and presumably heading for Enari. Rising above us on the right was a slick green hill, its forest pushed back by specially equipped bulldozers called Rome plows. On the left was a series of farms and rice paddies with their earthy smells. As we approached one of the last curves before breaking into the open of the valley that contained Blackhawk Firebase, we heard the unmistakable crackle of a light machine gun and then a tremendous thunder. Red braked and there we sat at the curve while wondering what was happening on the other side. A boil of smoke rose above the hill, followed by more machine gun rattles and more explosive thumps. We were next startled to see a man dressed in ragged shorts and a T-shirt come running out of the woods and down the grassy slope onto the road. He was carrying a rocket launcher I recognized as a B40 RPG. He didn't pay any attention to us but ran around the curve and then we heard another explosion and saw more boils of smoke and fire rose. That was when Red turned the jeep around, put the pedal to the metal, and we raced away, stopping after a couple of miles. To our astonishment, a jeep suddenly appeared from the direction of Pleiku. When I tried to wave them down, they ignored me and kept going.

We sat there for about an hour watching rising columns of smoke and listening to the thumps of explosions and the rattling and crackling of assault rifles and machine guns. Oddly, no phalanx of gunships passed overhead, only one Slick that orbited for a while before wandering off. When everything settled down, Red asked, "You think it's safe?"

Although tempted to wait another hour or maybe a day, I told Red to go ahead. We drove up to the curve and eased around it to behold an astonishing sight. The best way I know to describe what we saw is to reconstruct it according to a couple of Blackhawk lieutenants who, over coffee in their mess, were more than glad to fill me in on the action. It turned out the convoy Red and I saw was the main part without its tail, which had been slowed by a shaky old French-built concrete one-lane bridge. When a big platform truck carrying a load of rebar and other construction materials approached the crumbling bridge, its driver was afraid to cross it. A Cav guard post was situated there, and the NCO tank commander went under the bridge with the driver to make sure it was sound. By the time the driver was convinced to cross the bridge, the tail of the convoy was completely separated from the main part. Without the support of the armored-up escort trucks, it was on its own.

The tail passed Blackhawk Firebase without incident and then rumbled onto the road that led through the hills and farms and rice paddies that eventually led to Pleiku. When they reached a straight stretch, the lead driver was probably astonished to see a man in civilian shorts, shirt, and rubber sandals suddenly erupt from a ditch and aim a B40 rocket at him. It flew straight and true and the truck exploded, its wreckage blocking the road. From the bush high on the hill and the ditch line below, about a hundred men descended on the hapless convoy and began to blast the trucks while their drivers dived out of their cabs and tried to get away. Several were shot in the back while they ran. Before abandoning his truck, one of the drivers managed to get a call out to Blackhawk Firebase and, very quickly, a reaction force of M48A3 tanks equipped with 90 mm high-explosive rounds and fifty-caliber machine guns and M113A1 armored personnel carriers also with fifty-caliber machine guns rushed to the rescue.

What was later identified as Viet Cong—guerrilla fighters and not main force NVA—stood and fought bravely but never had a chance. They were simply massacred by all the heavy ordnance the Blackhawks unloaded on them. It was that sight that Red and I saw after rounding the curve, a huge mass of burning trucks and smoking wreckage and dead bodies and pieces of bodies and the Cav troopers securing the site in the meticulous, careful way they did everything. As I would later learn, the jeep we'd seen heading toward the ambush held a Transportation Corps lieutenant who was in charge of the convoy. When he realized he'd lost the tail, he'd rushed back to find it. Almost as soon as he made the turn into the ambush area, he had died, the victim of a mortar round.

The Blackhawks cordoned off the road, and Red and I had no choice but to turn around and try to find us a place to stay the night. We ended up at Camp Enari, put up by the Headquarters and Headquarters boys who knew enough to keep us secret from the head shed. When I sneaked down to the PX to buy a magazine or three, I ran across Rick Terrell, the lieutenant who'd taught me how to call in artillery on the flight over, which now seemed like a thousand years ago. "Used what I taught you?" he asked.

"Not yet" was my answer, but I was still glad I knew how. Rick told me he'd gone back to the States to accompany the body of a forward observer friend of his who'd been killed. Even though I'd only been gone less than four months, I asked him what it was like back in the States.

"I don't know," he confessed. "I just spent the time trying to do something for the family. They weren't proud, Sonny. They were bitter."

It wasn't much of a secret for us in Vietnam that we were not getting much support from the people back home. For that matter, Congress and the White House had more or less abandoned us. FTA—Fuck the Army—was appearing now on helmet covers or spray-painted on outhouses and hootches. There were reports of black and white troops in the base camps forming gangs and clashing over turf. Stabbings and suicides happened nearly every day. Moms and dads receiving their sons in coffins were no longer proud Gold Star parents. They were like Rick was saying, bitter and angry that while the politicians sat around and talked and talked, their sons were being murdered. And yet the war ground on.

When we returned to Blackhawk the next day, there was almost no evidence of the ambush except for a few burnt tires and some wreckage in the water of the rice paddy. A lieutenant I met in the officers' mess when I walked over for coffee and food turned out to be John Abrams, son of General Creighton Abrams, then deputy to General William Westmoreland who was head of the entire American show in Vietnam. A West Pointer, John wasn't entirely certain about the dirty, oil-stained Ordnance lieutenant that I was, but we struck up an uncertain friendship that mostly consisted of him complaining that I didn't fix his tanks and APCs fast enough and me snarking back that if his troops took better care of them, I wouldn't have to fix them at all. Anyway, I always knew I would get the straight skinny from him, and one of the things he told me was that we were going to get hit really hard in the next few months and the Cav might even need our lowly M88 to go on the attack. The way he told this to me, with such seriousness, I wasn't actually certain if he was pulling my leg, but I gave it some thought and told Specialist Flynn to do what he could to try to load up on fifty-caliber ammunition for our VTR. I also took him and the other mechanics and my radio guy out on the Blackhawk firing range to let them practice with their M16s and me with my M79 grenade launcher.

Lieutenant Abrams wasn't the only Blackhawk troop leader that got down on me for being slow to replace their engines and transmissions, so I thought about it and wondered what my dad would do. Putting myself into his head was always a good idea, as I could take a step back and assume his toughness and clarity of thought. What he would do, I decided, was to let the Cav know we weren't their punching bag. Accordingly, without asking anybody's permission in my chain of command or theirs, I formed teams and started to inspect their vehicles and give the troop commanders the results.

At first, nobody in the Cav liked these inspections, but then I started to get back reports that, afraid I might flunk them, the officers and crews were starting to pay more attention to looking after their machines. I was even called into his office by Colonel Gay and thanked and told that the percentage of his tanks ready for combat had increased considerably since I had started my inspection campaign. "Keep up the good work, Lieutenant," he said. "I'm going to let Major Looter know what you've done, too." Although I wasn't so certain that was a good idea, there was nothing I could do about it. However, like anything in the army, no matter how good a job you do, somebody will figure out a way to take advantage of it, the old "no good deed goes unpunished" wisdom honed to its ultimate by the US military.

It was the week after Christmas when I worked my way to the guard post that looked over the crumbling old bridge that had caused the doomed tail to get separated from the main convoy. To my surprise, I was met with enthusiasm by the master sergeant in charge of a Patton tank and two APCs sitting behind sandbag revetments. He even admonished his men whenever we found something that wasn't quite right on their machines. As I handed over my inspection slip to him with the advisement I'd also be giving a copy of it to his commander, he suddenly cupped his ear with his hand and said, "Did you hear that, Lieutenant? Specialist," he demanded of a trooper atop a tank, "what do you see down by the bridge?"

"Damn, Sarge. They're down there. I see 'em! They must be gonna blow the bridge!"

"Shit, Lieutenant," the master sergeant said, "we got NVA under the bridge. They're gonna blow it! What should we do, sir? You're the ranking officer here, sir. What should we do?"

Instantly, I knew what was happening. They were having their fun with me. After all, I was not in this sergeant's chain of command, not even close. Playing along to see what would happen, I said, "Whatever you think we should do, Sergeant, you should do." I might have even chuckled.

"Yes, sir!" the master sergeant said with a big grin and waved at the tank crew, who, to my shock, proceeded to fire three high-explosive 90 mm rounds into the bridge, which promptly collapsed into a pile of ancient French concrete rubble. A boil of smoke rose from it.

"They're on the run, Sarge!" the specialist on the turret of the tank reported while I stood openmouthed at what had just been done.

The master sergeant whipped out a salute. "I got to say, sir, it was a pleasure to serve under you, sir."

Numbly, I drove the jeep back while my inspection team of one, Spec Four Dale Loomis from Chicago, chewed over what he had just seen. Finally, he said, "You're in a world of hurt, ain't you, LT?"

"Yes, Dale," I replied sullenly, "I think I surely am."

Nothing happened until the next morning when the electrician in our electronics repair shop, which had a long-line telephone, woke me up. "Sir, got a call from Major Looter. You're to get your butt to Battalion right now, sir."

"Did he say why?"

"He said something about a firing squad."

That was enough information for me to know what it was about. Red drove me to Camp Enari, where I presented myself after a friendly wave from Tommy Matterhorn, who I noticed by the single stripe on his shoulder was no longer a Spec Four but had been demoted.

Major Looter was, shall we say, in a state. He declared me an enemy of everything good and fine in the world, a traitor to my country, a pathetic excuse for humanity, and, worst of all, an embarrassment to him and the Battalion. "Do you realize, Lieutenant Hickam, that the bridge you destroyed has been a target of the Viet Minh, the Viet Cong, and the entire fucking North Vietnamese Army for two decades and you—*you*, you bastard son of a bitch—knocked it down for them?"

Several responses occurred to me, mostly excuses and maybe an attempt to put the blame on the Blackhawk master sergeant, but I decided to just stay silent. After all, I'd done what he was accusing me of doing, and there was really no way around it. I didn't even say I was sorry.

After Major Looter wound down, he chewed on a stub of a cigar and said, "What should I do with you, Lieutenant?"

To this I was happy to respond. "Let me go back to work, sir?"

"You'd like that, wouldn't you?" He rapped his knuckles on his desk. "Naw, got to hide you away for a while. Where were you before you went out to the Blackhawks?"

"The Oasis."

He frowned. "Are you in Charlie Company? How in the hell did you get in Charlie Company?" When I chose not to answer, he shook his head, "Damn that Matterhorn. Get back out to the Oasis. Tell Orsenico to keep you there until I decide what to do with you. Keep in mind I haven't ruled out a court-martial or a firing squad."

Neither a court-martial nor a firing squad scared me more than having to stay on Camp Enari, so I saluted and took my leave. On the way out, I stopped to see Private First Class Matterhorn. "What happened?" I asked while pointing at his stripes.

"Got the clap at Sin City after Major Looter ordered me not to go there anymore," he said. "But better than committing treason, sir." He said the last with a smile.

"Guess we'd best clean up our acts," I said.

His smile was gathered up in a shrug. "I didn't really get demoted, just sewed on these stripes so Major Looter would think I was. But I did get a Purple Heart for the clap. Along with a pile of requisitions, the major signed the orders yesterday."

"You're too good for this army, Matterhorn," I said, and the boy, chuckling, chose not to argue.

Tet '68

Although I expected to get yelled at since I was the great bridge destroyer of the Mang Yang Pass who had incidentally embarrassed everybody in our entire battalion and surely reflected poorly on Charlie Company, Captain Orsenico instead greeted me back at the Oasis with something that approached wry amusement. He'd crossed swords with Major Looter numerous times for one thing or another and was glad that he could pretend to be on Looter's side for once. He'd also heard from an officer with the Cav who confided what I'd done was actually a good thing even though I didn't know what I was doing while I was doing it. He'd also learned the master sergeant who had perpetrated the scam on me was already back in the States, that it had been his last week in-country, and that he was ready to swear he really had seen NVA at the base of the bridge. The other Cav guys at the bridge were willing to swear the same thing and so any investigation as to what had really happened was quietly dropped. Or at least blamed on somebody nobody cared about—me. It had also occurred to me that the purpose for the bridge destruction was so a better one might be built in its stead. If that was the case, then I was happy to take the blame, especially if it was going to keep me in the field.

Still, to make sure Huey knew how sorry I was about the entire thing and that I was aware of how foolish I'd been, I assured him that I was never going to blow up another bridge in Vietnam. He thought that was a good thing and sent me back to the supply shed. Nick was glad to see me and so were Frank and Willy. Sergeant Hadley swung by to let me know he was glad I'd hitched a ride out to the firebase and left Major Looter's jeep at Blackhawk so Looter couldn't have it. The mechanics and other repairmen in Charlie Company one by one swung by to say hello and welcome me back. None of them indicated they knew I had returned in disgrace, although I'm sure it was common knowledge. The corpsman who owned BC came by and worried I might want him back but, after visiting him and seeing him fat and happy with the medics, I decided to let him stay where he was, although I enjoyed holding him for a little while.

With Shortround often joining us, Frank and I once more returned to our routine of snacks in our tent after our sixteen-hour days were done. As it turned out, I had been getting my mail at the Oasis and nobody had bothered to send it on, so I had a nice stack of letters from my mom and some also from the nurse at Dugway who was taking care of Gato. Mom said everything was fine in Coalwood except the coal mine was still on fire and putting it out was all Dad thought about and sometimes he had trouble breathing and Jim was doing great at his high school football coaching job in Virginia and she was going to Myrtle Beach every chance she got and Tiki was fine but his brother Tech had been run over just like my beloved calico cat Daisy

Mae was when I'd been a Rocket Boy and in almost the same place in front of our house.

The nurse wrote several long, chatty letters and said Gato was being a good cat but she was sure he missed me and it was going to be hard to give him up when I came home but please try not to get myself killed by doing anything stupid. There was also a stack of *Welch Daily News* and *Bluefield Daily Telegraph* newspapers that Mom had subscribed to for me. Nobody else wrote, which didn't entirely surprise me since I hadn't let much of anybody know where I was.

After reading my mail, I wrote Mom back and also the Dugway nurse, leaving out most everything that had happened since I'd arrived except I was fine and there was nothing to worry about. Poor Tech's demise bothered me most of all, and I spent a page recalling him to Mom and how much I loved him and I hoped they might keep Tiki inside more as that road in front of the house was just too tempting for our cats to cross because of the rabbits that played on the other side. After I wrote that, I discovered I was crying about poor Tech. Wiping my tears away lest anybody see me, I washed my underwear on a little washboard I had somehow acquired, hung them up to dry on the tent ropes, and went back to work while trying very hard not to think about anything other than the supply inventory and our requisitions until I couldn't stand it anymore and went over to the medics to hold BC for a little while but was surprised to find somebody else in his owner's tent. The medic had been transferred to the 71st Evacuation Hospital, I was told, and took his banana cat with him.

Somewhere along the line, it dawned on us that we were approaching the Vietnamese holiday called Tet. For the Vietnamese people, Tet was like Christmas, New Year's Day, Thanksgiving,

Valentine's Day, and the Fourth of July all wrapped up in one package. The day's festivities included giving gifts and lots of visits with the family and neighbors and also a little ancestor worship thrown in while celebrating the Lunar New Year and the beginning of spring even though for we North Americans it was closer to Groundhog Day in the winter. That year, 1968, Tet was on February 1, and if I recalled Lieutenant Abrams's warning that something big was coming at us, I don't remember being especially worried, perhaps because we received information that our generals had agreed on a truce with the North Vietnamese. Nothing was going to happen, we were told, and we should all relax and enjoy a couple of days off everywhere throughout the country, so we did.

Frank and I were lounging on our bunks the night of January 31 when a terrific din erupted outside. We emerged to see tracers streaking straight up toward the starry sky. Huey came out of his tent and told us it was probably just the South Vietnamese Army garrison in the ville near the Oasis shooting off their guns to celebrate Tet. This seemed reasonable and, before long, everything got quiet and Frank and I returned to our bunks.

It was approaching dawn when we heard more machine gun fire. With small arms fire thrown in and an explosion, this sounded serious so I swung out from under the camouflage cover I used for a blanket and quickly pulled on my fatigues, socks, and boots. Frank did the same and we grabbed our flak vests, plopped on our helmets, took up our rifles, and emerged to see our men, some sleepily rubbing their eyes, coming out from their two big tents and staggering into formation where they stood, looking confused. Off toward the ville we heard strange music like drums and the clanging of cymbals and singing. Captain Orsenico quickly apprised his mechanics of the situation. "We're being attacked, boys; that's all I know. Get into your combat gear." He also ordered our NCOs to choose a dozen or so of the ninety men we had to go on down to the bunker line and join the guards there. The remainder he'd keep in reserve until he had further orders.

Big explosions suddenly erupted from the direction of the ville, and the music abruptly stopped. Later we would learn that about a dozen Viet Cong with drums and cymbals and other noisemakers had marched at sunup down through the ville while singing patriotic songs followed by throngs of VC troops who were, in turn, followed by smartly marching uniformed North Vietnamese Army soldiers carrying flags of their country. Very quickly, the South Vietnamese unit in the ville were all killed and then anybody suspected of favoring or working for the Americans was hauled out of their homes and murdered.

While our men scrambled for their rifles and helmets and flak vests, I walked down to the perimeter. Our side of the Oasis faced a shallow valley that was covered with deep grass and bushes that served as excellent concealment. As I studied it, a bullet whizzed past me and I crouched down to study the situation further. On the side of the Oasis that faced the ville, there came the unmistakable crack of detonating claymore mines. I went from bunker to bunker and made sure our claymores were armed. When the men Huey had formed into a reaction team appeared, I told them to get on top of the bunkers and lie down and keep watch on the bushes. If anybody came out of them, they were to fire off a few shots but not go into a mad minute or activate the claymores until the enemy got close enough to be hit. We had some ammunition but weren't really prepared for a long firefight. We needed to conserve.

After running back to our area, I asked Huey if he minded if I climbed up on a CONEX container and kept watch on our rear. He agreed and I grabbed a spec four and we got up there. It gave me an excellent view of the entire firebase, which revealed, to my astonishment, that we were essentially empty of defenders. The mechanized infantry unit usually living there had been moved around mid-January along with the artillery unit. We were a firebase almost exclusively manned by mechanics, repairmen, clerks, cooks, and whatever colonels and other field-grade officers that were in the BTOC.

All morning and into the afternoon, there was confusion around the perimeter with the enemy choosing not to storm the wire but maneuver around it. What were they waiting for? Every so often they threw a squad of men at the wire, only to be beaten off. It occurred to me that they weren't certain what to do with us, that they had accomplished what they meant to do and that was to wipe out the South Vietnamese in the ville. Then we heard the whistle of jet aircraft overhead, and a flight of what I recognized as F-100 Super Sabre jets began to drop bombs and napalm in the valley on our side of the firebase. Then a Patton tank emerged from somewhere and made its way to our side of the perimeter, stopped, and leveled its tube and began to blast into the valley. This went on for about an hour until darkness descended. Although occasional small arms fire or the rattle of one of our machine guns could be heard, the battle, such as it was, seemed to be over.

Radio reports were coming in from all over. Pleiku and Hue and Da Nang and other provincial capitals were being attacked. Saigon, the capital city of the country, was being assaulted with the American Embassy and the presidential palace as the primary targets. Rockets and mortar fire were being directed at the big Tan Son Nhut Air Base, and troops everywhere were on the move. The next day came and went and nothing happened around the Oasis except we kept being reinforced by more armored vehicles and a few tracked vehicles called Dusters with twin 40 mm guns. It was clear somebody higher up thought we were going to receive a major assault. With our valley side the most likely approach, I asked Huey to let me construct a new bunker that could handle at least a dozen troops and have clear fields of fire. He gave me permission and I soon had it built, a long, low bunker that used scrounged aluminum culvert halves as firing stations that I capped with steel planks I found in bundles by the airfield. I also added several layers of sandbags and then asked for volunteers to go outside the wire. I got several and we placed trip wires that would activate flares and let us know if anyone was headed our way.

Three days later, while we continued to be reinforced, Huey called me to his tent. "The Cav's headed up to Kontum," he said. "The North Vietnamese have tanks up there and they're gonna go get 'em. They called and asked you to come back."

This was interesting. They wanted the disgraced bridge buster back? "Who was it that called?" I asked.

"I don't know and I don't care. Get your butt out there as fast as you can."

To get to Blackhawk Firebase meant, during the midst of what was clearly a countrywide major enemy offensive, traveling from the Oasis past Camp Enari and through Pleiku and thence along the always dangerous Highway 19. Since the Dusters had just arrived from that general direction, I went down to talk to them to get their advice. It consisted of "don't even think about it."

159

Once more, I tossed everything into my duffel bag and made my way to the BTOC, where there was a helicopter landing pad. None of the Slicks and gunships that landed there looked promising since they seemed to be overrun with colonels, major, and generals but when a little two-man helicopter landed, I ran out and asked the pilot if he'd mind taking me out to Blackhawk. It was a helicopter officially known as the Hughes OH-6 Cayuse but popularly called the "Loach." The Loach driver looked me over and, after delivering the packet of orders he'd brought with him, beckoned me to climb into the copilot's seat and off we flew.

As we climbed, I looked over the ville beside the Oasis. The concrete Arvin compound was smoking rubble, and about half the houses and shops were missing their roofs and some were still on fire. I didn't see any people at all. Along the dirt road that passed through the tea plantation were a number of burnt-out civilian trucks but otherwise no traffic. The pilot skirted around Dragon Mountain and followed the road until we got to Pleiku, which had several rising towers of smoke on the western side of town. There were people dead and dying out there, not only in Pleiku but all over the country.

A deep sense of helplessness swept over me for reasons I couldn't define and I wondered, not for the first time, about what I was doing in this place and why any of us were there. Even though everybody was being brave, and heroic deeds were being done, why were we at war in this country? I got all the politics of it, the domino theory that if South Vietnam fell to Communism, a political system that meant tyranny and the probable murder of millions of people, then all of Asia would fall beneath its awful control. But wasn't there some better way without all this pain and death in the grinding maw of combat where armies clashed and innocent people, caught between them, suffered? And why, rather than rolling up the enemy all the way to the border, were we instead spread all over the map, with most of our soldiers camping out in densely populated camps like Camp Enari or in exposed firebases like the Oasis? Most of our troops were never engaged in combat but shuffled papers and did other logistical stuff. Surely I didn't know enough, but something just didn't feel right about the entire plan to fight the war. For the first time, I began to get an inkling that maybe the people back in Washington, DC weren't as smart as they thought they were.

The pilot turned along 19 East. I didn't have any earphones so I didn't hear if he advised Blackhawk we were coming in but when we did, it was hot and hard. "Get out!" he yelled over the whine of the engines and the whopping of the blades and I yelled "Thank you!" at him and jumped out at almost the same moment he took off. Although there were some startled Cavalry troops watching me at the pad, I just waved at them and then, staying low with one hand on my helmet and the other carrying all my stuff with a rifle and a grenade launcher slung on my shoulders, ran to our house bunker and told the guys to saddle up.

Thunder Run to Kontum

We were told to get in the back of the convoy, that the Cav meant to make what they called a "thunder run" up to Kontum. Gladly, I accepted our place in the tail. The M88 recovery vehicle was armored and had a fifty-caliber machine gun on top, but it was really just a tricked-up slab-sided tow truck on tracks. If we were ambushed, I preferred the Cav armor take care of it. We also stole an S&P truck abandoned along the highway during Tet and loaded it up with engines and transmissions and other parts we'd need, plus our radio and electronics repair van. We painted over its bumper markings and hoped nobody would notice.

The Cav kept things moving until we got to Pleiku, where we bogged down at a military police checkpoint. Once that obstacle was resolved, we turned north on the highway and the Cav put it in high gear. This was a highlands road and was lined with both Montagnard and Vietnamese towns with plenty of bush alongside where the NVA or VC could hide. I sat up on top of the VTR behind the fifty caliber. Some of my crew chose to ride below, but it was so hot and noisy in there, they didn't last long and soon ended up with me where at least they could get some fresh air, not counting gas and diesel fumes from all the trucks and tracks ahead of us.

When the convoy suddenly stopped, I looked ahead and saw smoke rising, never a good sign. We listened to the Cav push but heard nothing that told us what was going on. After we sat for about fifteen minutes pretty much exposed to anyone coming at us from our flanks, I told my boys to sit tight, that I was going to walk ahead to see what was holding us up. I grabbed my M79 and trotted alongside the rumbling trucks and APCs until I reached a most remarkable sight. There on the side of the road was a Cav lieutenant with a pistol in his hand arguing with a major who wore the patch of another armored unit that had joined the rush to the north.

The crew of a Cav APC sat watching and so I asked them what in the world was happening. They told me the other armored unit had claimed to have received fire from the Vietnamese village a short way up the dirt road off to the right, and I realized the smoke I'd seen was a number of huts and buildings on fire. What I took at first for clothes on the ground on closer inspection proved to be bodies wearing civilian clothes. The non-Cavalry unit had turned into the village and proceeded to blast it and shoot anybody they could get in their sights.

"L-T's giving them hell about it, sir," the APC driver said. "Made them cease fire. Major there ordered his guys to keep shooting. That's when L-T pulled his pistol. Like something out of a cowboy movie."

As I watched, the tanks and APCs of the offending unit trundled out of the village and stopped. The major pointed toward us and some of the tanks swiveled their tubes in our general direction. "We may have to take them on," the APC driver said.

It was incredible that I was in a situation where American troops might turn their guns on each other but before that happened, the Cav lieutenant holstered his piece even while the major, his face cherry red, kept yelling. Unfazed, the Cav officer climbed up on their lead tank, slapped the gunner on the side of his helmet, and pointed north. When it was clear the tank crew had gotten the message to move out, the lieutenant got down, had a few more words with the major, and then came stalking back past us. After the miscreant unit turned up the road, the convoy finally started moving again. When the Cav tank trundled by with the lieutenant with the pistol, I looked up at him and nodded my approval. Looking back on it, I wish I had saluted him.

The thunder run turned into a crawl and, even though Kontum was only thirty miles from Pleiku, it was dark by the time we got there. The Cav sent a runner and told me to set up around some white concrete buildings that turned out to be old French Foreign Legion barracks, most with partial roofs, empty sockets for windows, and overrun with rats. My boys got out their shovels and started whacking the vermin that ran around chittering in panic, and it wasn't long before we had a little mound of rat corpses. "Bury them, boys," I said, "or the flies will carry us away." To demonstrate, I picked up an especially large rat, walked a little ways away, dug a hole in a patch of long grass, and dropped it in. It was part of my dad's leadership advice: never ask a man to do something you're not prepared to do yourself. We soon had a rat graveyard with little rocks painted white as tombstones.

For two months in Kontum, we kept the Cav on the road and in the field. The NVA mostly pulled back in our area while continuing to fight furiously all around the country, especially in a little place up north called Khe Sanh. When I had coffee with a Cav lieutenant, he told me they never found any enemy tanks. What they did find were bulldozers and road scrapers. Dozens of them. The North Vietnamese weren't building some paltry little road to bring in supplies and personnel. "They're building a damn superhighway!" he said and shook his head in both exasperation and no little admiration.

One night, while we were working under generator lights on some filthy mud-covered track or another, one of my mechanics turned on the radio and who should come on but our glorious president of the United States of America, Lyndon Baines Johnson. At the sound of his voice, boos from the Cav reverberated through the old barracks. LBJ blathered on until he reached the only important thing he would say: he wasn't going to run again. To that announcement came cheers.

Tired and dirty, I sat down for a minute on a rusty metal chair I'd found somewhere and, looking out over our rat graveyard, reflected on things and then came to a conclusion. It seems maybe like I even voiced it out loud. "Damn if they didn't beat us," I said of the North Vietnamese and Viet Cong. "Damn if they didn't."

Twin Events Still Hard
to Understand

After the Cav went back to Blackhawk, we went with them and set up shop again. A 175 mm Long Tom artillery outfit moved in beside us and every time they had a fire mission, their exploding thunder was like a million sonic splinters ripping through our bodies. We never got any warning. One second I'd be sitting at my desk and the next second I'd be quivering from the shock of those almighty bags of munitions exploding just a few yards away.

Other than being occasionally shattered and deafened by the Long Toms, those were good days. Everything had calmed down around us, the convoys were rolling in along the highway, none of them were being attacked, and as far as we could tell, the enemy was on the run. We hired two mamasans named Long and Hut from the neighboring ville to keep our house bunker clean and tidy and the laundry done. They were great girls and, even though they spoke little English and we less Vietnamese, treated us like they were long-suffering sisters who had to put up with dumb, dirty brothers. Hut was a funny sweetheart and loved to be teased and tease back. "You mop," one of the mechanics might say, meaning Hut was plump. She wasn't, of course, but they knew it got her mad. "You numbah ten!" she'd roar back.

This would start a back-and-forth. "You dinky-dow!" which sort of meant "You're crazy!"

"You numbah ten thou!" which meant you were awful, even worse than numbah ten.

Long was a lovely young woman with fine features and dark, luminous, expressive eyes. One of my boys said she was sweet on me, but I didn't know what to do with that information. One day, she came and sat down beside my desk and wanted to practice her English. "You marry?" she asked.

"No," I said. "You?"

This made her smile, a pretty smile. "No no. Numbah ten marry."

"Why?"

She batted her eyelashes. "Numbah ten marry Viet man."

"What's wrong with Viet man?" I asked.

"They butterfly." She made wings with her hands and mimicked a butterfly. "Go woman woman woman like flower flower flower."

It was the only real conversation I ever had with her, which I very much regret. At least I did my best to look after her and Hut. When I saw them climbing off a tightly packed deuce and a half that picked up the mamasans who worked on the firebase from the ville, I asked Red to take my jeep into town every morning and pick Long and Hut up and then take them back at night. He was glad to do it and had to fight with the other guys who wanted to do it, too. The word I got back was the other mamasans were very jealous and envious of our girls after that.

When we got time, I started up the inspections of the Cav's tracks and trucks again. This didn't make Lieutenant Abrams particularly happy, but he saw its value and didn't much complain. When I heard the Cav doctor was going on what was known as MEDCAPs—for Medical Civic Action Program—to the surrounding Montagnard villages, I signed on for a couple of trips. Montagnards were a native mountain people whose appearance was Polynesian. Dark-skinned and round-eyed, the Montagnards led lives that revolved around their families, tribes, and villages. It was said the Vietnamese disliked them and routinely harassed their villages or chased them off their land. It was also said they were fiercely loyal to the Americans, whom they saw, perhaps, as their protectors from the Vietnamese, both Southern and Northern.

The MEDCAPs consisted of rolling into villages and setting up a medical clinic and, if a dentist was available, a dental clinic, too. A long line of Yards would form, men, women, and children, and the Cav doc with his corpsmen would get to work on everything from broken bones to boils. The one time we had a dentist, I recall him marveling at how good their teeth were. "They don't have access to sugar," he concluded. Of course, the Cav guys protecting the MEDCAP would try to change that by giving out as much candy as they could to the kids.

On one MEDCAP, we were told a woman was having a baby and would the doctor like to observe? He did, and some of us followed him to see a naked woman hanging with both hands from a rope tied to the supporting beam of a native longhouse. Within a minute of our arrival, the baby plopped out, instantly carried away by a midwife. A basin was placed beneath the woman and out came the bloody afterbirth, which was also carried away. Our translator explained that the afterbirth was thought to be alive and was to be buried with many prayers said for it. The woman who'd just delivered let go of the rope and walked after her baby. Somebody said, "That didn't take long," and the doctor replied, "That's what wide hips will do for you. Our women have narrow hips and that's why having a baby is so painful." This was interesting information, although I've never used it for anything until now.

On one of our inspection trips, we saw a tired, dirty tank sitting high on the side of a hill that didn't look Cav to me and, sure enough, it belonged to another unit that had rolled in for a few days to guard a section of the road. Curious, I left my fellows to their inspections and drove up to have a look at it. After introducing myself to its somewhat seedy crew, I clambered around the vehicle. Other than needing to be washed off, it was actually in fairly good shape. After leaving a few notes with its crew, I started walking back to my jeep that I had parked about thirty yards down the road, and that, other than a strange whistle overhead that suddenly got louder, was the last thing I remembered of being on that hill.

What I remember next is that it seemed as if I was riding a roller coaster in and out of darkness. I was aware of being carried and then I was in a truck. That went on for a while. Then a light was shined in one eye and then the other and I recalled distinctly talking to someone, even carrying on a conversation although what about I couldn't say. When I came to fully, I found myself on a cot at what I recognized as the 71st Evacuation Hospital in Pleiku. Nurses and aides in jungle fatigues were walking by, and I smelled a strong disinfectant. For a moment as I lay there, I inspected myself mentally from head to toe and realized I mostly ached. I also realized other than the sheet covering me, I was naked. Pretty soon, an army nurse, a captain—I can still see her exactly as she was even though I only saw her once my entire life, short dark brown hair tucked beneath an army baseball cap with the black railroad tracks that denoted her rank, silver earring studs, brown eyes, long eyelashes, pixie nose, a corner of her pink lips turned up in a half-smile, and when I looked down, a gold wedding ring—swung by to see how I was doing. "Took a knock, did you?" she asked.

"What happened?"

"The bunch that brought you in yesterday said something exploded near you. They weren't sure what it was but thought maybe it was a short round. Artillery. Maybe South Vietnamese. You talked about it with Major Harriman. Doctor Harriman. Don't you remember?"

Yesterday? Although I did kind of remember talking to someone, I wasn't sure. My most salient thought was, at least for one fleeting moment, *I'm going home!* but she soon dashed that. "Major Harriman said you were good to go so we scrubbed you up, got out some splinters." She touched my forehead and I smelled her sweet, clean American womanly breath enhanced by Juicy Fruit gum. "Along your brow and some around your knee we couldn't get out without a lot of digging. They'll work themselves out over time. You feel good enough to sit up?"

I sat up, my sheet falling away. When I grabbed it, she smiled, her pixie nose wrinkling, and said with her Juicy Fruit breath, "Nothing I haven't already seen. Sit still. I'll get your things. We'll need you to sign a couple of things."

I was happy to sit still since my body hurt nearly everywhere. Before long, a spec four brought me my dirty, tattered fatigues and battered boots. No helmet or flak vest. After signing a form that I had no idea what it was and what it said, I dressed hurriedly right there with doctors and nurses and corpsmen walking by and then limped out of the hospital. There was a medevac chopper just landed, and corpsmen and nurses ran past me toward it. Once I got out on the road that led to the hospital, I started looking for a ride to Blackhawk. When nobody seemed to be going that way, I wandered into another building, a ward of some type, and asked the spec four at the front desk if he would call the Blackhawks and ask them to let my guys know where I was. After some obvious reluctance—as mentioned, calling anybody on the long-line telephone in Vietnam was a chore requiring patience and usually ladled with frustration—he did and a couple of hours later, Red showed up and helped me into the jeep that he'd retrieved from where I'd left it. My helmet and flak vest were in it. "Jeez, Lieutenant, what the hell happened to you?"

"I don't know, Red," I said and to this day, I'm still not sure, although splinters would work their way out of my body for the next fifty years. There was no Purple Heart. Probably Specialist Matterhorn would have given me one, but I didn't care enough to ask. After all, it wasn't the enemy who'd blown me up. At least, I don't think it was. I later heard there was an Arvin artillery unit practicing in the area who got their directions mixed up by 180 degrees, so it could have been them since there were other casualties reportedly caused by the errant shooters. The seedy tankers I was inspecting also had a man slightly wounded by the explosion that got me, so it was just one of those mysterious things that happened in a country loaded with weapons and explosives.

A few weeks later, Captain Orsenico called and told me he wanted me back at the Oasis, that it looked like the company was going to go somewhere else, and that since Nick and Willy were leaving soon and Frank was transferring to Camp Enari after putting in his six months in the field, he needed me back, this time to be in charge of the mechanics. It was assumed at this point that I had escaped the usual routine of six months in the field, six months in base camp. "Also," Huey added, "go to Finance and bring the pay when you come." This order, so casually tossed off, would nearly get me killed.

After saying goodbye to my team and also Long and Hut, both of whom cried and said I was a numbah one lieutenant, Red, who was transferring to the Oasis with me, drove us to Camp Enari but as soon as we got there, we were stopped by the MPs to look over the jeep's documentation. Since there wasn't any, they called Battalion and somebody there told them to secure the vehicle until further notice. We pretended to be chagrined about "losing" the jeep's paperwork and promised to head immediately to Battalion and get everything in order. The MPs thought that over and decided we weren't worth the trouble and waved us on. After Red delivered me to Finance, I told him to get himself and the jeep out to the Oasis any way he could without being caught. This he did, somehow, but that left me stranded after I picked up the pay slips and Military Payment Certificates, the funny money the American military used in Vietnam rather than real greenbacks.

There was about $10,000 in MPCs in the package handed over, which I carefully placed in an empty claymore mine pouch. At the airfield, I waited around until I caught a Slick headed out to the Oasis. I was the only passenger. There was also no door gunner, which I took as strange. The pilot called back over his shoulder that he had a brand-new, fresh in-country copilot and they would be "maneuvering" the chopper on the way out. What I'd caught was a test and checkout flight, so I shrugged and sat down with my duffel bag and rifle between my legs and the claymore pouch with the money hung over one shoulder.

The pilot chose the tea plantation to "maneuver" and we began to dip and climb and stop in midair and lurch to the left and then the right. On one of the climbs, I noticed it got kind of quiet but I didn't think anything much about it even as we slowly dropped out of the sky, rotating as we did. It was a massive shock when we struck the ground or, actually, a small, shallow lake. A torrent of water flushed me outside and I found myself floundering in the muddy water.

Disoriented, I tried to climb back onto the helicopter but I couldn't seem to get a purchase on it and kept slipping back. When I overcame the shock of the situation, I saw the pilot and copilot were already out and making their way across the tea plantation. When they turned around and saw me, they yelled something I couldn't hear and then kept going. I followed them until I remembered I'd forgotten my rifle and duffel bag.

Since it looked like the helicopter was thoroughly dead with no risk of fire, I searched around until I found my duffel floating near the tail and then when I looked under the bench seat, I saw my rifle, grabbed it, and, dripping mud, chased after the flight crew. When I caught up with them, they were standing beside an armored personnel carrier. The pilot was using the APC's radio to make a call. "We're going back to Enari," he said afterward and, numbly, I climbed into the back of the APC and sat down on one of the steel benches. It wasn't too long before it suddenly occurred to me that I didn't have the company pay. I yelled up at the driver, who stopped and let me out. My body was pretty well racked after being nearly blown up and now in a helicopter crash, but I ran as best I could back to the helicopter, which by then had gathered a gawking crowd of American soldiers and tea plantation workers. Without explanation, I handed my rifle and duffel to one of the enlisted men and, even though they yelled at me to stop, waded back to the chopper. After frantic but fruitless searching, I had to accept the claymore pouch was gone and with it $10,000 worth of MPCs, money I'd signed for.

After hitching a ride to Enari on a dump truck, I presented myself, still dripping mud, to Finance to tell them my sorry tale for which I received zero sympathy. A Finance major called me into his office. "We can't give you any more money, Lieutenant. About the best I can do is write up a report and see what happens. Honestly, you could end up paying for it."

"But it wasn't my fault. I was in a helicopter crash!"

"Look at it our way," the major said. "You signed for ten K of MPCs. Now you don't have it and you say you lost it and yet here you are."

The implication was if I had been killed, then maybe the loss of the money was understandable. But alive? Maybe not. Miserable and sore and filthy, I walked outside Finance and considered what to do. Finally, I trudged to Battalion to see Spec Four Matterhorn but was disappointed when I found a small, pimply faced, bespectacled spec four at his desk. "Tommy went home early, sir," the new admin clerk reported. "Somehow, he got orders, don't know how. Heard they had a parade for him in whatever little town he came from. Can I help you?"

Since he wasn't Spec Four Matterhorn he really couldn't, so there was little choice but to walk into the adjoining office and see Major Looter. When I reported, his expression was less than joyful and it didn't improve after I told him what had happened. He gave me a long stare and said, to my everlasting surprise, "You've done a good job for us, Hickam. Get out to the Oasis. I'll take care of it."

And somehow he did. I'll never know how but he did. The men were disappointed that they didn't get their MPCs to use at the Enari PX or Sin City, but most of them were at least sort of glad I hadn't been killed in the crash. A month later, the payment they'd missed was in their pay, and I never heard from Finance one way or the other. I didn't ask anybody about it. Sleeping dogs with sharp teeth are best left unprodded.

The Road to Ban Me Thuot

Captain Orsenico went home in August and Major Looter sent along another first lieutenant to take over the company. I'll call him Lieutenant Ted. Ted was a career officer and a nice fellow and had put up with Major Looter for a few months at Camp Enari, so he deserved the company even though some of the mechanics thought the command should have been mine. Personally, I didn't care; the position of executive officer I assumed was fine. Next up for the company was to move off the Oasis and, following the brigade, take up residence in the provincial capital called Ban Me Thuot, so how to do that was my main concern.

Ban Me Thuot was a storied old place. Bao Dai, the last emperor of Vietnam, kept a palace there and, at 7,500 feet of elevation, the air was nearly always crisp and cool. There was also tiger hunting nearby and Teddy Roosevelt, not the president but his son, stayed at the palace when on an expedition to hunt them. The French loved the area and planted huge farms of coffee, tea, rubber, and bananas. Some of the old French families were still there even in 1968. A Montagnard tribe known as the Rhade had lived there for centuries, but the war had brought in a lot of lowland Vietnamese. When they began to steal their land, the Rhade revolted but their ragtag forces were quickly crushed. When the Americans arrived, they took the Rhade on as allies and armed them, not to fight the South Vietnamese but the northerners. It was a complicated situation. Ban Me Thuot, threatened by the North Vietnamese Army that saw it as a soft target, was no longer a resort area but a combat zone.

We formed up our convoy just outside the Oasis. Ban Me Thuot was a hundred miles away, so we made sure we had plenty of gasoline and diesel. Although we were supposed to leave early in the morning, it was past noon when we finally got going and I sensed we were going to end up somewhere on the road in the dark, which was bound to be dangerous with NVA forces maneuvering in the area.

Before long, we reached a destroyed bridge. The only way to get across it was to descend down a steep bank and then up another steep slope to the road. This slowed everything down and when one of the trucks got stuck, it was up to me to get our M88 around the stalled convoy and pull it out. While we were worrying over that, the rest of the convoy kept going. When we got the truck out, it was too damaged to continue so its driver and shotgun hitched a ride in an MP jeep back to Camp Enari. This left the M88 crew and me and Red in our jeep all by our lonesome. I tried to call Lieutenant Ted but got no response so, with darkness rapidly approaching, I made a command decision and ordered the M88 to pull the broken-down truck back to a little artillery compound we had passed along the way. Red and I followed in the jeep. After it got dark, I had some C-rats and heated them up with the last of my C-4. Afterward, we tried to sleep in our vehicles, an almost impossible task since the mosquitoes did their best to eat us alive. We spent the night miserably hunkered down just inside the concertina wire.

As soon as there was any evidence of dawn, pink streaks on the horizon breaking through the monsoon clouds, I roused the M88 crew. When I spotted someone who looked familiar, I shouted out to him. It was my old friend Rick Terrell. He gave me the once-over. "You look like hell, Sonny," he said.

"Thanks," I answered. "How about yourself?"

His answer was casual. "Been shot a couple of times, the usual for an FO."

Although I started to tell him about being blown up and crashed in a helicopter and the thunder run up to Kontum, I decided to keep it to myself, as clearly he'd been through a lot. "Well, I hope you don't get shot anymore," I said.

Rick squinted as a thick, scarlet sun rose above the tree line, its hot light hitting him in the face. "Me, too," he said. "Startin' to think this place ain't worth dyin' for."

"Where you headed?"

He shrugged. "Back out there."

"You just said this place wasn't worth dying for."

He took off his helmet and wiped the sweat off his brow with the towel from around his neck. "Yeah, but the guys…us. I guess we're worth it." He plopped his helmet back on and frowned into the sun. "Don't you reckon?"

"Yes, Rick," I said with a catch in my throat. "I reckon."

After a handshake, Rick turned and walked away. I watched after him until he walked behind a ragged old bunker and tossed up a hope that he'd survive the war, after which I got busy figuring out what we were going to do to get ourselves down to

Ban Me Thuot. After consulting a map, I saw there was only one thing to do and that was to head there by ourselves and hope for the best.

After making sure all our weapons were clean and ready to rock and roll, Red and I took the lead and headed south with the M88 following. Before long, we caught up with a convoy of army trucks out of Camp Enari. Happily, it was supported by gun trucks covered with armored plate and armed with machine guns, including a couple with quad fifties. Every truck was individually tricked up according to the whims of their rough-and-ready crew, most of whom wore flak vests and no shirts. Although it was a couple of decades before the movie, they and their rides looked like something right out of *Mad Max*.

We didn't ask permission but just fell in with the convoy like we belonged. Nobody seemed to mind. The dirt road the convoy took passed through towns that were neat and clean and plaster white. The adults, dressed in their black pajamas or casual Western clothes, did their best to ignore us, but the kids seemed to be fascinated and came out on the road to wave and laugh. The drivers and gun truck troops tossed the essentially inedible tropical chocolate bars found in our C-rats to the children, who scrambled to pick them up. Any time we stopped, children emerged from seemingly nowhere to sell Coca-Colas or other soft drinks. They took the MPCs the guys had with no problem, which indicated somewhere in their chain of commerce was probably an American who was exchanging the military money for American dollars or Vietnamese dong. The good old black market always thrives during wars.

The towns reminded me in a way of Coalwood, also a small town filled with working people, and I wondered what we would have done if a roaring convoy of foreign military vehicles had passed through us. Somehow, I doubted our parents would have allowed us to go anywhere near it. On the other hand, these people had known nothing but war for years and maybe they'd come to terms with it in their own way. Mostly, I got the idea they didn't fear the Americans, although the experience during the thunder run to Kontum indicated to me that maybe that wasn't necessarily a good plan. After all, we were armed to the teeth and trained to lay down a lot of fire in a hurry. Our combat troops were often frustrated to have all that firepower and not be able to use it even while their buddies were being picked off by booby traps, snipers, ambushes, and sudden mortar and rocket attacks. For the most part the enemy was unseen but, in their stead, there were the Vietnamese civilians going about their lives. Or were they? Were they in fact enemy combatants, hidden in plain sight? It was that kind of war—they call it asymmetrical these days— that a big conventional army like ours wasn't designed to fight. It was also an army that could be worn down by stabs and jabs and carefully choosing the battlefield. We'd won a big victory during Tet, but it really didn't matter to an enemy who wasn't going anywhere and was willing to hang on while the resolve of the politicians who'd sent us there weakened day by day.

Our slow crawl down the road to Ban Me Thuot gave me time to think about a number of things. One of them was I was proud that I had learned how to be what the army apparently wanted me to be, a mechanical maintenance officer. Also, I was glad I had learned how to efficiently work my mechanics and other repairmen and also perhaps the most important part of an American army and that was how to get the paperwork done, how to use the bureaucracy when it suited me, and how to give it an end run when it didn't.

Besides all that, I had learned to use a variety of weapons. I had even somehow come up with a World War II M3 "Grease Gun" that was heavy as hell and could shoot with unerring inaccuracy a magazine of .45-caliber bullets. It was the worst weapon imaginable, but I kept it anyway. I could also put an M79 grenade right on target. In short, after eight months in-country, I was serious in my purpose, dedicated to keeping my men safe, was a bit of a tough nut to go after by either friend and foe, and knew my business.

When I reflected on it, I realized I felt so comfortable in my role that I began to think about extending my time in Vietnam. What, after all, did I have to go home to? I had Gato back in Dugway, but I guessed the nurse would keep him. I had the Porsche that was sitting in a garage somewhere in Salt Lake City, but I didn't much care anything about it, although it was still taking a big chunk of my monthly pay. I'd only occasionally heard from Mom, and her letters seemed a bit detached. She told me about going to Myrtle Beach but very little else. None of my classmates from Coalwood or Big Creek High School or Virginia Tech wrote, which wasn't surprising since I hadn't told any of them where I was. In a very real way, I had become untethered from my past with no sense of what the future could or even should hold. The boy who'd built rockets and the cadet who'd built the Skipper wasn't me. He had been replaced by someone I didn't know and was like a stranger I met every day. If I extended in Vietnam, I would stay where I was oddly most comfortable, a combat zone where nothing was normal except its abnormality, one that I had learned how to maneuver within. If I extended, I supposed that meant I would be making the US Army my career and why not? What else was I going to do with my life?

It would take most of the day but finally, we reached Ban Me Thuot. Just before we got there, gunships swept over us and made a run on a plantation of rubber trees. We didn't know why. We watched the tracers and rockets zipping out of the fast-moving helicopters, saw the rising smoke from the explosions, and just kept going. Somebody was dying out there. Who it was we would never know, and we knew we'd never know. It was simply none of our business.

We stopped along the road to ask for directions from an American MP, who sent us to an encampment close to the airfield. There, I found Lieutenant Ted, some new officers I hadn't yet met, and all our equipment set up in a circle around a field of mud. Our tents were up but there were no revetments around any of them. We had a new first sergeant just arrived in-country who, rather than stay at Battalion like the others, had for some reason been dispatched to the field. After talking to him, I got the idea he was going to do everything he could to get back to the relative safety of Camp Enari and after talking to the other NCOs, I knew they weren't too impressed and would just as soon he go back there.

Lieutenant Ted and the other officers were busily setting up our shop vans and trucks, so the first thing I did was to go after sandbags to fortify our camp. This did not prove easy. Finding nothing at Brigade, I had Red drive me all over Ban Me Thuot to poke into every military installation there to see what we could find. The first place that we had any luck was a Special Forces outfit on the outskirts of town set up beside a Montagnard village. The Green Berets had some sandbags, they said, but wanted to trade. "What we need," a corpsman assigned to them said, "is some way to light up our operating room when the generators don't work."

This was intriguing and I followed him into the camp, where there was what appeared to be an old hunting lodge where they had set up a kind of surgical ward. "Who gets operated on here?" I asked the corpsman while also wondering if this was where Teddy Roosevelt Jr. had stayed while hunting tigers.

"Ruff-puffs and sometimes our guys, too."

Ruff-puffs, which stood for Regional Popular Forces, were what the irregulars, mostly Montagnard warriors, were called. Since they were ineligible to officially receive American medical care, it appeared the Green Berets had built them a little unofficial clinic and surgery room using scrounged equipment. As to who did the surgery, I did not ask, but I suspected it wasn't anyone with a medical degree.

The lights in the surgery room were run off generators, which were a rusty mess, and it didn't surprise me they occasionally failed. "Made in France," the Green Beret corpsman told me. "And very old. We can't get parts for them. We just tinker with them until they run but they don't usually run long."

"Why don't you get some better ones from the army?" I asked.

"Because they'd probably ask us what they're for."

It occurred to me that if I could scrounge up some truck headlights, they could be wired to 24-volt batteries, which I might also scrounge, mainly by lifting them from our supply shed. After shuttling back to the mud hole that was Charlie Company and poking around until I stole what I needed, I went back to the Green Berets with headlights and batteries and some cabling and soon had lights dangling from wires over the surgical tables with a switch attached to turn them on during emergencies. Grateful for my poor but effective engineering, the Green Berets gave me two pallets of sandbags plus a bundle of steel engineering stakes that were helpful to support our revetments.

I called Lieutenant Ted and soon had a deuce and a half arrive to pick up the loot.

We followed the truck back, helped unload it, and, even though it was at the end of a long workday, I asked for volunteers to start filling sandbags. There was no good reason to go through another night without protection from mortars and rockets. When I was met with reluctance by our tired and dirty men, I simply got a shovel and started filling them myself. It didn't take long before I was joined by the men and the pile of sandbags started to rise. We worked long into the night and by morning had revetments around the tents for the troops and our shop vans. When the first sergeant came out with a mug of coffee in his hand and detailed four men to build a sandbag wall around his tent, I dismissed them and called him aside. "First Sergeant, you'll build your own revetment," I told him. "That's the way we do it in this company."

The man looked shocked. "I'm a first sergeant. I don't fill sandbags."

"If you want them around your tent, you do," I replied, which, if you ever wonder how to truly irritate your first sergeant, works every time.

It didn't take too long to hear from Lieutenant Ted that the first sergeant had complained first to him and then to Battalion. I gave the standard reply most of us long-timers in-country had learned to give. "What are they going to do? Send me to Vietnam?"

Lieutenant Ted laughed. He didn't really care. "It's good for that fat old fart to sweat a little," he concluded. The first sergeant managed to get a transfer to Saigon a few weeks later and we never heard from him again.

As it kept raining, the area our shops were circled around started to fill up with water until we were essentially arranged around a deep, muddy lake that was the only place we had to park the tired old trucks, tanks, and APCs brought to us for repairs. Every time we wanted to get them to work on, our M88 had to wade in and pull them out, which, because of the churning tracks, made our lake ever deeper. Stagnant bodies of water in the tropics tend to be unhealthy and it didn't take long before our men started to come down with dysentery and fevers. When I caught something, it made me feel like I had been run over by a locomotive. Knowing that the medical tent was overwhelmed, I asked Red to drive me over to the Special Forces camp, where I duly turned myself over to them. "Almost certainly malaria," the corpsman who I had traded with for sandbags announced. "You need to be medevac'd out."

"I don't have time," I told him while sweat soaked my jungle fatigues and ran off my forehead into my eyes and dripped off my nose. "What can you do?"

He shook his head. "I can cool you down with wet towels, maybe knock the fever back."

And so he did. It took three days of alternating wet towels and blankets and some kind of shots he gave me that I never asked what they were and I turned back up at Charlie Company. "Where you been?" Lieutenant Ted asked. "I started to call Battalion to see if you'd DEROSed when I wasn't looking."

DEROS stood for Date Eligible for Return from Overseas, and it was the date that most soldiers serving in Vietnam knew backward and forward. I was glad our company commander had not called anybody to find me. Actually, I think he knew where I was. Red probably told him, but Lieutenant Ted had a sense of humor.

"We've got to do something about this swamp," I told him.

"Then do it," Lieutenant Ted said and, taking that as permission to do whatever it took to dry the thing out, I worked up a somewhat nefarious plan.

When nosing around Ban Me Thuot, or BMT, as we tended to call it, I'd noticed a peculiar compound that had Americans in civvies hanging around outside plus some big earthmoving equipment and lots of CONEX containers stacked up all over as well as big black drums of something. There was also a sign over the doorway to the main building that said PACIFIC ARCHITECTS AND ENGINEERS. I went inside and found a fellow at a desk and explained my situation with the mud and disease my company was facing. The manager, a Mr. Hoyt, gave me a cold stare. "There's nothing here for you. We're a civilian outfit under contract."

"With who?"

"MACV."

MACV was Military Assistance Command, Vietnam, the big kahuna of all the organizations in Vietnam.

Mr. Hoyt went on to explain that PA&E had contracts to build roads, buildings, runways, and bridges throughout Vietnam. "I need a lake drained," I told him. "Could you add that to your list?"

"No."

"Well, do you have any pumps I could borrow? And peneprime?"

Peneprime was a liquidy tar used to cover and stabilize dirt road surfaces. I figured, with some ditching, it would help make the rain run off our mud parking area and maybe even kill the insects that had made themselves at home in the mess.

Mr. Hoyt considered my request. "What do you have to trade?"

"What do you need?"

"I could use a ring of tanks around this compound. I think one of these days the NVA are going to stroll in here and cut off all our heads."

"How about a couple M60 machine guns with ammunition? And a dozen claymore mines."

He laughed. "How about it?"

"I'll be right back," I said and, after a little time had passed, returned with the items I promised. Don't ask.

Mr. Hoyt admired the ordnance and called for a couple of his fellows. "Go drain this man's lake," he said, "And cover everywhere he tells you with peneprime."

Two days later, we were no longer set up around a muddy, disease-laden, filthy lake but around a tar-soaked meadow that, looking back on it, I recognize as an ecological disaster but at least wasn't making us sick and our vehicles could park on it without sinking up to their axles.

With this kind of success, which was kind of fun, I decided doing nefarious things in combat zones for good reasons in the United States Army was my true calling and therefore called Battalion, got hold of the new spec four who was running things there, and told him to extend me six more months in-country.

People Hanging Like
Clothes on the Wire

I didn't expect to be debriefed. I was just there to go through all the wickets needed to go home. At the S-2 office, I presented the sheet for the intelligence officer to sign. The spec four who sat at a desk in front told me to sit tight and went off somewhere. He didn't come back, but a captain did who beckoned me into his office.

The S-2 was housed in typical tropical army construction for Vietnam: wood with louvers in the sides, screened windows, and a plywood floor. The interior was filled with big gray metal desks and olive drab file cabinets. Mostly enlisted men sat at the desks with black typewriters positioned in front of them on which they languidly typed. There were a couple of sergeants E-6. The captain in a little cubbyhole in the back had a college diploma from a Midwest university hanging crookedly on the wall.

The captain was heavyset, baby faced, blond hair, clean uniform, shined boots, a base camp commando all the way, but that didn't mean he hadn't seen some action. Sometimes, junior officers in the combat arms went out and humped the hills and triple-canopied forests until they couldn't do it anymore or managed a transfer. This one, whatever his history was, which was none of my business, sat behind his desk and pawed out a manila folder from one of several metal trays. "Battalion said for me to debrief you on Ban Me Thuot and get your side."

It was news to me that I had a side.

"What made you call in the Cobras?" he asked.

Now I got it, or at least I thought I did. The attack through the concertina wire when I'd called up air support. The answer was easy. "We were about to get overrun."

He leafed through the forms in the folder. There were at least a dozen of them. I wasn't sure what kind they were, but I could see there were blocks on the tops that I presumed were for the usual name, rank, service number, date, the kind of information that headed most military personnel forms. I caught on that these were after-action report forms. He saw where I was looking. "I'm going to fill in one of these for you. You'll sign it."

"Am I in trouble?"

"I don't know. I was just told to debrief you."

"Does this mean I'm going to miss my DEROS?"

He blinked, my question taking him off guard. His answer was nearly sympathetic. "I'll get it typed up soon as we're finished and you can sign it and be out of here."

While I squirmed, he looked at the notes on a yellow legal pad. "How did you know how to call in the Cobras?"

It was easy to guess what he was getting at. A fellow like me, a noncombat arms officer, wouldn't necessarily know how to call in close air support. I had, however, a good answer, mainly because it was the truth so I provided it. "The sector we were responsible for was sort of a peninsula carved out by a creek. I could see us getting cut off there so I asked how to call for support from one of the Cobra guys and he told me."

"Do you recall who it was?"

"A maintenance sergeant over there. I think his name was Davids, Davidson, something like that."

"Were you expecting trouble?"

"I thought there was a good chance of it."

"Why would you think that?"

"The 173rd set up shop on the other end of the airfield. I was afraid the NVA would think we were them. It wouldn't be hard to mix us up. We were all dirty."

I was referring to the 173rd Airborne Brigade, a unit that had the reputation of being an NVA magnet. Wherever they went, it seemed the NVA went out of their way to engage them. I went on to tell the rest of my story, how a few days before the night in question, I had gone with our M88 crew to retrieve an M48A3 tank broken down in the boonies. According to its crew who had abandoned it, it had a burned-up engine. It took a while to find it since it was about two miles deep on the other side of a big rubber plantation. It made me wonder why an armored unit was out there in the first place. That particular outfit mostly guarded the convoy roads, not often barging through the countryside where they might be easily ambushed. It occurred to me after we got there that what I'd done was pretty dumb. Instead of rushing to the site, I should have asked for the tank's unit to send some support with me but, no, I'd just charged off and put us in danger.

When we got to it, I saw the tank was up to the top of its tracks in mud, which explained why it had a burned-out engine. It also made me doubt we could complete our mission. To pull a tank out of all that sticky red viscous goop would probably require two VTRs.

Still, we were there and maybe my assessment was wrong so I told the guys to hook up the tank. We were just about ready to see if we could pull it out when a young man stepped from the trees. I noticed him right off, mainly because he was carrying a rifle, and also because he was soon joined by a dozen other young men, similarly equipped. They were mostly wearing uniforms of dark green shirts and pants. My first thought (and forlorn hope) was these were ruff-puffs, but very quickly I had to accept what we had here was most likely main force NVA. This explained why the armor was out in those woods in the first place. They were looking for these fellows and now I had found them.

Nothing happened for the next few eternities (which were probably seconds), but then the Vietnamese simply melted back into the forest.

"Let's get out of here!" my VTR driver cried and I concurred. We unhooked the tank, jumped on the M88, and spun tracks with me on the fifty, swiveling it back and forth in case I heard that *flitttt* sound of passing rounds. The driver took a shortcut and about thirty tons of roaring armored vehicle threw itself up on the road on the outskirts of BMT like a crazed armored water buffalo while scattering Lambro motorized tricycles, motor scooters, mamasans, bicyclers, beer vendors, chickens, and pigs in every direction. We did not stop until we got back to Charlie Company.

Later on, the armored unit that it belonged to would go out and retrieve their tank with a couple of their own VTRs reinforced by three tanks and two armored personnel carriers with troops. They reported the tank untouched and one of the lieutenants came by and suggested to Lieutenant Ted that I had bugged out. When confronted by this, I calmly pointed out that when he'd gone out there, it was in force.

The S-2 captain took my story down, considerably abbreviated. "Did you tell anybody about what you saw?"

I had indeed. Within an hour back on base, I'd reported to the intelligence guys at Brigade what I'd seen and watched while they duly noted it and promised to be on the lookout, and then I went back to work. A couple of nights later, as I had feared, our little teardrop portion of the perimeter was violently attacked. At the call from men in the bunkers on our sector, I threw on my flak vest, grabbed my M79 grenade launcher, and ran down to the perimeter. Flares were being tossed up, tracers were flying, claymore mines were being detonated, and everybody was having a mad minute of shooting. I flung myself atop a bunker and started punching grenades out into the darkness. I couldn't see anything except flashes of light coming from the bush in front of us as enemy triggers were pulled.

It was a long night. Every time we'd stop firing, whoever was out there would start up again, bullets whiffing by or punching into the sandbags covering our field forts. Then we heard the rustle of clothing that people can't help but make when they're trying to be sneaky. We decided they were very close and probably intending to cut the concertina wire. That's when I used the knowledge I had of the call sign and frequency needed to call in close air support, meaning Cobra helicopters, and the topic the intelligence captain was so curious about. It turned out the Cobra drivers were apparently itching to get into the fight because within minutes of my call, there they came. They swept in, rockets spewing. It was crazy. One chopper zoomed right down our line of bunkers no higher than a few feet over our heads and cut loose with its rockets. Earth and steel crackled through the air.

After the choppers left, I called for a sitrep from my guys in the bunker. Their ears were ringing and one of them reported that his arm was bleeding but not too bad and he wasn't sure what had caused it. I scrambled over to have a look. It just looked like a scrape, but I put some salve on it and he said he was fine. After that, things quieted down. I began to think we were going to make it to sunrise without any more attacks, but then we heard somebody messing around in the wire again. I unlimbered my grenade launcher, punched out a round in the direction of the sound, it exploded and then nothing was heard again. When the sun finally came up, we began to see what looked like dirty laundry thrown on the concertina.

But it wasn't clothes. It was people.

"How many?" the captain asked, his pen poised.

I mentally unscrolled the scene in my head. "About eight or ten, I think."

One of the forms was consulted. "We got a hundred reported from Brigade. Counting blood trails."

"Eight or ten is what I saw," I said and he wrote it down. Or I think he did. He might have put down a hundred to match the other report.

And then, for some reason, I was moved to tell him there was something else in the wire, too. Where my last grenade had landed, I found a baby deer, its eyes fly-filled clots and blood dripping from its nose and mouth. I had killed it.

I went on to tell the captain that this had caused me to cry. And not just cry but sob, my dirty face with rivulets of tears that cut down my cheeks through the mud and sweat. Worse, even though I tried to get hold of myself, I couldn't stop. Turning my head away so nobody could see, I walked quickly into the firebase, got into my jeep, and drove into Ban Me Thuot, pretty much hiding from everybody for the rest of the day. I parked at a shot-up gas station and watched the Vietnamese people walk by, hating that they were caught up in this war. And then I started to think, really think, about who I was and what I wanted to be. The next day, I called Battalion and told the spec four to cancel my extension.

I realized I'd been blubbering about my blubbering over the little deer to the captain. "Wait here," he said.

I waited. I don't know how long it took but it felt like hours. It was shameful, my crying. My dad would not have cried. Looking back on it, I never saw a single man in Coalwood cry even after somebody they dearly loved died in the mine. They were stoic, you might say, or maybe they were just hard men. Me crying like a little baby to a fellow who was just trying to write down what happened in a report that would probably be filed and never seen again was a terrible thing for a West Virginia coal camp boy to do. When he came back, he slid a form across his desk. "Read, sign, and date," he said without a hint of emotion.

I didn't read but I did sign and date. He handed me a clearance form that he had already signed and dated, which was essentially my ticket home. After hooking a ride on a Chinook to Cam Ranh Bay, I climbed aboard a passenger jet, a gold Braniff, and sat down where they told me to sit down and flew to McChord Air Force Base and then was bused to Fort Lewis, Washington, there to process out and move on wherever life took me next. The flight was nothing like the boisterous flight over. The men inside sat quietly, spent. For my part, I looked down on the clouds over the Pacific Ocean and, for some reason, started thinking about writing. I wanted to write. But what about? Maybe, I thought, Vietnam. I could write about what happened there, what I'd seen, what I'd felt. But it would need to be fiction. That was the best way to tell it. Like *From Here to Eternity*, something like that.

The next day, as I walked through the airport in uniform, a young woman in tie-dye and bell bottoms spotted me, hissed something, and gave me the finger while applying the F word in my direction. I didn't care. My whole life was in front of me and what I did with it was up to me. She was on her own.

PART

3

The Purposeful Adventurer

Puerto Rico

If you'd asked me how I was doing during the decade after I came back from Vietnam, I would have wondered why you were asking and would've probably said, "Well, I'm doing fine," which would have been a total lie even though I didn't know it. Looking back now, I realize I was actually completely and totally messed up and there's not much else I can add to that except it's so.

My next duty station was Redstone Arsenal, Alabama. Gato and I headed to the South and Huntsville, the fabled Rocket City that was, in the flickering, dying flames of the Apollo program, suffering a severe economic recession. Engineers by the hundreds were out of work, so there was zero chance of me being hired to work in the space business, not that I was particularly inclined to do so. Building those rockets back in West Virginia seemed ancient history to me now, and I was decidedly no longer the boy who'd done it. In fact, I wasn't exactly sure who I was or what my purpose in life should be. Before long, the army promoted me to captain and sent me along to Fort Buchanan, Puerto Rico. Gato went into the belly of a jet and off we went to that storied island.

Once there, I found a cheerful, sun-washed apartment in Rio Piedras and bought a little VW Beetle that I drove into work every day. My work wasn't difficult. Essentially, I ran a motor pool and a garage and sometimes advised reserve units on the weekend when I was needed, which wasn't that often. Since the road in front of my apartment was busy, Gato could only go outside with me as a chaperone and so I taught him to walk on a leash. He usually did OK on it until he got tired or irritated about it and then would flop down. After that, I would take him for a "drag" rather than a walk, and he loved being pulled along on the rough sidewalk on his side for a few feet while flipping and flopping and purring.

Several houses away was what I gradually deduced was a high-class whorehouse with big, shiny limos parked in front of it day and night and some astonishingly beautiful women lounging on the porch fanning themselves. After a while, they took note of me and Gato. Although they didn't care anything about me—a poor soldier—they loved Gato and would often come down and sweep him up and carry him around cooing to him like he was their child. Once, amazingly enough, one of the women gave me twenty dollars, which I took as a rental fee for Gato, but I gave it back. Maybe she just felt sorry for this silly man who walked his cat, I don't know.

Sometimes, my duties led me over to the navy base at Roosevelt Roads, and there I got to know a couple of ensigns in the engineering department who were scuba divers. They kept insisting that they teach me to dive, and I finally gave in and joined them one Saturday in a Zodiac, which is essentially a rubber raft with an outboard motor, and allowed them to take me outside of the reef into deep water. Along the way, I realized two things: they were drunk, and there was exactly one set of scuba gear.

The two officers, whom I will call Rosie and Roads, stopped the Zodiac and one of them threw out an anchor. The line seemed to take a very long time to play out, but I only halfway noticed since I was studying the strange gear and wondering what it all did. Roads, who was from Mississippi, gave the explanation. "All right, Homer," he said, "this here is the tank." He patted it, his Academy ring making a clanking sound. "Gots air in it, compressed air."

"The oxygen tank?" I asked.

Rosie, who was from some Yankee state, laughed and I could smell the rum fumes on his breath even in the fair breeze blowing across the ridiculous little boat. "It isn't oxygen, dummy, it's air." He waved his hand and looked toward the sky. "Air!"

Roads gave Rosie a short glance and went on with his training, such as it was. "Now, this here's the regulator," he said. "You put it in your mouth and you just breathe." He took a draw off it and then handed it over to me. I wiped off the mouthpiece and breathed in. It worked. I followed the hose from it to another device clamped to the tank valve. "That's part of the regulator," Roads said without further explanation.

"This here's the weight belt," Rosie said and picked up, with a grunt, a strap that was curled through a bunch of gray metal things that turned out to be weights made of lead.

He handed me the belt, which felt like it weighed at least twenty pounds, and, under their direction, I strapped it around my waist and then let them strap the tank on me and put the regulator in my mouth. "If you get in trouble, drop the weight belt," Roads said.

"And never hold your breath," Rosie added. "It'll kill you if you do."

"Why will it kill me?" I wondered.

Rosie and Roads looked at each other. Finally, Roads said, "It just will."

After Rosie spit in it, they had me put on a mask and then pull on some rubber fins.

"Ready?" Roads asked.

Before I could answer, Rosie said, "Over you go," and rolled me right off the Zodiac.

I hit the water hard but kept the regulator in my mouth and started breathing, but no matter how hard I breathed, I couldn't catch my breath. I looked for the anchor line and swam toward it, but the weight belt dragged me down and I missed grabbing it by inches. One of my fins came off while I tried to kick my way back to the surface and when I looked down to watch it fall away, I couldn't see the bottom but just a never-ending blue turning to purple. Then some kind of fish swam by and, with amazement, I watched it while I sank. It was probably a tuna. When I hit the sand, it was with some surprise. Since I still wasn't getting enough air and, remembering Roads's advice on what to do if I got into trouble, I tugged on my weight belt to take it off. It took a few fumbles but I finally got the buckle unlatched and it fell away. Kicking with my one fin, I headed to the surface while blowing out bubbles because I remembered that I wasn't supposed to hold my breath. Along the way up, I saw the silvery fish again, which looked back at me with some curiosity before swimming off. I supposed it had never seen anything quite like me before.

When I broke through the surface, it was so fast that I almost came up to my waist before subsiding. After looking around, I saw the Zodiac and struggled over to it where my two friends were laid back against its pontoons, apparently dozing. After calling for their help without response, I took off my tank and regulator, which got away from me and sank and then, while I struggled to get back into the raft, I also lost my remaining fin and my mask, which also sank. Finally, with great effort, I flopped into the bottom of the boat, which caused Rosie and Roads to blink awake and stare at me. Finally, Roads asked, "How did it go?"

"I saw a fish," I reported and decided right then and there I was going to be the best scuba diver anybody ever saw.

Aquaspace

After a year in Puerto Rico, it was decision time. Should I stay in the army or try civilian life again? Weighing against staying was the fact that the army was still in Vietnam and I suspected it wouldn't be too long before I would be sent back there. This was at a time when the federal government was tearing itself apart with daily battles between Congress and President Nixon about the war, and most Vietnam vets were being called baby killers and generally scorned.

By then our forces were awash with drugs and from what I could tell, our soldiers didn't trust their officers and our officers didn't trust their men. Anybody with half a brain at that point had to know Vietnam was not going to turn out well. After bouncing it around in my head and flipping a coin or two, I decided it was time to leave active duty but, since I had so much experience in the military and the country was in an economic recession, I hedged a little, applied to be a Department of the Army Civilian (DAC), and was accepted.

As it turned out, not because of any decision of my own but where I apparently was needed, I went back to Huntsville and took a job with the Army Missile Command on Redstone Arsenal. Since I had a knowledge of the computer language FORTRAN, I was tasked to program an IBM 1620 computer and produce a spreadsheet that tracked how maintenance and repair was accomplished on Redstone-managed facilities and missile programs. Many hours were spent writing code and punching the commands on cards with a keypunch and running the programs again and again until I worked out the bugs. This was in the early 1970s, so I was on the cutting edge of a computer revolution, although I didn't see it that way. The 1620 was just a tool I happened to know how to use.

At home, I read a lot and got to thinking about writing again. This led me to join a local writers club that met once a week in a meeting room in the back of a bank. It was exactly what I needed, and I loved the camaraderie of the group and the help they gave me as I struggled to write my stories. Gato was my biggest and only fan since I usually read my stuff to him before going off to the bank. When I came home after work, he was always there at the door waiting for me. We were pals.

Even though my work was satisfying and I enjoyed the writers club, I still felt as if I needed something else in my life, some great challenge. When I saw a handwritten note on a bulletin board at work, I was instantly interested. "Learn to Scuba Dive," it said. "Become an underwater explorer. Call Aquaspace." At the bottom of the note was a local number and, remembering my promise to myself after my diving experience in Puerto Rico, I called right away. The woman who answered the phone said they had a class starting next week and I should come down and sign up. The shop proved to be a tiny plywood hut with a tin roof in an otherwise vacant lot, but it was there my passion for the sport of scuba diving and the sea came alive.

Aquaspace was owned and operated by a couple named Cliff and Bobbie McClure, childhood sweethearts who were working hard to make a living with a dive shop several hundred miles from the nearest seashore. Huntsville, however, had thrown off its post-Apollo blues and was growing with a lot of young people who had disposable incomes. Bobbie was a clear thinker and a careful businesswoman. Cliff was a natural-born leader, dynamic, charismatic, and enthusiastic. Before Huntsville and Aquaspace, he'd been an air force fighter pilot and a pre-astronaut in a program called Manhigh.

Manhigh required its pilots to strap into a tiny aluminum gondola beneath a huge helium-filled balloon and soar aloft into the stratosphere. It was an important precursor to NASA's Mercury program that would put the first Americans in space. After two other Manhigh pilots successfully reached the edge of space, Cliff's turn came in October 1958 and it almost turned into a disaster. After a successful launch and a flight to nearly one hundred thousand feet, the gondola's cooling system failed and Cliff's internal body temperature rose to an astonishing 108 degrees. Concerned for his life, the project managers ordered him to descend, but a stuck valve caused the dumping of helium to be much slower than normal. Communications was also sparse and then stopped altogether as the balloon very slowly came down with its overheated passenger.

When the gondola finally landed in a cornfield, there was fear that only a corpse would be found inside but when the hatch was opened, the ground crew found Cliff wearing a big grin. He assured everybody he was fine and climbed out of the gondola on his own power. The doctors who examined him were amazed there were apparently no ill effects even though he'd spent hours with a body temperature that should have killed him. Such stress on the human body can be subtle, however, and perhaps that was why Cliff would suffer from occasional bouts of deep depression for the rest of his life.

After Cliff separated from the air force, he and Bobbie moved to Huntsville where the space program was going great guns with the Wernher von Braun team at Marshall Space Flight Center. Cliff found a job as an engineer with a NASA contractor, and the couple settled down and had two sons and a daughter before Cliff got restless. After meeting some people in the new, growing industry of scuba dive training, he decided to quit his job and open Aquaspace. Bobbie took over the management side and Cliff became the instructor. In 1973, he would teach me to scuba dive, and I could not have possibly had a better instructor.

Intrigued and enamored by the sport, I got serious about it, enough that two years after being certified, I went to an instructor's school in San Diego, got my Open Water Instructor's certification, and started teaching for Aquaspace. Kismet being what it is, I earned my OWI rating on April 30, 1975, the day South Vietnam fell to the NVA.

At their shop, Bobbie taught me the business side of the dive industry and Cliff became kind of an older brother, although one who was a bit unpredictable. He had super highs and super lows and when he wore a certain worried expression, I learned to leave him alone. Eventually, I would go my own way as an independent instructor, but I was always grateful for everything Cliff taught me. He's gone now, a stroke taking him in 2000, but I think of him often and am grateful that I knew him.

Even with my new passion for diving, I kept writing. With the encouragement of my writers club, I began to submit my short stories to a variety of magazines. The very first story I had published was in a magazine called *Appalachian Heritage*. Although fiction, my story was based on a flood that happened when a dam behind a coal dump failed in Buffalo Creek, West Virginia, and killed people downstream. My fellow club members praised it and told me I should send it off for publication. The bible for freelance writers at that time was the annual reference book *Writer's Market*, and I studied it to see if there were any magazines looking for stories about life in the Appalachian hills and coal mining. *Appalachian Heritage* seemed a good fit and I sent my story off to them with, of course, the required self-addressed stamped envelope for a reply. A few months later, to my astonishment, they published my story and sent me ten copies as payment. Proudly, I sent off a copy to my mom, but it wasn't her that I heard from but my very unhappy father. "Your mom showed me your story," he said on the phone. "You know that magazine is run by radicals? I thought you were smarter than to let yourself get used like that."

I really didn't know what to say except what I did. "Dad, I was just happy they published my story."

"You used my name on it, too," he complained. "You realize how embarrassed that makes me? People think I wrote for that damn Communist rag."

I realized Dad probably didn't know I'd been going by "Homer" since Vietnam. "It's my name, too," I pointed out, but he probably didn't hear me as the next voice I heard was Mom's, who proceeded to change the subject. She talked about how things were in Myrtle Beach and how Jim was doing great with his coaching and then got around to asking how I was doing, too. "I'm fine," I said and left it at that. Although I was tempted to ask Dad to come back to the phone to talk out his objection to my publisher, I didn't. I also wanted to ask Mom what she thought of my story but since she didn't volunteer, I didn't do that either. She ended our conversation by telling me that Coalwood was still going downhill. "The water's gone bad here," she said. "It stinks and I'm afraid to bathe in it. Your dad's been driving all over to get us drinking water. He brings it in big old cans that I can't lift. He has to pour it into mason jars and put it in the refrigerator. Electricity keeps going out, too."

At the writers club, I made Dad's call into a funny story and, after being asked about it, also told them a little about what it was like growing up in a mining town deep in the mountains of West Virginia. One of the members, a young woman who taught English in one of the local high schools, said that maybe I should write about Coalwood, that it sounded like an interesting place. Although I pretended to give her suggestion some consideration, I thought she was wrong. Who, after all, would care about a dying old coal town?

The group also encouraged me to write about Vietnam, but I claimed not to be interested in that either, although the truth was I'd already written a novel over a thousand pages long that was based on my experiences in Vietnam. It had just come pouring out of me. After studying *Writer's Market*, I picked out a well-regarded agent in New York and sent along my manuscript titled *The Ivy Patch*. Three months later, it came back with a handwritten note. Paraphrased, it said, "You write well but it is too soon for a novel set in Vietnam." Disappointed, I set the manuscript aside and wondered if I had the tools to ever be a successful writer. There were some glimmers of hope, but there were also indications that even if I had talent, maybe it wasn't enough. All I could do was keep trying, and that's what I did.

Guanaja

From the mid-1970s and across the 1980s and even into the 1990s, I kind of led a triple life. One of them was as a scuba instructor, one as a writer, and the other as an engineer. Carl Spurlock, a friend at the time, observed all I was doing and called me "the Purposeful Adventurer." I liked that. All three lives were not only filled with purpose but kept me busy. Eventually, the combination of scuba and writing carried me to a special Caribbean island inhabited by some marvelous people whom I came to cherish.

As a scuba instructor, I naturally read everything I could on the subject of diving and that included a lot of scuba magazines. The quality of writing in those magazines varied, and I thought I could do at least as well if not better than some of their correspondents. Accordingly, I submitted a number of travel articles to magazines like *Skin Diver* and *Sport Dive*r and was rewarded by having several of them published. Another was a magazine called *Aquarius*. John Gaffney, the publisher of the magazine and also the president of the National Association of Skin Diving Schools (NASDS), didn't pay me for my article but instead sent a proposal that I go to Honduras and write a piece about a live-aboard dive boat that he just happened to own. If I would go and write an article about the boat, he said he'd repay me for whatever it cost and so, with that promissory note, I agreed.

The Republic of Honduras was a complete mystery to me except I was pretty sure it was south of Mexico. After I called around to some airlines on how to get there, I learned New Orleans seemed to be the hub for anyone headed in that direction. So it was in July 1974 I found myself climbing aboard an aircraft flown by the Servicio Aéreo de Honduras, the national flag carrier Honduran airline. We were barely off the ground before I heard one of the passengers say that SAHSA, the airline's acronym, actually stood for "Stay At Home, Stay Alive." The Electra turboprop we were on was an aircraft well known for losing its wings but, fortunately, they stayed stuck to the fuselage all the way to the sleepy coastal banana town of La Ceiba.

As we flew in, I saw vast plantations of banana trees. As I would learn, United Fruit, in effect, owned the country (or at least its politicians) and were a somewhat benevolent dictatorship as long as you didn't get too much out of line. I had no interest in doing anything but getting on out to the island of Guanaja but, since that was with another airline named Lineas Aéreas Nacionales SA (which some said stood for Lost and Never Seen Again), I had to spend a night on the mainland to catch its morning flight.

La Ceiba was an interesting town. It reminded me a lot of towns in Vietnam. It was hot and tropical and there was a lot of noise and gas fumes from scooters, motorcycles, and taxis mixed in with the smell of sweat and frying grease. Drivers paid no attention to street signs, so there was a lot of honking of horns and swearing. The chaos was somehow inviting. People on the streets were either yelling or singing, little kids were racing around selling chewing gum, and there was a bar on every corner that blared American rock and roll or South American salsa. From my time in Puerto Rico I knew a little Spanish, enough that I could at least order food and a beer. The people swirling around me were warm and friendly. Instantly, I fell in love with the place.

Martel, the taxi driver who drove me in from the airport, made a recommendation for a clean hotel that cost all of four lempiras, or about two dollars a night. I dropped off my dive bag in a room that had a single bunk, a table, a sink, and a toilet in a corner behind a plastic divider. As far as I was concerned, it had everything I needed. Soon I found a small, friendly bar, had a cerveza, and then walked around to absorb the sounds, smells, and feel of the place.

An ancient black Buick rattled by and then stopped. "Hey señor!" It was Martel. "You set up?"

"Si, gracias," I replied. "How about coming by at five in the morning? My flight's at six."

He laughed. "That plane, she won't fly before noon. I pick you up at ten. Hokay?"

Well, when in Rome and all that, so I agreed and sought out a little restaurant that served fried plantains, spicy rice and beans, and cold beer. Since I had been warned on the flight down to avoid the water in La Ceiba or anywhere on the Honduran mainland, I drank only beer. I even brushed my teeth with it. When it comes to things that have to do with the digestive tract in tropical countries, I have always been cautious. Still, as I sat on a plastic chair on the patio of the little restaurant, I was delighted by the colorful, boisterous people passing by on the street. It was there I felt something that I hadn't felt in what seemed forever: a taste for life and a sense that something good was going to come my way.

The next morning at ten, exactly as promised, Martel arrived at my hotel and off we went to the airport. At the LANSA ticket counter, a young Honduran woman in a tight and revealing uniform (not that I noticed) didn't blink a mascaraed eye when I presented myself four hours late for my flight. She stamped my ticket and pointed toward a door that I went through, where I expected to find a waiting room. Instead, I found myself outside on the runway tarmac beneath a beating sun where there was parked two ancient twin-engine DC-3s, a small jet, and a few smaller prop jobs. Passengers were getting on one of the DC-3s so I followed with my dive bag and got in line. "Guanaja, si?" I asked the stewardess standing at the door.

"Guanaja, si!" she chirped. She pointed at the tail of the plane where the other passengers had stacked up their baggage and I added my dive bag to the pile. After I climbed up the rusty steps into the plane, I glanced in the cockpit and saw a silver-haired pilot wearing aviation-style sunglasses. He looked American and when I heard him say something to his copilot in a midwestern drawl, I knew indeed he was. My guess was he was probably a veteran of World War II or Korea who'd somehow ended up in Honduras. This made me feel confident about the flight. Even if we crashed and burned, I figured it would be done with old-fashioned skill and professionalism.

The DC-3 was a tail-dragger, which meant once inside, it required going downhill to find a seat, none of which were apparently assigned. The seats in front were filled with passengers who all seemed to be locals, the women in colorful frocks and the men in pressed slacks and ruffled guayabera shirts. Held in the laps of their owners were also several chickens and a pig, the creatures all looking rather pleased with themselves. When I spotted a fellow dressed in white slacks, white shirt, white sports coat, a black string tie, and a panama hat, I thought he looked like a man who had a good story so I sat down beside him. As it would turn out, he had a very good story indeed.

His name was Jules Verne Hyde and he had been born on Guanaja, left the island when he was a teen, made a great deal of money in the construction trade in Pennsylvania, went through a nasty divorce, and was going home to raise cattle, build himself a grand house, and take up with a local woman if he could find one. Verne, as he preferred to be called, told me a little about the island I was about to visit and of the unique society that existed there. Guanaja was one of a group of islands off the north coast of Honduras known as the Bay Islands or, in Spanish, Islas de la Bahías. The predominant language spoken there, however, was not Spanish but English. How that occurred was a lesson in Caribbean history and politics. I shall make it short.

Before the Europeans came, the Bay Islands were home to a variety of people, the last being the Paya, an offshoot of the Mayan civilization. They were mostly peaceful fishermen and had a relatively easy life, the ocean around their islands teeming with fish, conch, turtles, and manatees. These laid-back folks were, however, doomed. Coming up through the Caribbean was a tribe known as the Caribes, a bloodthirsty lot often given over to cannibalism. The Caribes had already raided the islands a few times before Columbus, who while enduring his fourth voyage in 1502 and still forlornly looking for India, showed up off Guanaja, which he called Isla de Pinos, the Island of Pines. The great explorer and a few of his fellows went ashore but found nothing of interest except a plant called cacao, the source of chocolate. Even a potential Hershey bar wasn't enough to convince Columbus to stay and, after speaking to a few local inhabitants and sharing some food with them, he and his landing party rowed their way back to their ship but not before leaving behind a few diseases, including smallpox, which proceeded to wipe out most of the indigenous people. Slave raids by the Spanish finished the rest of them off. For many decades afterward, Guanaja and the Bay Islands were unpopulated, with only occasional visits by transient fishermen and turtle and manatee hunters.

Eventually, it was the very remoteness of the islands that earned them attention, this time in the 1600s by English, French, and Dutch pirates. Sallying forth from their hidden Bay Islands lairs, they caught Spanish treasure ships and then returned to divide up the spoils. To the north of these pirate-infested islands was British Honduras, also known as Belize. The Royal Navy cast a covetous eye on the Bay Islands, and it wasn't long before the English sent a fleet not to fight the pirates but to cut down the many old-growth trees there for ships, masts, homes, and furniture.

After the islands were denuded and the British warships withdrawn, the pirates swept back in to harry Spanish galleons, but the Spaniards, tired of the attention, landed and wiped them out. Once more, the Bay Islands were abandoned until the late 1700s when a few Spanish settlements were established. A half century later, however, the mainland wrested its independence from Spain, which left the status of the Bay Islands unclear. The English sent a party from the Cayman Islands to occupy the islands but the United States, under the Monroe Doctrine, forced the British to cede the Bay Islands to Honduras, and there the matter has rested ever since.

But had it? Verne explained that the people of the Bay Islands mostly considered themselves independent of the mainland government and a number of families on Guanaja pretty much ran the show. The Hyde family was one of them, along with the Bodden (sometimes called Borden), Wood, Tatum, Merren, Forbes, Powery, and other families, most of whom claimed to be of old English stock and not Honduran.

While Verne happily chattered away, I looked through the window of the old plane and saw the woman from the reservation counter and a helper load the bags on the DC-3, which I supposed meant we were finally ready to take off. This proved a good assumption as the engines coughed into life and our silver-haired pilot steered us in a zigzag path through the other aircraft, bumped up on the runway, turned around to face the beach, and firewalled the throttle. As we gradually gained speed, the tail of the plane began to lift and then we climbed into the air, banana boats flashing beneath us as the wheels thumped into their recesses and we took to the open sea at a low altitude, the ocean so close it looked like a big wave could slap us in the nose.

The chickens got down from their owners and strutted up and down the aisle and then the pig got loose and scrambled around in something of a panic. Perhaps thinking I was its owner, it jumped in my lap but when it looked up at me, it was clearly horrified and ran away. I soon heard its owner talking to it in a consoling way and a woman, either the man's wife or girlfriend, got up and patted the pig and also talked to it. I wasn't sure if it was a pet or a future meal, but the couple seemed to love it and it them.

Our first stop was the big island of Roatan to let a few people off, and then we proceeded still at low altitude on out to land on Guanaja's small crushed-coral runway. Verne had a map of the island and showed it to me on the way. The seventeen-mile-long island was dragon shaped, its head separated from its body by a canal, and was about five miles at its widest. There were no roads on the island, so most people had some kind of boat, mostly dugout canoes called cayucas. The island had dozens of lagoons or bays, and there was a chain of small islands or cayes off the southern coast. Verne pointed at one of the cayes that was closest to the runway and said that was where most of the people of Guanaja lived. He also said that Guanaja was sometimes known as Bonacca but so was the main town but, then again, sometimes people called the village Low Key. "You'll figure it out," he said.

After we deplaned, I wished Verne well, traded addresses with him, and then caught a waiting skiff out to the live-aboard dive boat where I was to spend the next week, the *Aquarius II* or, as it was also known, *The Good Neighbor*. On board, I discovered a film crew from Santa Barbara, California, who had taken John Gaffney up on a similar deal as mine to make a documentary about his business.

The week that followed was amazing as we dived on pristine reefs in a sea of crystal-clear water. Visibility was easily three hundred feet and probably more. It was like diving in gin. Huge shoals of grunts, snappers, angelfish, surgeonfish, and silversides hovered over endless varieties of healthy corals. In the caverns were fleets of copper sweepers, their coppery scales flashing in the sunlight filtering inside. Munching on the coral were Technicolor parrotfish, their scat the bleached-white sand of the island beaches. Big green and spotted morays slipped in and out of the coral heads while sleeping nurse sharks rested beneath the ledges. Damselfish flicked along the gardens they tended, brazenly nipping the hair on our arms if we got too close. Occasionally, a great hammerhead shark could be seen soaring along the edge of a drop-off, its massive head slowly swiveling back and forth before descending into the endless purple below.

The film crew were Mal Wolfe and Buzzy Rohlfing. Mal owned the Diver's Den dive shop in Santa Barbara and employed Buzzy as a divemaster and underwater photographer. Buzzy and I immediately struck up a friendship. He was a cheerful fellow with blond surfer-dude looks and attitude. Between dives, while we cleaned our diving gear and cameras, we sat around and talked about this and that. Buzzy let me borrow his Nikonos underwater camera and strobe and taught me how to take photos of undersea life.

When any of the local crew took the skiff into town, I often asked to go along. Bonacca town or Low Key was a fascinating place. One of the crew said it was called the Venice of the Caribbean because of the canals, but it was considerably less grand than that ancient Italian city on the Adriatic. Mostly, it was brightly painted wooden shacks that sat over the water on stilts with boardwalks that connected them. The canals, if such they could be called, were the openings between the shacks that were so narrow only the cayucas could navigate along them. Every shack had a toilet that consisted of a board with a hole in it above the sea so, even though it harbored some huge barracudas and banks of silversides, it was no place to go snorkeling.

One evening with the skiff crew off visiting their girlfriends or family, I found myself alone on Low Key making my way along the boardwalks and peering into the storefronts, which were mostly open windows with a clerk, usually an elderly member of the family that owned it, holding court with a few of its wares displayed such as bottles of rum or chewing gum or chips or whatever it was that was being sold. There was only one glass storefront where I saw displayed for sale a derby hat, a pair of old button-up women's shoes, and on a cracked plastic mannequin missing a head an ankle-length dress I thought would have been perfect for a gussied-up pioneer woman on a Conestoga wagon. When I heard some salsa music, I made my way to a bar called the Blue Wave and sat down on a stool to listen to the music and watch the locals take in the setting sun. Since I was in the Caribbean, I ordered rum.

There was only one representative of the mainland government on the island, a fellow everybody called the Soldier, and I'd seen him patrolling around the boardwalks with a menacing expression on his mustachioed face. He had a flashy gilt badge that looked like it had come in a cereal box and wore a khaki shirt and shorts that were patched and dirty and a crushed officer's cap slightly askew. He was also armed with a .45-caliber pistol carried in a brown leather holster on a green web belt.

As it happened, the Soldier chose to come into the bar while I was sitting there. He stood glaring at the men around one of the tables and I watched his hand stray to rest on his pistol butt. "Elon," he said loudly, "you are arrested!"

One of the men, handsomely round-faced with a big black moustache, briefly looked up from the table but then went back to his beer.

"Elon!" the Soldier barked again. "You are arrested!"

The man looked up again but this time turned his blue-eyed gaze to the Soldier. He was a big fellow with muscled arms, wide shoulders, clearly a rough character. He scraped his chair back, stood up, and, without a word, walked over to the Soldier and, in a deft move, slapped his hand away and grabbed the pistol. The Soldier fell back. "Elon," he squeaked, "you are arrested for breaking and entering another man's home!"

"I did not break and enter, Soldier," Elon replied. "I was let in by his wife so that we could bounce on the bed together."

"She does not have that right," the Soldier said. "Only a man can invite another man into his house."

Elon tossed the pistol over his shoulder to be caught by one of his friends and then, starting a little game, they tossed it from man to man while the Soldier madly tried to catch it. Finally, apparently tired of playing, Elon grabbed the Soldier and, with the help of the others, tossed him through an open window into the sea and then went back to their table and took up their drinks. Before long, the Soldier, dripping wet and his cap on backwards, came stomping back inside. Taking note, Elon got up, put the Soldier's pistol back in his holster, slapped him on the back, and then handed him a beer. After a moment of hesitation, the Soldier took the beer and sat down with Elon and the others at their table. Before long, they were singing some kind of sea shanty that had to do with shagging mermaids. My thought during all this? *I like this place!*

As gloriously beautiful as the Caribbean is, it can also be fickle. After my week aboard the *Aquarius II*, Hurricane Fifi struck Honduras and its Bay Islands. In a desperate attempt to get away, the dive boat was caught out on the open sea and sunk. Low Key was devastated with almost every house damaged. Dozens of people died.

As for Jules Verne Hyde, the house he was building on the northeastern part of the island was completely destroyed, a big timber falling on his legs and breaking one in two places. With no roads on the island and his boat sunk, Verne fashioned a raft out of the remnants of his house and, over the course of two pain-filled days beneath an unforgiving sun, paddled his way down half the length of the island and into the village of Savannah

Bight. There, he was taken in by a widow. A year later, I received a letter from Honduras with no return address. Inside, I found a water-stained square of notebook paper with almost indecipherable handwriting. After I studied it for a while, I got the gist of its message. It said, "Dear Homer: Island destroyed. Please come back. Tell us if reefs are OK. I am in Savannah Bight. Ask for Enola Gay. —Verne"

The *U-352*

When I heard over the scuba grapevine there might be the wreck of a World War II German U-boat off North Carolina, I didn't know if there was anything to it but, if so, decided it might make for a great article. To find out more about it, I called some dive shops on the coast but none seemed to know anything until I called a little shop in Morehead City. The man who answered the phone was friendly until I mentioned the U-boat. Instantly he became cagey and then abruptly hung up. More calls led to more stonewalling. Finally, after ordering a copy of the Morehead City phone book, I found an ad for a dive boat that said it specialized in diving on wrecks in the Graveyard of the Atlantic, the storied area off the Outer Banks where the U-boat was supposed to be. I called the number and got a fellow who called himself "Captain Dunn."

"Heard about it, never been out to it," Captain Dunn said of the U-boat. "But I know where it is. Hey-yup, I'll put you on it pure as pie." I scheduled a trip with him the following weekend.

Morehead City was a quiet town set along a wild coast of brown sandy beaches pounded by a foam-flecked surf and strewn with seashells and torn nets and floats from the fishing boats that sailed from its port. A diver friend, a captain in the army named Dave Todd, went with me along with John Harkins, a fellow Aquaspace instructor. We found Captain Dunn at his house on an inlet several miles out of town. Tied up to the dock was what appeared to be a small landing craft like in movies about D-Day.

Captain Dunn didn't look much like a sea captain. He wore bib overalls tucked into rubber boots and had white, shaggy hair peeking out from under a greasy ball cap. "Hey-yup," he said. "I'll find that sub for ya," and trusting a promise supported only by the captain's confidence and our ignorance, we carried our dive bags and tanks on board his peculiar little boat and off we went.

It was a rough ride. As soon as we got past a protective jetty and across a line of churning surf, we were plunging and rising through a sea of three- to five-foot waves. Luckily, neither John nor Dave nor I was particularly prone to seasickness so although we got cold and wet, we at least kept breakfast down. After a couple of hours of wallowing through seas that only got rougher, I climbed the little pulpit where Captain Dunn stood with his hand on the wheel. All I could see was the sea. "How will you find the sub?" I asked, which was a question I perhaps should have asked earlier in our relationship.

"We'll fish for it," the captain said and pointed at some tackle. "On this heading, we should be near yer sub in 'bout a half hour. There's fish all over it. We'll cast out a line, see if we can reel in some. That'll tell us where it is."

This seemed kind of nebulous if not dubious to me, but I reported Captain Dunn's plan to John and Dave, who rolled their eyes and made various hand gestures that indicated they were somewhat skeptical of the plan. Nonetheless, when the time came, while my buddies watched with interest but it must be said also doubt, I cast a line and, for the next two hours, while going back and forth in a zigzag pattern I caught absolutely nothing until finally I hooked a little barracuda that I let go. After handing the fishing rod over to John, I climbed into the pulpit to consult with Captain Dunn, which consisted of, "We don't think we're going to find the sub this way."

"Hey-yup. Think not," the captain said with no hint of an apology. "Know a wreck I can find fer ya, though. World War II freighter. Ain't got a name for sartain but buoy on it's marked WR-2. Torpedo hole in her side. Want me to take ya?"

After consulting with my buddies and recognizing that Captain Dunn was not going to find the sub and figuring something was better than nothing, we gave in. About an hour later, we pulled up to a buoy that was, sure enough, marked WR-2. John hooked us on, and Captain Dunn dropped the anchor and lowered the ramp. "Deep here," he said. "Hundred feet, mebbe more."

Having an idea of the depth is important information for scuba divers. Normal air—and that's what most scuba tanks are filled with—consists of only about 20 percent oxygen, the rest mostly nitrogen, which is soluble—meaning it dissolves in liquids. This is a problem because as a diver goes deeper, more nitrogen than normal ends up in the blood or tissues. If a diver comes up too soon or too fast, it's like shaking up a bottle of soda and taking the top off. Bubbles spew out. After consulting the navy decompression tables for the amount of time we could safely spend at a depth of a hundred feet plus or minus twenty feet, we strapped on double tanks and stepped off to swim around the boat to use its stern anchor line as a guide down to whatever waited for us on the bottom. As a backup to the tables, I wore on my arm an Italian-made device called a DeComPressimetro, or DCP. Theoretically, if I could keep the little arrow on its dial from pointing into the red crescent along its circumference, I was not in danger of decompression sickness or, as it is also known, the bends. That's why the device was also called a "Bend-o-matic" since they were not considered particularly reliable.

At the bottom of Captain Dunn's anchor line, we found what appeared to be the wreck of an old freighter, its broken hull resting in the sand almost exactly at 120 feet. We worked our way around it, our lights penetrating the gloom of its corrupted structure. Sand filled the holds and fish swam in and out of rusty steel caverns formed by collapsed bulkheads. A giant barracuda rose from beneath one of them, its silvery scales flashing in the sunlight. It circled us, its large intelligent eyes taking us in and then, apparently losing interest, it wandered away.

While John and Dave worked their way to the bridge, I dropped along the hull and looked at a massive hole in its side. The way the plates were bent, it appeared like it had been punctured by a huge spear. A torpedo hole? I swam down the side until I happened upon a row of portholes. Armed with a small crowbar, I scraped at the porthole and saw, to my delight, a golden metallic gleam. I couldn't believe my luck. It was every wreck diver's dream, a brass porthole! Using a small pipe wrench from a pouch of tools I carried on my belt just in case such an artifact presented itself, I cranked at the big nuts holding it down.

So absorbed in my work on the porthole, when something pushed me from the back, I ignored it, but then came another push, this one so shockingly hard that I dropped my wrench. When I turned around, I saw the retreating crescent-shaped tail of a very large fish. When it turned, I saw it was a shark and when it turned again and headed back toward me, I saw its mouth was filled with what appeared to be barbed wire. Since I had become a diver, I had tried to learn to recognize and identify fish, including the large varieties of sharks. This was a sand tiger shark at least ten feet long but because of the magnification of water, it looked even bigger.

Sand tigers have been known to be man-eaters, but everything I had read about them indicated the jury was out on whether they deliberately attacked people or just took advantage of an obvious situation such as a drowning victim. Since I presumed this shark was illiterate, I supposed it just did whatever it wanted to do despite the debate on its menu proclivities. In any case, it certainly seemed interested in me. The porthole forgotten, I held my crowbar in spear fashion and pressed my tanks back against the hull. The shark swam with deliberate purpose at me but swerved just as I jabbed at it. As it soared effortlessly away, I saw another sand tiger emerge from around the stern of the wreck. It joined the shark that had menaced me and they both disappeared into the blue gloom for a few seconds before reappearing and heading straight at me. It was time to leave. I kicked my way up to the deck and looked for John and Dave. That didn't take long because they had also been menaced by sand tigers. Following their point, I saw four of the massive creatures orbiting the wreck like miniature submarines.

While occasionally looking back to make sure we weren't followed, we swam to the anchor line and started up. Despite the adrenaline flushing through our bodies, our training took over. We couldn't hurry up the line. We had to remember our body tissues had soaked up nitrogen like sponges. We had to ascend slowly and then hang at ten to fifteen feet for at least a half hour to breathe off the excess nitrogen before we could safely go to the surface.

The anchor line thrummed in the stiff current that made us into human pennants as we climbed hand over hand until we could rise no farther and there we hung, every exhalation we hoped doing the job of removing the excess nitrogen. Flashes of movement came from below and then we saw rising from the depths some small sharks that were clearly coming up because of us. They were gray and sleek and had mouths that looked like they could take a grapefruit-size chunk of flesh. We turned our backs to each other to create a circle of defense and, for the next twenty or so minutes, kicked the sharks off us. They were lemon sharks and were like wolves, circling, darting in, and snapping their jaws. One of them was bit by another one and fled downward trailing blood with a couple of its fellows after it. More lemons came until it was like a carousel of them going round and round, their unblinking, staring eyes always watching for an opening to dart in and take a mouthful of prime American flesh from one of our legs.

Finally, the time passed and we could safely go to the surface. John went first, followed by Dave and then me. While keeping an eye on the sharks, I swam around the boat lifting my head only when I grabbed hold of the ramp. Just at that moment, a lemon bit one of my fins and, with a powerful wrench, tore it off my foot. Even with heavy double tanks strapped on my back, I flung myself up on the ramp and crawled like the world's fastest turtle until I was sure I was completely out of the water. After I caught my breath, I looked up and there stood Captain Dunn. He made no move to help. "Captain," I gasped, "there's sharks down there and they tried to eat us!"

Captain Dunn hooked his thumbs beneath the straps of his bib overalls and rocked in his rubber boots. "Hey-yup," he said, "that's what all the divers I bring out here say."

The weather on the coast of North Carolina being what it is, storms descended on us and we were chased back to Huntsville before we could do anything else to find the U-boat. Before trying again, some basic research on the World War II wrecks and the battle that had put them down in the sand was in order. *Iron Coffins*, a memoir by U-boat captain Herbert Werner, was a good resource, as was *Das Boot* by Lothar-Günther Buchheim. A journalist, Buchheim spent several wartime months aboard a U-boat, and his description of life aboard gave me my first inkling of the hell endured by the crews of these submersibles. Duke University had a chart of wrecks off North Carolina that I ordered, and one of them showed a U-boat wreck designated the *U-352* that seemed to be in the area Captain Dunn thought the mystery sub was located. The only historical reference I could find about this particular submarine was in a book by author David Stick titled *Graveyard of the Atlantic*. His account, although interesting, was sparse but mentioned the *U-352* was sunk by the United States Coast Guard cutter *Icarus*.

Fortunately, the Freedom of Information Act had recently been passed so many of the previously secret documents from World War II were now declassified. This allowed me to start hunting for the *U-352* in the National Archives. After many calls and explanations to the clerks and historians there about what I was looking for, I received a microfiche that contained the *Eastern Sea Frontier War Diary*. This was a daily account of the goings and comings of the warships of the US Navy and Coast Guard along the East Coast during the war. As I read it, my eyes were opened to a huge battle I had never heard of, a frightful tale of death and destruction of merchant marine and American and British warships by German U-boats after the Japanese attack of Pearl Harbor. The archivist I worked with said during his twenty-plus years of employment there, no other writers or researchers had asked for this microfiche. He also told me the archives had original U-boat logs taken from Germany after the war. Although it was expensive, I paid the fee for the researchers to make microfiche copies of hundreds of logs and mail them to me. As a writer, I sensed I was onto something special. Before long, I was obsessed with uncovering not only the story of the mystery U-boat but also the entire battle against German U-boats along the East and Gulf Coasts. Such obsession is a tendency of mine that has gained me both success and trouble over the course of my life, and this one would prove no exception.

Although I was getting enough new information to write a number of articles about the nearly unknown battle that had claimed the U-boat, I still needed to dive on the *U-352*, if that's what it was, to gain firsthand knowledge about it. A few months later, through cold calls to dive shops and pretending to be a local diver, I finally found a dive boat captain who said he could put me on the wreck. He said he knew the location because it was his brother who was the skipper of the fishing trawler that had recently found it. He had tangled his nets in the thing and sent down divers to see what it was. They had returned to say they thought it might be a German submarine. Before long, more local divers descended on it to strip it of souvenirs and artifacts. Outsiders were not welcome but after I confessed who I was accompanied with a little begging, the dive boat captain said he'd take me and a couple of others to the wreck if I promised not to tell anybody. Fingers crossed, I promised.

John Harkins, Dave Todd, and I headed back to Morehead City. As it would turn out, the dive boat skipper was truthful. He had the right location through a set of coordinates known as LORAN numbers that was at the time the standard for seaborne navigation based on radio signals. When I pulled down the anchor line, I thought we were surely at the wrong place because I could see the sandy bottom, not likely at the location where the wreck was supposed to be. To my surprise, it wasn't sand but a vast, seemingly endless mat of small silver-sided fish, probably sardines, pierced by the line. As I neared them, they opened up like a hole in a doughnut, closing over my head as I passed through.

I found the anchor dug into the sand at 110 feet and beside it, a long, narrow wreck that was decidedly a submarine. To confirm its type, I swam directly to the conning tower but that didn't prove much help. Rather than the sleek airfoil shape of U-boat conning towers I'd seen in photos, I found a dark stub with a couple of sponge- and coral-encrusted tubes rising from it. After going in closer and running my gloved fingers around its ragged circumference, I decided that much of the steel shroud that should have covered it and gave it its distinctive shape was gone, with only some of the support structure left.

Peering into the remaining recess, I saw an open hatch surrounded by sand and silt. Dropping headfirst to look through the circular opening, I saw that the interior of the vessel was filled with sand. When my eye caught sight of what looked like the bottom of a small bowl sticking out of the silt beside the hatch, I reached for it and, with a cascade of muddy debris flowing out of it, brought up a human skull absent its jaw. After a moment of surprise, I put it back and tried to cover it up. The U-boat, I realized, was a grave. When I rose from the conning tower, I looked for its deck gun but saw only a hole where it should have been. After only a few more short minutes, we scampered up the anchor line, there to hang for a while. Unlike the WR-2 we were not threatened by sharks but instead were joined by a school of amberjacks, beautiful torpedo-shaped fish, that circled us endlessly, pausing only occasionally to soar down into the layer of sardines over the wreck to snatch a meal.

Our surface interval was a couple of hours, as required by the navy tables, to breathe off as much nitrogen as possible. After checking our gear, John, Dave, and I sat on the deck and talked over what we had seen. They had spent most of their dive on the stern where they had found the submarine had two bronze props. I asked them to go forward this time and count torpedo tubes if possible. I wanted to study the hatches and see if there was a way to get inside to find a serial number on any of the equipment that might definitely identify the wreck, although I was already pretty certain that it was the *U-352*, especially after finding the skull and the missing 88 mm deck gun. My research made those two finds fairly indicative that this was that U-boat.

On the second dive, I went directly to the open aft torpedo-loading hatch and looked inside. The interior revealed more sand and silt, although I supposed it was possible for a determined diver to make his way inside. Moving a little toward the conning tower, I found a smaller hatch, this one closed. It was undoubtedly the galley hatch. To get any hatch open that I found closed, I had brought along a come-along, which is a handheld winch device. I set about using it.

It was common knowledge, at least according to the tales and legends that we divers shared, that the one thing you never did on a U-boat wreck was open a closed hatch. This was because, so the legend went, the Germans always booby-trapped the hatches before scuttling their submarines. The skipper of the *U-352*, however, had not done that and the reason I knew was because I was corresponding with him. This I had managed by going to one of the many German families in Huntsville who'd come over with the von Braun rocket team after World War II and asked them if they could help me find the whereabouts of former U-boat *Kapitanleutnant* Oskar Rathke. Their relatives in Germany were glad to help and it wasn't long before I had his address.

My research had already revealed that Rathke was not a successful U-boat captain even though he operated during a time when most German submarines were having tremendous success in American waters. After being on station off North Carolina for a month without hitting anything, he finally spotted a small freighter one morning in May 1942 and, desperate for success, sent a spread of torpedoes at it. The only problem was it wasn't a small freighter at all but the United States Coast Guard cutter *Icarus* fully armed with a load of depth charges, a three-inch gun, and a half dozen big fifty-caliber machine guns. After the cutter's crew spotted the torpedoes that missed them by a wide margin, the captain of the *Icarus* began a systematic search that soon found the *U-352*. Multiple depth charge explosions shook the submarine and tore off its deck gun and the shroud around its conning tower. With water pouring inside, Rathke ordered his U-boat to the surface where he intended to fight, but as soon as he threw open the conning tower hatch, he realized he had no deck gun, only a big hole where it was supposed to be.

With no other choice, Rathke ordered his crew to abandon ship. When the first crewman climbed up, a three-inch shell from the *Icarus* struck the conning tower and killed him instantly. This was probably the man whose skull I had found. Still, even though the cutter kept firing, Rathke urged his crew to risk it and jump into the sea. Many of the Germans were killed by the wildly firing crew of the cutter. Rathke was the last man out, jumping into a sea of blood while the *U-352* slipped beneath the waves forever. Still, the Americans kept firing their machine guns and rifles at the screaming men in the water. They only stopped when the cutter, whose captain was career officer Maurice Jester, sailed on toward the horizon, leaving the Germans dead, dying, and alone in a bloody sea.

A couple of hours later, after some of the enlisted crew aboard the cutter disobeyed their captain's orders and called headquarters in Charleston, South Carolina, to let the upper echelon know what had happened, Jester was ordered back to the scene to pick up the U-boat crew. Although glad to be rescued, Rathke was furious that his men had been killed and wounded while obviously surrendering. He and his crew would eventually end up in a POW camp in Texas, where he would spend the rest of the war plotting impossible escapes and trying to get Jester tried as a war criminal. Instead, the Coast Guard skipper got a medal for sinking the second U-boat in American waters at a time when the Germans were well on their way to sinking nearly four hundred of our ships.

Despite his unhappiness about the *Icarus*, Rathke's response to my letter was gracious. No, he wrote, there was no time to set any booby traps on the hatches and, yes, he would be open to an interview, either in person or by mail. He appreciated that I was researching the sinking and was intrigued that I was diving on his U-boat. There was, he said, perhaps a dead man in the conning tower. His name was *Maschinistmaat* Gerhard Reussel.

With Rathke's assurances that I wasn't going to blow myself up by cracking open the galley hatch, I used the come-along to pull it open and then looked inside at pots, pans, and dishes strewn across patterned deck plates. My time at depth was dwindling. Even with double tanks, I had to make sure I'd have enough air to decompress. Still, I really wanted to get something to positively identify the *U-352*, which is why I plunged headfirst through the galley hatch, my hands outstretched to grab what I could. With my trembling fingers just inches away from what looked to be a dinner plate that might have an identifying mark, I was stopped short when my double tank rig wedged into the small opening of the hatch and no matter how I squirmed, I couldn't get free.

To find where I was caught, I walked my fingers back to the aluminum bands that held the two steel seventy-two-cubic-foot tanks in place. They proved to be the culprits, both snagged on the hatch rim. Only one solution presented itself, which was to unbuckle the straps on the backpack, slip out of them, turn around inside the U-boat galley, push the rig up and through, follow it, and strap it back on. It wasn't exactly a maneuver I thought I was ever going to have to do, but I had no choice other than to try. My air was rapidly dwindling and, even if I could have headed up the anchor line at that moment, I was going to have to go into a lengthy decompression hang.

After unbuckling the backpack buckles, I pushed down and turned a tight somersault which caused the silt in the galley to turn into a storm of debris that cut visibility down to inches. As I did, my regulator suddenly stopped providing air and, before I realized it, I breathed in some water. Coughing and blowing bubbles, I desperately pushed the rig up and out of the hatch and followed it, gratefully seeing the crystal-blue water of the Gulf Stream. The regulator problem was due to its mouthpiece coming off. The solution was to switch to what is known as an octopus regulator, a second stage carried along as a spare. After switching, I fought the buoyancy compensator built into the backpack which, without me in it, was too buoyant. Settling back to the deck after I got the gear strapped back on, I looked up just in time to see John Harkins kicking languidly toward me. To my astonishment, he was carrying an 88 mm round, which was about the length of a baseball bat. From my research, I knew it was still capable of being detonated, especially by a sharp blow, so I waved frantically at John to put it down. Well into nitrogen narcosis, also known as the rapture of the deep, he looked at me quizzically and then, to my horror, nonchalantly tossed the lethal device in my direction, which sent it along on a slow trajectory. At the end of its flight no more than a yard from me, the big bullet-shaped artillery shell struck nose-first on a steel plate, bounced once, and then rolled off the sub into the sand.

I looked at John. John looked at me. I gave him a thumbs-up, not to say he'd done a good job but to say it was definitely time to get up the anchor line. He returned the signal, saying the same. When Dave appeared tapping his watch and looking a bit frantic, we ran from danger, not from the U-boat or even the deep water, but from ourselves.

Back to Guanaja and
Another U-boat

A year after I received the plaintive letter from Verne Hyde to come back to Guanaja and dive the reefs to see about their condition after Hurricane Fifi, I convinced Dr. Bob Froelich, a Huntsville physician and friend who was also an accomplished pilot, to fly me to the little island. With his son Win and daughter Krisan plus Dave Todd and his wife, Ann, Bob did just that aboard his twin-engine Piper Aztec. We flew from Huntsville to New Orleans and thence to Merida, Mexico, and from there to La Ceiba on the northern Honduran mainland. Although we started before sunrise, the sun was low when we gassed up at the La Ceiba airport. Bob's flight charts and maps were not much use for what lay out on the ocean, but I thought Guanaja should be easy to find. It was the third island out so how could it be missed? Bob was worried about being caught out over the ocean in the dark but, after the airport manager told him he could not guarantee security at night, he decided to head for Guanaja. As we flew over the Caribbean, the airport lights behind us blinked off and all communications ceased. The La Ceiba tower was closed down and we were on our own.

We flew by Utila and then Roatan, easily identified islands, and then scanned the sea ahead to see Guanaja. When we saw an island, Bob lowered the Aztec but what I saw didn't look right. This island was too small and too flat. Bob continued on until, finally, and with great relief, we saw rising from the sea a big mountain of an island I recognized. Guanaja!

Bob pulled back the throttle, lowered the flaps, and down we went to make a perfect landing on the short runway. As the sun set and night crept over us on the lonely strip, we walked down to the dock and, seeing the flickering lamps come aglow on Pond Caye, yelled for help but nobody came. The only thing to do was to wait for morning and sleep in the airplane and that we did, although we were attacked mercilessly by sand fleas and other no-see-ums all night long. In the morning, there was a knock on the Aztec's door and I was thrilled to see Verne. "Thought you were flying in tomorrow," he said in apology and then led the way to his little dugout cayuca that had an outboard on the stern. With our heavy scuba gear bags, it took two trips to Verne's house in Savannah Bight, there to meet his girlfriend Enola Gay and her daughter Venus. Enola had plenty of rice and beans and Verne had a cabinet packed with local rum so we were set.

After contracting for a boat with a young fellow named Gilbert Wood and using scuba tanks rented from some lobster divers, we began to explore the reefs that proved mostly un-harmed by the hurricane. One of the places we dived was the prettiest little lagoon I'd ever seen. It turned out Verne owned it and he offered to sell it to me. Even after all those years, I still had the Porsche I'd bought for Sherry. When I got home, I sold it for just about the same amount I'd paid for it and used the funds to buy the lagoon and so it was that I, the son and grandson and great-grandson of Appalachian coal miners, became the owner of a beach on an island in Honduras. Of all my fates, that might have been the last one I could have imagined, but there it was.

My research and dives on the *U-352* paid off when *American History Illustrated* bought an article I wrote about it and then *Sport Diver* magazine also bought a story about the sub wreck illustrated with my underwater photographs. *Skin Diver* next bought an article about another wreck—a Russian freighter off Pensacola. When *Trailer Life* brought my article out about flying to Guanaja and diving on its reefs, my writing club was thrilled at how many articles I was getting published, all except for the English teacher. "When are you going to write about that mining town where you grew up?" she demanded. Although I kept telling her I would, I didn't mean it. What I was aiming for was to eventually write a book about the battles against the U-boats along the American coasts. To help that out, I kept making the long drive to North Carolina, carrying with me a number of Huntsville divers. My most consistent dive buddy was Dave Todd. Also joining was Buddy Stokes, a well-known underwater photographer from Tampa, Florida, who helped me learn the techniques of taking well-lit and properly framed pictures beneath the sea. Before long, I was winning underwater photography contests.

In May 1977, Dave and I drove once more to Morehead City, intent on getting aboard the *U-352* again. For time frame purposes, I was thirty-four years old that month, Jimmy Carter was still president, and the first *Star Wars* movie premiered. Since the sub wreck was starting to become a tourist diver destination, it wasn't hard to find a dive boat to take us out there. I was also interested in diving on some other wrecks, and the dive skipper suggested one that was kind of unusual. It wasn't a World War II wreck but a much more recent one, the oceangoing tug called the *Marjorie McAllister*. It was an intriguing wreck that had gone down at night in 1969 during a storm off Cape Hatteras. Her captain was in contact with the Coast Guard and reported some difficulty but didn't seem worried. After his last transmission around midnight, the tug simply vanished. There was no sign of her for three years until some scuba divers decided to see what was causing a mysterious and persistent oil slick about twenty miles off Hatteras Island. At the bottom of their anchor line they found the *Marjorie McAllister*, still leaking fuel and apparently a tomb for its six crew members.

As Dave and I descended on the tug, we saw what looked like a giant bleached-white dead whale. The wreck was upside down. Swept by the warm, blue Gulf Stream, vast schools of mullet and jacks covered it. Dave and I switched on our lights and descended through some open hatches to explore within and, seeing nothing of interest, came out and cruised around the hull. Eventually, we made it to the stern where I examined the hatch that led to the engine room. Interestingly, it was wired open. We swam through it and into an upside-down world where the stairs led upward to the engine room deck. I took photographs and Dave poked into the silt with a small crowbar. When he spotted a blue checked shirt, he picked it up. In a swirl of silt and sand, the shirt came up and with it human bones. Dave instantly dropped it and made for the engine room hatch and I was right behind him. It was a creepy dive, but I felt like we'd solved the mystery on why the tug sank. Because the engine room hatch was wired open, probably to cool it down, a big rogue wave, not that uncommon in the Graveyard of the Atlantic, could have crashed atop the stern, flooded the engine room, and sent the *Marjorie McAllister* to the bottom within seconds. Interestingly, soon after we dived on her, she was raised, the remains of the crew removed, and a year or two later put back into service.

After a few more dives on the *U-352* and other wrecks off Morehead City, I decided to move my diving operations to the Outer Banks. It was my first time to that glorious line of shifting shoals covered with sea oats and populated by colorful people, many of whom were descended from so-called wreckers. To survive at a place that was beautiful but not so bountiful, the people of Hatteras Island, Ocracoke, and the other islands along the banks took whatever the sea delivered up on their beaches, which included thousands of wrecks caused by the shoals and foul weather. They were also fully engaged in assisting when they could the shipping that passed along their dangerous shores. They manned the Coast Guard vessels, light ships, and lighthouses and saved countless lives. Their unofficial motto was, "We have to go out but we don't have to come back."

Reviewing my dive logs now, it is clear I was completely and utterly consumed with finding out what happened in the battle against the U-boats on the American coasts. For three years, from 1975 to 1978, I drove an average of once a month to the North Carolina coast from Huntsville, a twelve-hour one-way drive. Since the weather was unpredictable, sometimes I would have to turn around and drive all the way back without diving on anything. My social life, already nothing to brag about, dwindled to nothing. I worked at the Missile Command Monday to Friday and then either taught scuba on the weekends or drove to North Carolina. To help pay for diving off North Carolina, I put out the word I was willing to work as a divemaster. That got around and a few dive boat captains took me up on my offer. Sometimes I would go out with local spearfishermen who were only interested in filling their freezers for the winter. Although most of them were experienced divers, there was a subset who ignored anything approaching safety, even hanging bloody strings of fish off their waists while sharks circled about. It was my job to watch out for them, so I swam a big circle to ward off sharks that came sniffing around. Bull sharks were the worst. One of them bowled me over to take a fish off a spear and then came back, intent on attacking the spearfisherman. When I used a crowbar to push the bull away, I got no thanks from the diver. Instead, he complained to the captain that I should have acted quicker. Divemasters didn't get much respect from the spearfishing crowd.

Tourist divers, often ill-prepared for the rough waters off Hatteras, also made me work hard to keep them safe. Within seconds of him stepping off the boat, I once had to go in after an overweight diver who, caught in a vicious surface current, spit out his regulator, began to scream for help, and proceeded to drown. After finding him thirty feet down with his mouth wide open in hopeless supplication, I released his weight belt, inflated his buoyancy vest, and dragged him back to the surface. While he floundered around, kicking and screaming, I dodged his grasping hands and unwound the camera lanyard that had twisted around his neck and took it off him. With great effort, I managed to tow him and his camera against the current back to the boat and see him pulled aboard and stripped of his gear. His response was to get up, demand that I hand him his camera, tell the captain I owed him a weight belt, and head below. If he ever thanked me for saving him, I don't recall it mainly because it didn't happen.

One day, I was shepherding a group of six or seven spear-fishermen somewhere out in the Gulf Stream and I looked over and there was a bull shark looking back at me. It had kind of a sad expression on its face, and I felt sorry for it. It was hungry and nobody was letting it eat. It was also as if it just wanted to say hello, how you doin', you seem nice, and here we are living creatures in the sea alive at the same time, who woulda thunk it? To this day, I can see that shark looking at me and I think there was a connection between us. Sharks live for a long time. That little bull might still be swimming around out there in the Gulf Stream and as long as it does, I guess a little part of me is out there, too.

My primary purpose in shifting my diving to the Banks was to get aboard another U-boat, this one the *U-85*, the first U-boat sunk by American forces in American waters during World War II. Bob Estep, a well-regarded local diver and skipper, was the first captain to take me to the wreck. Unlike the *U-352*, which lay inside the Gulf Stream and was covered with warm, clear water, the *U-85* was within the Labrador Current. It was a cold and murky dive, but I still got a good photographic record of the wreck. On the way back to Huntsville, I stopped at the home of Admiral Hamilton Howe, the skipper of the US Navy destroyer *Roper*, the ship that sank the *U-85*. Howe's willingness to talk about it was the first step in sorting out what had actually happened that deadly night that, up until then, was shrouded in some mystery. Bit by bit, I began to unravel the story, although it would take me years to fully understand it.

My diving obsession continued in other places, too. I documented everywhere I went, photographing underwater and topside, and wrote more articles. Key Largo's Pennekamp Park was a favorite dive where I met the famous diver Steve Klem. Steve was perfect for underwater photographers, as he had a number of pet fish, including barracudas and moray eels and sharks, who came to him to be fed on a gorgeous outcrop of coral called Molasses

Reef. Crystal River in Florida was another favorite because we could swim with the manatees and photograph those gentle creatures. Panama City and Pensacola in Florida were also favorite dives, usually with my scuba students for their open water checkouts. My bottom time, as the amount of time underwater on scuba is called, was starting to add up into hundreds of hours and my experience levels and abilities in all kinds of diving from reefs to wrecks transcended normal sport diving. With my freelance writing and scuba instruction proceeds increasing every year in the 1970s, I considered getting out of engineering and opening my own dive shop somewhere to make scuba diving and writing my full-time profession.

After a few more trips to Guanaja during which I mapped the island's reefs and left my charts and notes with the folks who were operating the new resorts of Bayman Bay and Posada Del Sol, life took a sudden turn. With the economy crashing under the well-meaning but sadly incompetent President Carter, I chucked the idea of opening a scuba shop and, even though I was selling lots of articles, began to doubt I'd ever make enough as a writer to quit government work. In a moment of frustration, I tossed out an application to the army for a job overseas just to see what would happen. The next thing I knew, which surprised even me, the purposeful adventurer was headed to Germany.

A Travelin' Man

My three-year contract was with the Seventh Army Training Command in Grafenwöhr, a sprawling American base in Bavaria north of Nuremberg and close to Czechoslovakia, which was then a Soviet client state trapped behind the Iron Curtain. As a civilian, I wasn't eligible to live on base so I moved into an apartment in a Grafenwöhr suburb with a large living room encompassing a dining area, huge windows that let in the sun, a tiny but useable kitchen, and a second bedroom that was perfect for an office.

My job required me to come up with a system to keep track of engineering work orders for the training command, similar to what I'd done for the Army Missile Command. Our office was in a quaint old chalet-style house deep into the woods of the base that had once trained Wehrmacht troops during World War II but now trained NATO infantry and armored personnel. Called the Directorate of Engineering and Housing, my office was headed up by a US Army major who was in charge of several

American civilians as managers. German nationals were our assistants and secretaries except for mine, who was a pert Doris Day look-alike named Fran Mayle. Fran was the wife of one of the army sergeants who worked out on the training ranges and the doting mother of two young children. We got along great. Ours was an efficient little office, and it didn't take long before I really liked everybody in the DEH.

To bring us up to date and make records-keeping much easier, I started researching what we could afford in the way of a computer system. This got me out of the office to visit trade shows in Frankfurt, Hamburg, and Berlin, where I learned about something new called word processing that used a small computer to take the place of electric typewriters. It was amazing to see how a document could be produced on a computer screen through an electronic keyboard, corrected there as necessary, and then printed out with as many copies as required. This was revolutionary, and I got it in my head that maybe I could combine a work order system with a central computer that also provided word processing to my office. If that was possible, we'd have the most efficient organization in NATO. Happily, the major in charge told me to see what I could find and, if he liked it, he'd look for the money to install it. As it turned out, the Massachusetts-based Wang Company had a German division that could provide exactly what I was looking for, a small package computer that I could program while also networking with word processors throughout our office. Before long, our little operation way out in the sticks of Germany was a pioneering hub in office computerization. Not only were we getting requests from NATO commands to see what we were doing, but Department of Defense officials flew from the States to observe my new system.

Once I had established myself in Germany, it was time to bring Gato over. A friend of Dave Todd's in Atlanta had kept him and, coincidentally, Dave and his wife, Ann, were assigned to Germany and stationed in Nuremberg. Dave agreed to pick Gato up at the airport in Frankfurt. When he called to tell me Gato was there, I immediately dropped everything and headed for Nuremberg, a two-hour drive. As soon as I entered their apartment, Gato, his tail up, came running down the hall and leapt into my arms with a purr that was as loud as a locomotive pulling a train through Coalwood. I held him close but was dismayed to find him just skin and bones.

"He wouldn't eat the whole time he was away from you," Dave reported. "They kept hoping he'd start but he never would. He hasn't eaten for us either."

I'd brought along some Gerber beef baby food, which I knew Gato loved. He went through three jars and then chomped down the dry food the Todds had gotten for him, too. I spent the night with them and Gato climbed under the blankets with me and, in the crook of my arm, purred us both to sleep. Back in Grafenwöhr, he soon fattened up. He loved the apartment, especially a marble shelf that ran along under the big living room windows that faced out on our street. Not only did he get the warmth of the sun but the lines of a hot water radiator ran under the shelf and he had a great view of the German countryside in warm comfort, no matter how cold and snowy it was outside.

The years in Grafenwöhr were magical and filled with travel adventures. While Fran kept Gato for me, I explored Spain in my VW bus with a friend who was a teacher for the Department of Defense school system. We camped out some of the time and stayed in little hotels here and there. Everyone was very nice and accommodating. When I got thoroughly lost in Madrid while looking for a museum that had Montezuma's feathers in it, I accidentally hooked my bumper on a tiny little car parked at the curb and pulled it out into the road. When I got out to find a policeman to make a report, some fellows sitting in an outdoor cafe got up, lifted the car off the ground and put it back where it had been and, laughing, sent me on my way. Because my friend sometimes sang in amateur Broadway shows, we took a detour to the rural province of La Mancha. Just like in Cervantes's novel *Don Quixote* and the musical *Man of La Mancha*, there really are a lot of windmills dotted across the farmland that might be mistaken for giants from a distance. We hopped over a fence so she could stand in front of one and belt out "The Impossible Dream" from the show. At the time, no dream seemed too impossible.

In Portugal, we camped beside a former French Legionnaire who, over wine, told me about fighting in Algeria in the desert and chopping up the enemy with an axe. He asked me if I wanted to see the axe but I respectfully declined. Portugal is the home of Vasco da Gama, who first sailed around Africa to India. The Portuguese still honor him, and it was interesting to visit his tomb and recall the first time I heard about him in the old Coalwood School, probably around the third grade.

Greece was a lot of fun. Never one to take an organized tour if I could avoid it, I rented an apartment in Athens with the same lady friend who went with me to Spain, and we made day trips around the country in a rental car. We sat on the porch of Poseidon's temple at Cape Sounion and contemplated Lord Byron's name where he'd carved it into the marble. In Delphi, it was amazing to be able to walk amongst the dozens of small temples built on a hillside that are still in good condition after two thousand years. The guide we found to take us around said most of the damage, not counting earthquakes, was from shepherd boys rolling down rocks over the centuries. I could see that. We used to roll rocks down in West Virginia, too. If there had been some targets like a bunch of Greek temples, what fun that would have been!

To visit Egypt required a tour group so I chose to go with a German one just to see what it would be like. Along the way, I got to know my German companions well and was amused at their frustration with the Egyptians, who were disorganized and had an *insha'Allah* or "as God wills" attitude about most everything. I liked that the tour leaders gave us a lot of free time. When nobody objected, I climbed the big pyramid nearly all the way to the top. It took me most of the day but the view was amazing. In the Valley of the Kings, we got to explore the tombs on our own when the tour guide took part of the day off. We were respectful but it was nice to just hang out in some of the chambers all by ourselves. In Upper Egypt, which paradoxically is the southern part, I rented a little boat and we floated up and down the Nile like Mark Antony and Cleopatra. The ruins in and around Luxor and at other places were amazing.

The fun of going with the Germans did not include the time in Luxor when their frustration finally boiled over at the airport. After the flight was delayed again and again, when our transport finally landed, they burst out of the terminal and stood beside the airplane and demanded it take them to Cairo. Finally, stairs were rolled up and we all got on board and there we sat for a few hours until a pilot arrived. Just the pilot. There was no copilot or attendants. The pilot, a young Omar Sharif look-alike, grinned, stuck a copy of the Koran on the cockpit door with a strip of duct tape, and took off. The cool thing was he left the cockpit door open and we could see his view. Did you know that at night

Cairo is so big and bright it can be seen from two hundred miles away? Neither did I until then.

My VW bus was also my transport several times on ferries to the United Kingdom. London became one of my favorite cities in the world. My favorite spot was Westminster Abbey and hanging out at the graves of the likes of Chaucer, Darwin, and Isaac Newton. In Scotland, I spent two days roaming around Loch Ness looking for the monster. Although I didn't see it, I did find a tick on my side at the hotel so I did discover sort of one. There wasn't a corner of the British Isles that I didn't love. On one trip, I crossed over to Ireland and drove all around the Ring of Kerry and kissed the Blarney Stone, although my friend along with me said if I had any more blarney, she couldn't imagine what I'd do with it. Along one lonely road, we came across a car wreck with a couple pinned inside their little car after being struck head-on by a big lorry. We got them out and I applied pressure to the split forehead of a lovely redheaded woman who was in the passenger's seat while my friend attended to the husband who was stuck beneath the steering wheel. Before long others showed up, including, finally, an ambulance. We were thanked profusely by all concerned.

There was also Paris, which was just a long weekend trip from Grafenwöhr. Although Parisians are supposed to be unfriendly, I never found that to be true. We got along great. Mostly, I opted to go off the beaten tourist track and just roam some of the back streets and sample the food and wine.

Since I was so close to the border, it was also possible to go across to Prague. It was a mostly depressing city because it was so dirty and unkempt, scarcely cleaned up at all from World War II. The people were great, though, and I got to know quite a few folks there. Years later when I went back at a time when the Communists were banished, I found Prague transformed into a bright, modern, and cheerful city. It's amazing what a little freedom can do for a place.

Of course, I also loved Grafenwöhr and the surrounding area. There were paths behind my apartment that led into a magical forest that reminded me of the ones in illustrations of *Grimms' Fairy Tales* with majestic oaks, lofty firs, and rocks dripping with moss. Deep in that forest was a limestone formation that someone had fashioned into a Christian shrine with crosses carved in the stone. On the other side of the forest were turnip fields that turned into snowy pastures during the winter where I could practice my cross-country skiing. The *gasthauses* in the area served amazing schnitzels and sausages that melted in your mouth. At one of them set along a small lake, I developed a taste for *schnecken*—snails in garlic-laced butter sauce. Of course, the local beer was amazing served up by Fraus and Fräuleins in Bavarian frocks. It was a place of gorgeous women. One GI said every time he walked down a street in Bavaria, whether it was in Grafenwöhr, Weiden, Nuremberg, Munich, or any of the towns and villages amongst its hills, valleys, and majestic mountains, he fell in love two or three times with women he never met.

Since I was still very interested in scuba diving, I organized two treks to Israel to travel down the Sinai and dive the crystal-clear and glorious reefs of the Red Sea. At the time, the Sinai was occupied by Israel and the expeditions were led by a man named Serge Buki, an accomplished diver and well-known Israeli explorer. His approach was to camp out along the shore of the Red Sea as we journeyed ever south all the way to Ras Mohammad on the southern tip of the Sinai. When we weren't diving, we explored the vast desert. Once, while out alone, I spotted the shadow of a ledge far above that looked like an artificial opening of some kind. To get to it, I climbed a steep cliff, worked my way along its face, and found a tomb inscribed with odd carvings that held a complete human skeleton. I led Serge back to it and, after investigation, he decided it was not recent but probably thousands of years old. I immediately wondered if it was one of the Israelites coming across from Egypt or maybe Moses himself. A recent earthquake had perhaps dislodged the hill enough that a part of the cliff face hidden for many centuries had fallen away to reveal the tomb.

"Homer, this is the problem," Serge told me. "We occupy the Sinai but Egypt owns it and eventually Israel will have to give it back. If we announce this find, it could cause a diplomatic argument on who should come study it. I think it's best we not tell anybody."

After considering Serge's advice, I agreed to cover up the tomb. I wonder to this day if it was ever rediscovered, but my guess is it's unlikely. It was high up on a nearly vertical cliff. To get to it took a curious fellow from West Virginia willing to make a difficult climb, and I doubt there's been many back there since who might try it.

Even with all the travel and work, I kept writing. I had decided to set a novel on a Caribbean island similar to Guanaja and make it a modern version of *Treasure Island*. A German U-boat wreck was worked into the plot and lots of scuba diving, so I was getting in all of my avocations and obsessions. With the thought I might yet write a book about the German U-boats in American waters, I also tracked down some U-boat crewmen and interviewed them and then spent some days in Flensburg to study the Type VII-C U-boat that was there as a memorial.

As the summer of 1981 approached, my contract with the US Army in Germany began to wind down and I needed to figure out what was next. On a whim, I decided to apply for a job with

NASA. Since I was thirty-eight years old and had no experience in the space business, I didn't expect there was any chance but thought it would be fun to have a rejection letter from NASA to go with the one from Vice President Nixon. I filled out the necessary forms and mailed them off with no expectation of success.

Unhappily, as the summer drifted by, Gato, now fifteen years old, started to show signs of kidney failure. There was a veterinarian in the nearby little town of Pressath who was excellent. He and his staff of white-starched nurses doted on Gato. They weren't familiar with Siamese cats and thought he was the most marvelous creature they'd ever seen. The vet told me that there wasn't much that could be done except to keep Gato comfortable. His last week, I never left his side. I sat beside him on the couch by day and had him in bed under the covers at night. At last, when it was clear he could go no longer and I had to say goodbye, I took him to the veterinarian to send him on his way. Afterward, I made a little casket out of an army ammunition box and wrapped him in the camouflage cover I'd brought back from Vietnam. My banana cat BC at the Oasis had slept on it and it was also Gato's favorite. I dug a grave in the garden of my Grafenwöhr apartment and there I placed him.

Although I know many people can't understand such emotion for a pet, Gato was my best friend. After he was gone, I hurt so much I couldn't go to work for nearly a week. When I finally did, I found a letter waiting for me from NASA with a number for me to call. When I called it, I found myself talking to a fellow named Jerry Richardson, who was the deputy in what he called the Spacelab Program Office at Marshall Space Flight Center in Huntsville. Would I be willing to come to work for him and his boss John Thomas? Vaguely recalling that Coalwood boy who used to build rockets, I said yes.

PART

4

NASA Man

Rocket City

When I called to tell my mom that I had a job with NASA, she allowed a soft chuckle and said, "Well, don't blow yourself up."

"Tell Dad," I instantly replied.

She was quiet for a moment and then said, "Actually, he's not here. He's at the church. I swan, Sonny, he's doing everything but writing the preacher's sermons for him and that's probably next. He's running that church like he did the coal mine. He's appointed committees of those old men and their biddies to clean the church and rake the grounds on a schedule. He's down there right now supervising."

Although tempted to remind Mom that it was she who kept insisting over several decades that Dad should move to Myrtle Beach, I didn't because we both knew he hadn't done it for her. My father had left Coalwood for the simple reason that his men refused to lower the manlift with him on it. His black lung—officially and medically called pneumoconiosis—had gotten much worse during the years I'd been in Germany. Without warning, sudden attacks caused him to collapse and gasp for breath. There was little anybody could do when that happened except administer oxygen and wait for the attack to subside. About his beloved Coalwood, Mom said it was only a shell of what it had once been. I knew Dad had to be depressed about that. If the little South Carolina church was providing an outlet for him, I was all for it.

As for my situation, changing careers midstream is usually not a good idea and I was keenly aware that what I'd done was risky. Although they are both part of the federal government, the United States Army and the National Aeronautics and Space Administration aren't much alike. They have different cultures, different approaches to problems, different management styles, different budgets, and different technologies. Although it's got helicopters, the army mostly rides on tracks and wheels through mud and dust while NASA flies on Newton's third law of physics through the air and into a vacuum. My learning curve about NASA was steep. Fortunately, my job was familiar and it became clear why I was hired. The Spacelab Program Office wanted me to install a computerized management system similar to what I'd done in Grafenwöhr.

Although I knew very well what to do in terms of office computers, I still wanted to learn as much as I could about the space business. To do that I turned to books. Fortunately, there was a fine library in the basement of the Marshall Space Flight Center's headquarters building. Since I was assigned to the Spacelab Program Office, I thought it wise to begin my studies to understand it.

When the space shuttle was designed back in the 1970s, it had one primary job and that was to deploy satellites into orbit, but its designers suggested it might also be used to carry science experiments into space and bring them back, something that had never been done before. NASA Headquarters thought that was a fine idea and told the engineers at Marshall Space Flight Center (MSFC) to start playing with some designs. The result was a plan for pressurized modules and unpressurized pallets in the shuttle cargo bay, the modules designed to contain racks and power for experiments, the pallets for attaching science payloads outside in the vacuum. When the word got out about this idea, universities, private companies, and other federal agencies sent word that if Spacelab was built, there would be plenty of experiments to fill it.

Although it had a lot of enthusiastic potential customers, the problem was Spacelab existed only on paper. Congress was at the time busily starving NASA, an ongoing situation after Apollo, and the space agency barely had enough funds to build and fly the shuttle, much less a laboratory in its cargo bay. That's when the brand-new European Space Agency (ESA), eager to learn how to operate in space, stepped up with a bag of money. Pretty soon, contracts were signed and ESA took over the construction of the modules and the pallets. To make sure the job was done right, the Spacelab Program Office in Huntsville was given the job to keep track of the fabrication of every nut, screw, valve, and deck plate of the equipment. That was the organization I had joined and why my expertise in designing computer logistics tracking systems was of interest.

Within a month of hiring on, I also became a diver in MSFC's huge water tank known as the Neutral Buoyancy Simulator. The NBS was where astronauts learned how to cope with the weightlessness of space. They did this by going underwater with weights strapped to their space suits. Once balanced by the buoyant force of water, the experience closely simulated zero gravity.

The NBS had an interesting history. Long before the shuttle or Spacelab, NASA engineers came up with the idea of building a space station from an upper stage of the Saturn V rocket. The idea was to fly it into orbit and then have astronauts pull out its fuel tanks and other hardware and install laboratory equipment. But could astronauts actually do that kind of work in space? Nobody knew.

In Huntsville, Charlie Cooper, a young engineer from Indiana who'd recently learned to scuba dive, decided to find out. After adding floats to a heavy steel ball to make it neutrally buoyant, neither sinking or floating, he pushed the ball around in a shallow water tank used to form sheet metal. He found moving it was easy. After borrowing an old pressure suit from the navy and adding weights and a homemade air system, and with the help of other MSFC scuba divers, Cooper entered the water tank and went underwater with the ball and again had no problem moving it around. Hearing of this, Wernher von Braun, then the director of MSFC, provided Cooper with a bigger metal-forming tank to further test how to work in low gravity. Before long, Huntsville had a team of neutral buoyancy space simulation experts.

MSFC, because of Cooper's work, was given the lead on neutral buoyancy simulations by NASA Headquarters even though Johnson Space Center (JSC) in Houston took a dim view of it. Training astronauts was Houston's specialty, and it surely didn't want those hicks and Germans up in Huntsville doing it. Before long, they began to lobby for their own water tank. Von Braun decided to leapfrog the competition by building a giant, sophisticated tank that Houston couldn't match. Without congressional approval, he simply declared the tank a tool, took the money he already had in an account for rocket tooling, and, using in-house labor plus a small contract with Chicago Bridge & Iron, built the Neutral Buoyancy Simulator.

NBS divers were divided into the categories of utility divers, safety divers, water safety divers, and swim camera operators. Except for a few permanent employees, we were all volunteers allowed to take time off from our normal duties to support the tank. Utility divers set up the mockups and simulators prior to the run and stood by to fix things. Water safety divers stayed on the surface to observe everything that happened below. Safety divers got to work directly with the person in the space suit or, as we called him or her, the suited subject. As soon as the suited subject got in the water, two safety divers outfitted in double tanks took him or her and proceeded to add or subtract weights to reach a state of neutral buoyancy. This was as much an art as a science, and not every safety diver was good at it. Since I was asked very often to be a safety diver, I guess I was at least adequate. Upon reflection, it was truly astonishing that somehow, without planning on it, Kismet had put me precisely where I needed to be to combine two of my obsessions, scuba diving and space.

The NBS had cameras set up around the tank to videotape the proceedings within and also a camera that could be moved around. It was called a swim camera and was inside a big, heavy box trailing an umbilical that fed its signal back to the control room. Swim camera operators were among the first women who worked in the tank. Over time, they would graduate on to be utility divers and water safety and safety divers.

Working in the NBS was fun. They paid us hazardous duty pay but the truth was most of us would have paid NASA to work there. When they came up from Houston to train, I got to know some of the astronauts, including Kathy Sullivan, the first woman to take a spacewalk, Jerry Ross, Ellison Onizuka, and Story Musgrave, among others.

In the evenings I taught scuba diving and on weekends traveled to Florida's Gulf Coast for open water work. I also started to jog and kept at it until I'd even run a marathon. My writing career was also going well. I sold articles to *Skin Diver, Sport Diver, American History Illustrated, Air & Space/Smithsonian*, and a variety of other magazines. I wasn't making very much money, but I was developing my own style and I still had in mind writing a book about the battle against the U-boats.

The first Spacelab module flown was on a mission appropriately called Spacelab 1. Launched on November 28, 1983, aboard *Columbia*, it included in its crew Owen Garriott, a veteran astronaut, and Byron Lichtenberg, one of the new breed of space fliers who didn't work for NASA but were scientists called payload specialists. Both Owen and Byron would ultimately become good friends of mine. Happily, Spacelab 1 proved itself to be an excellent platform for all kinds of scientific experiments.

As successful as the science was, I would later learn Spacelab 1 still had to be rescued by its commander, the former moonwalker John Young. As *Columbia* was nearing reentry into the atmosphere, Young routinely fired the reaction control system thrusters to properly orient the spacecraft. Warning lights flared in the cockpit that alerted him and pilot Brewster Shaw that two flight control computers had gone belly-up. Young and Shaw worked frantically to get one of them back on line in time to reenter. Then an inertial measurement unit (IMU), necessary for precise navigation, also failed. Mission Control called up and told Young to go ahead and land anyway. Young thought that advice over and elected to let the shuttle drift for a while to give everybody time to figure things out. After an extra orbit and a thorough analysis of the situation, including some reprogramming of the working computers, Young was satisfied and brought the shuttle in. Later, it was learned that if he had flown the shuttle into the atmosphere as recommended, *Columbia* would have probably broken up with the loss of spacecraft and crew.

NASA was in a dangerous business but sometimes that was easy to forget, especially when the agency was trying so hard to make spaceflight routine. My life in Coalwood and my experiences in Vietnam should have made me fully aware that danger often arises when you least expect it but if I had forgotten, I was about to get another awful reminder.

Death on the Tennessee

It was 1984. For context, President Ronald Reagan was in the White House, the Winter Olympics were held in Sarajevo, Yugoslavia, the HIV virus was discovered, the Soviet Union announced it would not go to the Summer Olympics in Los Angeles, and Metallica released its second album. In the NBS, I was thoroughly involved with supporting the training of Kathy Sullivan, Bruce McCandless, and other shuttle crew members slated for space walks. Before the astronauts came up from Houston, engineers were often put in the Extravehicular Mobility Unit (EMU) space suits to check out the procedures. The suit made a lot of folks claustrophobic but, maybe due to my scuba training or my coal miner genes, it never bothered me in the least so I got to make a number of test runs.

Other tests in the tank included some early space station ideas such as putting up micrometeoroid shields on a module mockup and studying what it would take to gut a shuttle external tank (ET) and turn it into a space station. We had an exciting time with that one. The first time we went underwater to show we could open the ET hatch, we were met with a rather large reminder concerning buoyancy. It turned out that the foam that covered the ET was extremely buoyant so when we unbolted the hatch in forty feet of water, it headed for the surface like a crazed flying saucer. I was a water safety diver that day floating above the utility divers and the next thing I knew a screaming circle of orange foam-covered aluminum was punching up through the water straight at me. My frantic kicks got me just clear of it as it burst out of the water like a Poseidon missile, ricocheted off the steel roof supports of the NBS, and then took another shot at me on the way down. Fortunately, it missed again!

Eventually, we were able to show that it was possible to clean out an ET and reconfigure it as a space laboratory, but it was a lot of work. After seeing the results, NASA administrator Jim Beggs chose not to go that route and most of us who worked on the project agreed with him. By the time you flew all the missions needed to clean out an ET and then install all the partitions, racks, and life-support equipment into its shell, it was cheaper and more effective to send up modules already outfitted and ready to go. Still, we learned a lot about what was possible in space, not to mention we had a lot of fun in the process.

Besides my coworkers with NASA, my work as an independent scuba instructor widened my circle of friends, including the staff at WAAY-TV, the local ABC affiliate television station. Announcer Carl Spurlock became one of my best friends, as did cameraman Bruce Hutson. Carl was a tremendous talent on the local stage and starred in or directed a number of Broadway shows that were incredibly well staged, acted, and produced. Not only was Huntsville full of engineering and scientific talent but there was decidedly an artistic side to the city that included such vibrant stage productions. The sets designed and operated by the same people who built the giant Saturn V booster and the engines on the space shuttle were truly amazing. As often as I could, I joined the set designers to help with the carpentry work and anything else I could do. Once, for the show *Sadie Thompson*, these astonishing amateur designers even built a water-filled ocean lagoon on stage!

When Bruce and his girlfriend invited me to go water skiing one hot July Saturday morning, I accepted but first made a cross-country flight as part of my pilot training. In a Cessna 150 rented from the Redstone Arsenal club, I did a touch-and-go at the Muscle Shoals airport that morning and then turned around and ran for Huntsville in front of an oncoming storm from the west. It was a scary sight, a deep black anvil with clouds rolling over one another like a massive airborne tidal wave. After landing and tethering the plane, I headed for the Tennessee River to meet Bruce but before I got far, the storm hit with a battering rain and high winds. When I reached the harbor, I found Bruce by himself at the gas station pier. His girl had opted out because of the storm. He told me that he'd just heard a boat had sunk and there were people in the water. We jumped into his boat and sped out onto the river and, near a tiny riverine cay called Hobb's Island, found several people standing on the pontoons of some kind of large boat that had turned over. We were told to stay away by the men on the pontoons, one of whom was a county deputy sheriff. "What boat is it?" Bruce asked him.

"Paddle wheeler," the deputy said. "The *SCItanic*. Don't know how many are on it. Maybe a dozen."

"I know the *SCItanic*," Bruce told me. "Owned by SCI. They have it for their employees."

SCI was a local computer manufacturer, its employees mostly assembly line workers. Bubbles were still coming up from the wreck, which made me think about an air pocket that might be down there, a place where trapped passengers could have perhaps found refuge. "Look, Sheriff," I said. "I'm a scuba instructor. Let me dive down, see if I can get anybody out."

The deputy thought that over and then agreed. Instantly, I dived in and swam to the wreck. There was another fellow in the water whom I recognized: "Mick" Roney, the coach of a local swim team. Somebody from another boat tossed me a snorkeling mask and Mick and I kicked into the murk below. Before we went very deep, I spotted an upside-down walkway running along the port side and followed it until I came to a door with a window. When I looked inside, I saw a man's legs hanging down. He was wearing jeans and tennis shoes. After we wrestled the door open, Mick grabbed the man around the legs, pulled him out, and we headed for the surface. The man's face was dark blue. Mick wanted to give him mouth-to-mouth resuscitation right there in the water, but I said best to get him up on the pontoons where there was a hard surface to work. The deputy took him, laid him out, and said, "He's drowned, boys. I'm sorry."

Mick and I dived again. We searched a little more on the same side but saw nothing else. In order for us to do more, we would have to get inside the boat. Just then, a boat with three scuba divers arrived. I gratefully accepted that my part in the tragedy was at an end. Those divers would get the rest of the people out if there was anybody trapped.

The trio of divers were underwater for only a few minutes before they were back up, saying that the water was too dark and cold. "Can I borrow your gear?" I asked one of them.

After a moment of hesitation, he stripped off his gear and handed it over and down I went all the way to the bottom, where I worked my way around the inverted boat. When I came to a window that was partially broken, I peered inside and saw a young woman. Apparently of Indian descent, she was wearing a green sari and white slippers and was floating peacefully with her head up. She looked so calm and peaceful, as if she were asleep. The window had horizontal glass slats. To get hold of her, I grabbed a slat and pulled it until it broke and then broke some more. When I had an opening big enough that I could reach inside, I took her by her hand and she came through easily, her long ebony hair streaming behind her. As I took her up, bubbles escaped through her partly open lips. If she still had air in her lungs, I had hope for her. After surfacing, I called to the people standing on the pontoons to take her and then dived back down and began to tear more of the window out, slat by slat, until I could finally squirm through to go inside.

As soon as I entered, I saw a man lying on the floor which, since the boat was upside down, was actually the ceiling. I swam him out just as Mick free-dived down to get him. After I made sure Mick and the man had gotten to the surface, I went back inside and looked around. Soft drink cans were rolling around everywhere. Stuffed furniture was floating overhead. Tables and chairs were lying about. An umbrella, still rolled in its case, lay on the floor and even then, the irony did not escape me. These gentle people, just out for a nice day on the river after working in a factory all week, had brought an umbrella in case of rain.

Before long, I came across a young woman floating faceup between some stuffed furniture. She had her arms crossed on her chest. A life vest floated nearby. I took her by the hand and carried her to the window and up to the surface. Mick was still busy with the previous body. I left her with him and dropped down and entered the window again and found another man and then another. With two bodies this time, I struggled my way back to the window to hand them off to Mick.

After bringing out the body of another young woman, I returned one last time and searched some more but found nobody else. I was starting to get very cold, enough that I was shivering. Still, I hunted. When I had covered everywhere I could get to, I finally swam to the surface. All the people I'd found were stretched out on the pontoons. Nobody was working on them. When I doffed the scuba gear and crawled up on the pontoons, somebody pointed out the gashes in both my hands with rivulets of blood still pouring from them. Somebody else handed me a towel to wrap my hands and then placed a scrap of tarp over my shoulders. A police launch took me back to the pier, where I was sutured up by the paramedics, six stitches in my right hand, two in my left, and then I went home.

After an investigation by the Coast Guard, it was determined that the same storm that chased me back home in the Cessna was the cause of a microburst that turned the *SCItanic* over. The survivors, all outside on the deck when the storm struck, reported that a ferocious sudden wind flipped the boat over. Fourteen passengers, just trying to have a nice holiday on the river, were trapped inside. A month later, the governor of Alabama, a fellow named George Wallace, presented Mick and me with an award that said we had performed meritorious service to the state for our part in the *SCItanic* tragedy. Although we accepted the award, I looked Mick in the eye as we stood for photographs and I could tell he was thinking the same thing I was, that we hadn't saved anybody and that we were just part of a terrible tragedy.

The sinking of the *SCItanic* had at least one positive thing come out of it and that was the realization there was a need for professional search and rescue divers in the area. When a few paramedics asked me to teach a course on it, I recruited Joe Dabbs, another Huntsville scuba instructor, to put one together. Over several weekends, we taught the course with the latest techniques for searching underwater for drowned victims. On our first training dive at a remote boat launch area, we discovered eight stolen cars dumped in the murky water. This provided another imperative for the police and other teams to be able to search the many rivers, lakes, and quarries in north Alabama. Eventually, based on the training Joe and I gave, professional search and rescue dive teams were formed that are still active today.

Challenger

After finishing my job of automating the Spacelab Program Office, I was moved upstairs with the mission managers who supervised Spacelab flights from construction through orbit. Tony O'Neil, one of the mission managers who thought I had some potential, took me under his wing and started teaching me the ropes of handling these complex flights. Before long, I was handed more responsibilities and was on an upward trajectory into NASA management. Mission Manager, Program Manager, even Center Director, all were at least feasible possibilities if I kept going on that track.

When I heard that NASA had picked a teacher to fly aboard the space shuttle, I naturally thought of Miss Freida Riley, that special teacher in my life back in West Virginia, and how much she helped me and the other Rocket Boys in our quest to build rockets and go off to the science fairs. I was certain she would have been thrilled about the idea of a teacher in space. Maybe she would have even applied. Although Miss Riley passed away in 1969 from Hodgkin's disease, she never left my mind or my heart.

The person who was selected to be the first teacher in space was named Christa McAuliffe. She wasn't from West Virginia but New Hampshire, another small, mountainous state. As Kismet would have it, I got to meet her. As part of her training, she made a tour of all the NASA centers, which naturally included a stop at our giant Neutral Buoyancy Simulator. When she came topside to the NBS, I was one of the safety divers standing on an underwater platform waiting for our astronaut to enter. As it happened, the suited subject for the day was Ellison Onizuka, who would be on her crew. After sharing a word with him, Christa took note of me standing with my head and shoulders above water and asked, "What are you doing?" She was pretty and cheerful and I liked her immediately.

I told her what we were doing and why and then made a suggestion. "Go get a swimsuit and come on in for a closer look. The water's great!"

She provided me with a huge grin. I don't mean this in any disrespectful way but Christa McAuliffe was a very nice-looking woman. I also knew my fellow divers would have absolutely loved having her in the tank.

To demonstrate how nice the water was, I splashed a little Christa's way, which made her laugh. "Can I?" she asked one of the Houston people. Their response consisted of frowns and heads firmly and negatively shook.

"Too bad," I said.

"Next time," she said while providing that amazing grin in my direction.

"That's a promise," I told her and then turned to my duties as Astronaut Onizuka entered the water.

That was the first and only time I would see Christa McAuliffe.

After its crew was at the Cape, for various schedule and weather reasons, the flight that included Christa was delayed four times. Dan Rather on the *CBS Evening News* called the delays "high tech low comedy" and most of the rest of the media jumped on NASA about it. With the criticisms ringing in their ears, the decision-makers within NASA were determined to get the launch off no matter what. On January 28, 1986, the coldest day any shuttle was ever launched, *Challenger* roared off the pad.

As the shuttle climbed into the sky with her excited crew aboard, I was not there or even in Huntsville but asleep in a Tokyo hotel. I'd been sent there to meet with the members of Japan's National Space Development Agency (NASDA) because the Japanese were very interested in flying a Spacelab mission. With me was Ken Smith, who represented the training branch in Huntsville's Mission Operations Lab.

The flight across the Pacific to Japan felt strange. The last time I'd crossed that big pond from east to west, it had been on a troop carrier bound for Vietnam. I sat and watched the endless clouds unscroll below and wondered if I was perhaps dreaming. Maybe I was still in Vietnam and would wake up and have to grab my flak vest and M79 grenade launcher to face death. This was all fancy on my part but on Pad 39-A at Kennedy Space Center, death was truly gearing up.

From the first, I liked Japan. I liked the hustle and bustle of Tokyo, I liked how well dressed everybody was and how polite they were, and I liked their energy. Every morning before meeting with the Japanese, I went out for a jog and weaved through the crowds on the streets while taking in all the sights of that amazing city. Burning calories is a lot of fun if you can chase it with donuts, so each morning I stopped at a pastry shop. The proprietor took note of my NASA T-shirt. "You NASA man?" he asked and I confessed indeed I was.

"*Columbia, Discovery, Atlantis, Challenger,*" he said, proudly naming the four ships in the shuttle fleet while adding an extra donut to my order without charge. He added, "*Challenger* tomorrow," and pointed upward.

"You're right," I said, although the truth was that I hadn't paid much attention since it didn't carry aboard a Spacelab.

At about two in the morning, the phone in my hotel room rang. It was Ken. "Have you heard about *Challenger*?" he asked. "It blew up after launch." There was a tremor in his voice and I could tell he was working hard to keep an even strain. "Everyone on board was killed. I don't know any more than that. If a reporter calls you, don't say anything!"

Those were easy instructions. After all, what was there for me to say? I knew nothing about it. The next morning, the story was all over Japanese television. The shuttle had exploded but why it had wasn't certain. When I stopped at the bakery after my morning run, the proprietor's face was clouded. "No more *Challenger*?" he demanded.

"No more *Challenger*," I confirmed.

After he gave me my donuts, he refused to take my money. A woman, perhaps his wife, came out from the kitchen. They both bowed to me and said, "Sad, we sad, we sad you."

"*Domo arigato gozaimasu,*" I replied in what was surely an awful accent but they kept their bow and I returned it as best I could.

Ken and I met with our Japanese counterparts at NASDA headquarters and were surprised when Dr. Hiroyuki Osawa, the head of the Japanese space agency, walked into the meeting room. Osawa-san gave a little speech that offered sympathy and any support that might be needed from the Japanese people to

NASA and the American people. Ken and I were touched by the gesture. After all, we were fairly low-level guys. To have the head of Japan's space agency take the time to talk to us was amazing.

After the meetings that day, we were told by our bosses in Huntsville to pack up and come home. Once home, I opened the door, pitched down my bags, and sat down on my couch and just kind of stared at nothing. Not only was I thoroughly jet-lagged, I was worried. For all I knew, the shuttle would never fly again. Maybe NASA would be shut down. Nothing was certain. In that dark moment, my cat Paco, a fluffy black-and-white boy, jumped on my lap to be cuddled. He was a comfort. The next day, I gave Mom a call. "Your dad wants to talk to you," she said after she'd ascertained that I was still alive.

"What happened to the shuttle?" Dad asked without preamble.

"I don't know, Dad," I said.

Dad was quiet for a moment. "Did you know any of the astronauts?"

"Two. I worked in the tank with El Onizuka a few times and I met the teacher, Christa McAuliffe."

"You need to figure it out, Sonny."

"Dad, I work on the Spacelab, not the shuttle. I don't have anything to do with—"

But Dad was gone and it was Mom back on the phone. "He's been a puddle of worry since that thing blew up," she said. "But I heard him tell one of his buddies at the church that Sonny would figure out how to fix it if anybody could."

Tears crept into my eyes. My dad had kind of almost said he was proud of me, so proud he'd told a friend that his boy would fix the shuttle. That's why I answered what I did. "Tell Dad not to worry. We'll soon have it flying again."

Despite my bravado with my parents, the one certainty after *Challenger*'s explosion was the shuttle fleet was grounded and it looked to be years before the spaceplanes would be operational again. John Thomas was assigned to figure out how to make the solid rocket boosters (SRBs) safe, and I volunteered to be on his team. He had a full complement of engineers, he said, but suggested I come on over anyway. This I did, being a gofer when required, and also worked through piles of paperwork and documentation as a technical editor, making comments whenever I spotted something I thought could be written a little better or didn't mean quite what the engineer had really meant to say.

One of the things that gradually became clear as I went through the documentation was that it was an accident that didn't have to happen. It was the joints lined by rubber O-rings between the segments in the solid rocket boosters that were the villains. Hot gas being produced by burning propellant had torched through one of the joints to play across the external tank until it burned through. Temperature sensors at the base of *Challenger*'s SRBs that morning read below freezing. When interviewed, Thiokol engineers who'd designed and manufactured the solid rocket boosters told John's team they had zero experience with flying at such low temperatures. This was, as it turned out, critical since the rubber O-rings were too stiff to seal, which gave the flames from inside the rocket a path to the outside.

Even though there was evidence that the seals had failed to close properly even during normal temperatures, Marshall Space Flight Center managers on the morning of *Challenger*'s liftoff pushed the Thiokol engineers to put aside their reservations. There is a phenomenon in the space business known as "launch fever." Frustration leads to poor decisions and the order is to push that button and let's go! The result of launch fever for *Challenger* was an American disaster.

Eventually, John Thomas and his team of engineers, both NASA and Thiokol, would figure out a better field joint for the SRBs and never again would the solids cause a problem on a shuttle flight.

Things were subdued at work. We had no real deadlines, nothing to aim for. Although I liked everybody in the Spacelab Program Office, I gave my situation some thought. Ken and I had bonded during the trip to Japan, and I really liked what he told me about his branch. On the flight back, when he suggested I might consider becoming a Spacelab Crew Training Manager, I was intrigued. After all, I already knew a number of the astronauts through the Neutral Buoyancy Simulator, and my work as a scuba instructor required me to know how to train people for complex and potentially dangerous situations, not so dissimilar as astronaut training. I talked it over with Chuck Lewis, Ken's boss, who said he'd be glad to have me.

My next stop was with Tony O'Neil, who said I should go with my gut, that if I was going to make a change, now might be the time to do it. After we got flying again, he said the office wouldn't want to let me go, that there would be too much to do and I'd be involved in too many actions to just walk away. I told him my gut was telling me to go train the astronauts. Tony smiled. "I thought you'd say that."

And so it was that I became a Payload Crew Training Manager, my first assignment to train the crew for Starlab, a Department of Defense Spacelab. When Starlab was canceled, I was reassigned to be the training manager for the first Japanese Spacelab, the very one I'd been talking to the Japanese about when *Challenger* had gone down. This would begin a remarkable period in my life, but first I had something else to do and that was at the world-famous Space Camp.

The Underwater Astronaut
Trainer and David Letterman

Space Camp, which is a vital part of the US Space & Rocket Center in Huntsville, Alabama, is a program designed to teach young people about space in as close to the actual environment as possible. It has an interesting history that included my boyhood hero, Dr. Wernher von Braun. In 1965, when the von Braun team was up to their eyeballs building the Saturn moon rockets, there was a great deal of public interest in what they were doing. To satisfy that interest, both Marshall Space Flight Center and the Army Missile Command dragged out some of their old rockets and put them on display at a couple of sites on Redstone Arsenal.

Getting on the army base wasn't easy, however, so not too many tourists got the chance to come out and look at them. The governor of Alabama at that time was none other than George Wallace who, when he wasn't standing in front of schoolhouse doors blocking racial integration and saying stupid racist stuff, was a fairly good governor. Wallace thought maybe something could be done to increase tourism to his state, so he and the legislature created an entity called the Alabama Space Science Exhibit Commission that evolved into the museum known as the United States Space & Rocket Center. In 1968, with money secured through the sale of state bonds, a big concrete and glass facility was built to house the exhibits, which consisted of mostly donated military and NASA rockets. Ed Buckbee, at that time an assistant chief of NASA public affairs, became its first administrator.

Once the museum was up and running, von Braun came up with another idea. "We have band camps and cheerleader camps and football camps," he told Buckbee. "So why don't we have a space camp?" Buckbee took the idea and the first Space Camp opened in 1982 and was an instant success. Tens of thousands of students, some of them future astronauts and leaders in the space business, have since passed through the Space Camp gates.

It was in 1986 when I read in the *Huntsville Times* that a swimming pool was going to be built to teach Space Campers and high-school-age Space Academy students the principles of weightlessness. The picture showed a drawing of what appeared to be a small pool and I thought to myself, why not a real neutral buoyancy simulator? I didn't know Ed and he didn't know me, but we had something pretty important in common: we were both from West Virginia. I worked up a proposal and made my pitch to him for a tank that not only could train his students but might even be rented by space companies to give the center a little added revenue.

Ed was a bit dubious. For one thing, the concrete pad was already poured for the pool so anything different had to fit the footprint. He also said his budget was small. When he named the number, he asked, "Can you do it for that amount?"

"You bet I can!" I promised, even though I had no idea if I could. Somehow, though, I did it by designing a thirty-foot diameter, twenty-five-foot-deep steel cylinder with portholes that could be easily fabricated and welded together. I even had enough money left over to purchase scuba gear. Along the way, I also designed a simulated underwater space suit that included a bubble helmet made by the Lama company in France. Ed named the tank the Underwater Astronaut Trainer (UAT) and, with permission from NASA, I formed a company called Deep Space to train the students. Deep Space hired a team of experienced divemasters and assistant scuba instructors from the Huntsville area whom I had worked with before. They included Linda Terry, a young Huntsville woman who became a divemaster while living in the Cayman Islands for a couple of years, plus Carl Spurlock, Bill Revelez, Cindy Walker, Wes Hoopengartner, Al English, and Brenda Bradford. Ed hired a recent East Tennessee State University graduate, Lori Kegley, to manage the tank and we worked very well together. After installing a mockup of a portion of the Hubble Space Telescope in the UAT, we established a quick and safe methodology to teach teenaged Space Academy students to go underwater on scuba to learn what it was like to work in the weightlessness of space. The UAT became a great success and one of the most popular simulators at Space Camp. Besides the students, we also trained real space fliers in the UAT, including Ron Parise and Sam Durrance, astronomers who orbited on the two Astro Spacelab missions, plus Byron Lichtenberg, who went into space aboard the first Spacelab flight and also Spacelab ATLAS-1.

It was a period of my life that was not only filled with interesting work but was a very happy time. My Deep Space divers plus a few others formed a loose-knit group we called the Shallow Divers. Our motto was "The deeper we go, the shallower we get!" We had more fun than you can imagine. One of our running jokes was, for a price, we carried around spare air for any diver who was getting low. We also had a change-maker on our weight belt. After an evening of working with students at the UAT, we'd often go to a local pizza joint and eat and drink and tell stories and laugh a lot. If I could go back to any part of my life and just stay there, I think it would be to the era of the Shallow Divers.

One of my divemasters, Linda Terry, probably had more hours in the Lama helmet than anyone outside of France and maybe inside it, too. When we simulated swapping out an electronics box on the side of a space station, she usually put on the helmet and the boots, gloves, coveralls, and backpack of our wet space suit and demonstrated to the chosen students how to do the work. She was a breathtakingly beautiful blonde woman of Scandinavian descent on her mother's side, spirited, and came with a love of adventure. Naturally, we hit it off, although our relationship was often a bit rocky because we both enjoyed our independence. It would take some years to fully develop and neither one of us was in any hurry.

In 1988, a call came in to my NASA office with an unidentified voice on the other end wanting to know if I was Homer Hickam, the expert on the Lama helmet. I said I was and the reply was, "How would you like to come up to New York and teach David Letterman how to wear that helmet underwater?"

"Who is this?" I demanded. I was suspicious it was Carl Spurlock, my jokester buddy who was a man of a thousand voices. "Is that you, Carl?"

It wasn't Carl but really was a producer of Letterman's NBC late-night program who said, "Look, we're thinking about doing an underwater show. Can you come up here and spend some time with Dave?"

At that time, David Letterman was a young, up-and-coming television personality whose show came on right after *The Tonight Show* with Johnny Carson. I'd only seen Letterman's show a couple of times but I heard he was funny. Still, I wasn't entirely thrilled at the idea of traveling all the way to New York to teach him how to breathe inside a French plastic bubble. "I don't know," I told him. "I'm pretty busy."

The producer was a little astonished at my lack of enthusiasm. He sputtered a bit, then said, "We'll pay you."

My response was typically American. "How much?"

He named a number that sounded good, and that's how I ended up flying to New York to train David Letterman how to scuba dive and wear the Lama helmet. For the first time in the entire history of my life, I had a first-class ticket and sat beside a fellow I thought looked familiar. We shook hands. "I'm Jay Leno," he said. "Where you heading?"

I told him and he laughed. "Well, try not to drown him."

"You substitute for Johnny Carson," I said, the truth of whom I was sitting beside dawning on me.

Leno smiled. "What do you think? I do OK?"

"Sure," I answered. "You make me laugh."

"Well, Homer Hickam," he said, "have fun in the big city!"

"I guess I will," I said and then we chatted about NASA for a while and then about the book I was writing that told the story of the U-boat battles along the American coasts during World War II.

"Sounds interesting, although not very funny," he said. "Still, you get it published, call me and I'll see if you can come on my show." Not having any clue on how marvelous such a thing would be for a book, I told him I would. He gave me his card, which, before the weekend was out, I managed to lose.

Once in New York, I was put up at a midtown hotel, then chauffeured across the bridge to New Jersey to a Red Roof Inn, which had an indoor swimming pool. Buckbee had shipped them one of our Lama helmets and NBC provided a crew to record everything, including a diver with an underwater camera. I was introduced to Letterman, who was casually dressed in nice slacks and a shirt. "Are you ready to get in the helmet?" I asked.

"What am I supposed to do?" he asked, his voice betraying a little nervousness.

"Well, it's just like diving except you won't have a regulator in your mouth."

"What do you mean regulator?"

"The thing you breathe through when you dive," I replied.

"But I don't know how to dive," he said.

"You don't know how to dive?"

"No. Are you going to teach me?"

"I guess I am now."

While David went off to get into his swimming trunks, I called the producer over. "You didn't tell me he wasn't scuba certified."

"What difference does it make?"

"He could die in the Lama helmet if he doesn't know the rules of scuba."

"Aren't you a scuba instructor?"

"Yes."

"Then teach him."

"How much time do I have?"

He looked at his watch. "Two hours. Including getting him in the helmet."

"A normal scuba diving course usually takes about forty hours."

He clapped me on my shoulder. "Well, son, good thing you and Dave aren't normal!" And then he wandered off.

Of course, I had brought along my own dive gear and, happily, there was another set of scuba gear the underwater photographer had brought along. To train David, I decided to treat him like a Space Camper. Once I had him in the water, I said, "All right, David, here's what's going to happen. You're going to listen to me and do exactly what I tell you to do when I tell you to do it. There are three Homer Hickam rules of scuba diving. First one is never, never, *never* hold your breath. You do that, you can embolize."

"What does that mean?"

"It means you'll spit up blood and then die."

His eyes widened. "Got it. What's the second one?"

"Come up slowly."

"If I don't, will I die?"

"Probably. The third one is if it hurts, don't do it. If you feel pain of any kind and that includes mental pain, stop what you're doing. OK?"

"OK. I think I want to get out of the water now."

"Are you in pain?"

"That mental pain thing. What do you call it? Fear?"

I laughed, which I think was actually his purpose. "Your producer paid me a lot of money to train you in two hours to wear a bubble helmet, so you've got to stay in here and do what I tell you."

"How much is he paying you?"

I told him and this time it was David who laughed. "I could pay you more than that out of my wallet."

"I also gave him my word."

"You're from the South, aren't you?"

"Pretty much."

"What's with all that honor stuff down there, anyway?"

"We're just stupid, I guess. You ready?"

"Boy, howdy, I reckon."

"Here we go."

And there we went. In two hours, I not only taught David Letterman how to safely scuba dive, at least in a New Jersey Red Roof Inn swimming pool, but I had him in the Lama helmet in the deep end. The underwater cameraman moved in and captured it all. After we got out, David pulled me aside. "I really had fun," he said. "You know your stuff. What's your favorite dessert?"

"Brownies," I said.

He snapped his fingers and an assistant came running. "I want the best brownies in New York City for my buddy Homer."

Afterward, sitting beside a pyramid of the lushest, richest brownies I'd ever seen, David and I chatted about a little of everything, including Jay Leno. "You sat beside him?" he asked. "I wonder what he's doing in New York? The Carson show is in Los Angeles."

I was sure I didn't know and said so. "I wonder if he's visiting NBC suits," David mused. "They like him more than me."

I still didn't know. After David went off with his girlfriend, his producer came over. "Good job," he said. "You definitely earned your pay."

"David said you didn't pay me enough."

"Did he? Well, that's why he's the talent and I'm the producer."

"So what are you going to do with David in the Lama helmet?"

The producer went over his plan. They were going to build a set that looked just like Dave's regular one but it would be immersed in the Mystic Aquarium. Dave would be in the Lama helmet and so would all his guests. They were hoping to get actress Teri Garr as one of them.

"What's the water temperature in the Mystic Aquarium?" I asked.

"I checked on that," he said. "It's around sixty-five degrees, which is great. David likes the studio cold."

I factored in that temperature and said, "OK, here's the deal. By the time David finishes his monologue, his teeth will be chattering."

"Why is that?"

"His body temperature is 98.6 degrees or thereabouts. The human body has about two gallons of blood. The Mystic Aquarium has about a million gallons of water. That water will pull the heat right out of David, trying to get him down to 65 degrees, too."

"Teeth chattering? We can deal with that," the producer replied.

"By the time he has his first guest on, he will also be shivering uncontrollably..."

"Maybe if we gave him some hot chocolate...or brandy. That's it, we'll give him brandy!"

"...and by the time the second guest comes on, he will be unconscious. By the end of the show, he will be dead. It's called hypothermia. Don't take my word for it. Ask a doctor."

After being allowed to view *Saturday Night Live* from backstage where Jon Lovitz wanted to talk about NASA and almost missed his cue for a sketch, I flew to Huntsville, my adventure complete. Although the underwater show never happened, I at least left David Letterman thoroughly enamored with the idea of being a scuba diver. He'd later get certified and enjoy lots of diving adventures.

Many years later, I met David again. This time, I was a guest on his show because of the movie *October Sky*. Before I went on set, one of David's people approached me and asked if it would be all right if they showed footage of us that day in the New Jersey Red Roof Inn swimming pool. They also said if they did, they wouldn't have time to show a clip of the movie.

I gave that some thought. "Let's do it," I said out of homage to David and to the young fellow I'd been a decade before on an adventure in New York.

The interview went great, David and I had a lot of fun, our underwater training was shown, the clip from the movie wasn't shown, and the Universal Studios folks weren't very happy about the entire thing. After the show, I met bandleader Paul Shaffer backstage and asked him how I did. He gave that some thought and said, "Purely cosmic," which I took as high praise.

The *U-85*

And then there was that time when I was driving at night through the construction site of an overpass in Huntsville that would eventually connect Memorial Parkway and the spur known as I-565. There were concrete barriers and orange barrels everywhere and there were several sharp curves to get through them. All of a sudden, a compact car flew past me, traveling at a high rate of speed. It proceeded to swerve into one of the barriers, swipe another with sparks flying, roll over twice, and burst into flames. Most drivers kept going but not me. Without pausing to change into my Superman costume with cape flying, I stopped, jumped out, and ran to the car, which was boiling with flames and smoke. A woman was hanging by her seat belt through a half-open door. With the heat blasting my face, I reached inside, unlatched the seat belt, and pulled her free. When she fell to her knees, I picked her up and put her arm over my shoulders and, with my arm around her waist, pulled her away. Behind us, the car exploded, a shower of burning debris sent soaring aloft like

288

embers from a crackling fire. Pieces of it fell around us as we stumbled away.

I steered her toward my car while the woman kept hanging on to me to keep herself upright. My thought was maybe she had suffered a concussion. With cars whizzing past us in the darkness that was illuminated only by her burning wreck, I was able to get her safely to my Honda and in the passenger's seat. Cars continued to fly by, some dangerously swerving past the burning vehicle. I waited until one skimmed past nearly hitting me and then quickly opened the door and lunged into the driver's seat. "I'm taking you to the hospital," I told her as I got my first look at her. She was young, pretty, but with long, unkempt hair that looked like it hadn't been combed for a while.

When I pressed on the accelerator to pull out and match the speed of the other cars, she sat quietly until she said, "I don't wanna go to the hospital."

Her words were slurred and I smelled alcohol. The first inkling of the truth started to slowly seep into my brain. "You need to go to the hospital, get checked out," I insisted.

"No. I can't go there! Take me home. I'll show you."

Cars were still thundering past way too close for comfort. In the rearview mirror, I could still see her burning car. I assessed the situation and did what I thought was best and that was to take this woman wherever she wanted to go. Although she had trouble enunciating, she was able to tell me how to get there, which turned out to be not a house or an apartment but a cocktail lounge on the seedy side of town. "Why'd you do it?" she asked. "Save me, I mean."

"I thought you needed saving."

She chuckled. "Tha's what all you men say, honey." She leaned over, kissed me on the cheek, and got out and walked unsteadily into the lounge whereupon, my duty accomplished, I drove away.

Once home and after giving the situation some thought, it occurred to me that maybe leaving the scene of an accident that included a burning car on the parkway and where I had taken the driver, the *drunken* driver, to a bar might best be reported to the police. So, meaning to stay anonymous, I called 911 to tell them where I'd last seen the driver of that burning car they had maybe noticed. The woman who answered listened while I explained that I had rescued a young woman from that car because she had gotten trapped in her seat and then afterward sort of, you know, took her to a cocktail lounge and named said lounge. There was a slight pause on the part of the 911 operator and then she asked, "Is that you, Homer?" On the line was Tina McDonald, a policewoman I had trained to scuba dive who obviously had a good ear for voices. "We've been looking for that driver!"

Although I received no award for my act of heroism and altruism, I wasn't arrested either. Forever too embarrassed to ask Tina, I don't know what happened to the poor woman in peril, although I've often wondered if the police went to the cocktail lounge to arrest her for drunken driving only to realize she had the perfect alibi since, well, of course she was drunk because she was in a bar courtesy of Homer Hickam! Still and all, I'm glad I saved that young woman and I hope she got her life together.

As busy as I was with NASA and the UAT and saving drunken women whether they liked it or not, I was still obsessed with discovering the truth behind the U-boat battles along the American coasts during World War II and began to focus on the *U-85*, the first German sub sunk by American forces.

The *U-85*'s battered hulk rests on the sand some fifteen miles off Nags Head. After several dives on it, I had a good picture of it in my head and some fair photos taken with my trusty Nikonos II and Subsea 150 strobe. Compared with the *U-352*, it was a beat-up wreck. Sand covered a lot of it and filled its interior. Its deck gun was in place, its barrel covered with cold-water corals and sponges. A small spotted moray's head poked from the gun, where it watched with interest whenever divers swam past its home.

Over a couple of years, I teased the story of the *U-85* out of the archives and from the captain and crew of the destroyer *Roper* that sank it. *American History Illustrated* published it under the title, "The Night of the Roper." My article, thoroughly documented, showed that Captain Hamilton Howe, the *Roper*'s skipper, was so worried about the U-boats that he kept his destroyer at a high pitch of readiness that left the crew little time to sleep. Frustration, fatigue, and fear permeated the old destroyer.

On the night of March 13, 1942, Lieutenant Kenneth Tebo had the *Roper*'s con. On board was a primitive form of radar. When the radar operator reported a contact just ahead, Tebo ordered the *Roper* to catch up with it. Before long, a white, glowing streak passed by the destroyer's port side that Tebo thought was a torpedo. Howe arrived on the bridge and ordered general quarters. Searchlights played across the water and then—there!—a U-boat was spotted to port, its crew scrambling out on deck to man its deck gun. When the destroyer tried to beat the U-boat men to the punch, all of its guns jammed except one, a three-inch gun commanded by Seaman Harry Heyman, who aimed and fired and later reported he struck the U-boat just beneath the conning tower. The submariners abandoned ship and yelled at the destroyer crew to help. Instead, Captain Howe dropped depth charges, which killed all the Germans.

The next day, the bodies of the U-boat crew were carried into Norfolk, where the FBI took over. Since the battle along the coast was still a state secret, the federal government quietly interred the Germans in the Hampton National Cemetery. One of them was Erik Degenkolb, who'd kept a diary that I managed to acquire from the National Archives. The archives also led me to Harry Heyman, the *Roper*'s gunner, who lived in New Jersey. When I interviewed him, I found out he was upset that the official history by the navy said the *U-85* was scuttled by the Germans even though he was sure it was his three-inch round that had sunk it. Obsessed with discovering the truth for Mr. Heyman, I decided to dive on the *U-85* and focus on the base of the conning tower to see if there was a hole there deep enough to have penetrated the inner hull of the submarine.

I was accompanied by Carl Spurlock, Bruce Hutson, and several other Huntsville-based divers. After visiting the Hampton cemetery to inspect the graves of the *U-85*'s crew, including Erik Degenkolb's, we made our way back to Nags Head for the night and then set out for the *U-85* aboard a dive boat I'd used before named *Sea Fox* captained by a local character named Doogie Dugan. I'd divemastered with Doogie a couple of times before.

At the buoy that marked the wreck, we descended into a swirling gray maelstrom. The water was ice cold. When I reached the deck of the U-boat, I headed for the conning tower to inspect it along its base on the starboard side. Since Heyman's gun had been on the *Roper*'s port side and the U-boat and the destroyer were pointed in the same direction, it made sense that if the round had hit, the hole it left would be there.

I wormed my way into the wreckage until I spotted what looked to be a puncture right where one should have been if Heyman's claim was correct. Since I knew the thickness of the outer shell and inner pressure hull, I worked my hand into the hole to see how deep it went. I kept pushing until my arm was all the way in up to my shoulder. There was no question that Heyman's round had blasted through the *U-85*'s pressure hull. When I pulled my hand back, my thumb encountered a jagged steel edge that sliced it to the bone. Since blood isn't red at depth but green (warm colors are filtered out by the water), there was a lot of green flowing out of my hand.

After the dive, Carl drove me to the local clinic where my injury was thoroughly cleansed by a nurse and then the cut sutured. Carl's version of the story was that he sat in the waiting room while beautiful nurses, hearing of the handsome diver needing help, hurried in and out of the surgery room. He heard bits of my conversation as the doors swung open and close. "There I was on this U-boat wreck, and then…" [swish, swash] "I'm a writer and a NASA engineer…" [swish, swash] "Sharks to the left of me, sharks to the right of me…" [swish, swash] and so forth. Of course, I don't remember it that way at all. What I do remember is how happy Harry Heyman was when I made the trip to New Jersey to tell him he had, indeed, sunk the first U-boat ever by the United States Navy.

An Author at Last

After years of working on the history of the World War II U-boat battles up and down the East and Gulf Coasts of the United States, I thought I had enough to write a book about it. But how to find a publisher? As it turned out, I knew a writer who'd already written a book about submarines. When I first met him, he was an insurance broker in Maryland who called me to talk about submarines after he read one of my articles in *American History Illustrated*. We had several nice chats, although his interest was in nuclear submarines and mine was on old 1940s German submarines. He seemed like a nice fellow but he'd never published anything, not even an article, so I doubted he would ever be published. That insurance broker's name, by the way, was Tom Clancy and the book he wrote was titled *The Hunt for Red October*. It was published by the Naval Institute Press. If they liked Tom's book, I figured they would like mine, too, so I set about attracting their attention.

Completely ignorant of the best way to approach them, I took the simplest. I boxed my manuscript up, put their address on the outside of it, and mailed it off. A few weeks later, it came back with a curt note from an editor saying that he had looked it over and, unfortunately, it wasn't right for the NIP. I thought about that and, because I didn't know any better, did the unthinkable. I sent the manuscript back, without a word changed, and asked for someone else to read it. What happened next was astonishing because someone else did read it and the next letter that came back was a note of acceptance. In April 1989, *Torpedo Junction* was published and went on to become a military history bestseller. It is still in print.

One of the greatest pleasures of becoming a published book author was to imagine the effect it would have on my parents and especially my dad. I shipped off a copy of the book to them in Myrtle Beach and waited. And waited. Days went by, and then a week, and then another. Although I talked to Mom once a week, she never mentioned the book. Finally, unable to stand it any longer, I got up the courage to ask her if she and Dad had read my book. "I haven't yet, Sonny," she said. "Your dad has it."

"Has he read it?" I gulped.

"Oh, yes, several times."

"And…?"

"He said it was well researched." While I absorbed this, Mom added, "He ordered a dozen copies for his friends at the church."

I was thrilled! As far as I was concerned, "well researched" was high praise from my dad. And ordering a dozen copies? That was amazing to hear.

Mom said, "Your dad's been published, too. He wrote an article about Coalwood. It got published in *Coal* magazine."

This was news for a couple of reasons. First, I had no idea that Dad could write and, second, I was surprised anyone would want to read about Coalwood.

"I'll send you a copy," Mom said.

When I received Dad's article, I was impressed. It was really good! His writing was crisp and told the story of Coalwood from the time Mr. Carter founded it until the closure of its mine, a moment that must have broken Dad's heart, once when it actually happened and again when he wrote about it. I put his article on my list of things I wanted to talk to him about, but every time I called, he was somewhere else. "You know what you should do, Sonny?" Mom said. "He's not much for visiting on the phone and when you're here. I've never seen you talking much, so why don't you write him a letter and tell him what you want to say?"

It was good advice and I also put that on my list of things to do, but in September of that year, while I was visiting Guanaja, Dad suddenly died, the black lung finally getting the best of him. Because there were no telephones on the island, I didn't know he was gone until I got back, a week after the funeral.

I made certain Mom was settled back into the house she loved, near the great brown strand of beach that runs along the Atlantic, and then I came home. The list of things I wanted to tell my dad was long, but now there was no way to say them and I had waited too late to write them down in a letter. It was a weight on my heart and, rather than diminishing as the years passed, it seemed to get ever heavier but I had no clue what to do about it.

Ease Your Bosoms

From 1989 to 1992, I was the training manager for Spacelab-J (also known as SL-J), a mission that was designed to carry Japan's first official astronaut into space. The Japanese people were enamored with spaceflight, and to see its space agency join the great American NASA, conquerors of the moon, was a hugely popular and closely followed event. The three Japanese chosen as astronaut candidates, two men and one woman, were treated like rock stars. Since only one of them would be picked to fly, it was also something of a game. Who would be picked? Who was the best? There was endless talk about it in Japan. Would it be Dr. Mamoru Mohri, the solid scientist and family man, or Dr. Takao Doi, the handsome, dreamy astronomer, or Dr. Chiaki Mukai, the surgeon who had held beating hearts in her hands? Although it was the last thing I ever expected, I would end up helping to make that decision.

In terms of a basic job description, my role as the NASA payload training manager of SL-J was to see its crew trained on how to operate the instruments and experiments aboard the Spacelab module. There were two phases to training on Spacelab missions. The first was what we called PI-site training. A PI, in NASA parlance, was the principal investigator who was usually a top scientist but could also be a university, a company, or even a country. PI-site training meant the astronauts would go to the location of the PI for initial training. The second phase was for the crew to come to the Payload Crew Training Complex (PCTC) in Huntsville where simulators representing all the experiments were combined in high-fidelity Spacelab modules for what was called integrated training. This two-tiered training plan had worked perfectly for the three Spacelab missions prior to SL-J. There was no reason to expect it wouldn't work perfectly for my mission either.

My first duty was to go to Japan with the three American astronauts who were assigned to SL-J. The only direction I got from my various supervisors was to help out where I could with the schedule and accommodations but not to interfere with the Japanese. Collecting information on the Japanese experiments and their simulators was also on my list so they could be later integrated into the PCTC. The Japanese, I was told very clearly, were to have full responsibility for the training, every facet of which had been approved by both NASA Headquarters and Japan's National Space Development Agency (NASDA).

Although I read the documents carefully, nothing in all the stacks of papers that were given to me on the Japanese experiments gave me much insight into how the training would be conducted. All I knew was NASDA wanted the American astronauts to spend a total of nine months in Japan broken up in three segments, the first from October to just before Christmas in December 1989, the second the following spring, and the third to be determined by the shuttle launch schedule. When I laid out this plan to the three American astronauts in a meeting in Huntsville, they gave no objections. In October 1989, I flew with these same three to Japan with great expectations for a very interesting, productive, and enjoyable time in a foreign land. Instead, on the very first day of training in the very first class, I found myself in the middle of a diplomatic crisis that threatened the entire mission.

At first, it didn't seem like much. During the couple of days we had to recover from jet lag, I got to know the three American space fliers by having meals with them and walking around together and gawking at downtown Tokyo. They apparently didn't know each other very well and all were from very different backgrounds, and my thought was that training away from Houston was just what they needed to weld them into a team.

Our initial set of classes was at the NASDA headquarters in Tokyo. Joining us were the three Japanese astronaut candidates, even though they were thoroughly familiar already with the experiments. The idea was for them to get to know the American crew and to assist in any way they could during the training.

The first class was conducted by one of the most honored and respected scientists in the country from the Tokyo Medical and Dental University, an elderly man I will call Dr. Yamaguchi. When Dr. Yamaguchi began the class, it was clear his English was not very good. Immediately, I noticed squirming by one of our astronauts, who then proceeded to turn around and glare at me before slumping back into his chair with his arms crossed. I wasn't sure if he wanted me to do something but since it wasn't my class but NASDA's, I just paid attention to what the learned scientist was trying to say in his somewhat broken English. When Dr. Yamaguchi asked our astronauts, one by one, to read aloud from a book that described the science of his experiment, the squirming by that particular astronaut got worse and I got more dirty looks. Although the other two NASA astronauts read the book as they were told, when it came the turn of the squirmer, there was an adamant refusal. After a confused and nervous Dr. Yamaguchi asked the astronaut again and was refused again, he asked for everyone to please close their books. He had some flip charts and used them to continue with his class, although, with his limited English, not much of what he said was understood. I made a note to suggest to the Japanese that they provide an interpreter for future presentations by their scientists and perhaps not ask the crew to read aloud. I figured that would be the end of it. What I didn't anticipate was the explosive reaction of the Japanese to what had just occurred.

After the crew went back to the hotel, I was asked to visit with my NASDA counterparts. In a meeting room, Mr. Suzuki, the lead NASDA training manager, and a half dozen of his training staff waited for me. They were grim-faced and their heads were bowed. After I sat down, there was silence until I finally asked, "Is something wrong?"

"Why you not like read in classroom?" Mr. Suzuki demanded.

It was late, I was still somewhat jet-lagged, and also of the opinion that this was a small matter. I tried to explain the situation logically. "Reading aloud isn't commonly done in the United States except in primary schools" was my answer, which might have been logical but it wasn't enough.

"We are ashamed," one of the trainers said.

"You shame us!" Mr. Suzuki reiterated in no uncertain terms.

"Look," I said with a smile while holding up my hands in a gesture meant to slow things down, "it was just a little misunderstanding."

The grim faces around the table told a different story. "Dr. Yamaguchi was dishonored," Mr. Suzuki said.

The seriousness of the situation was finally sinking in. "I'm sorry," I said. "We're all just tired, that's all. Everything will be better tomorrow."

Before I could say anything else, not that I had anything else to say, Mr. Suzuki and his team rose as one and filed out of the room except for a young woman. Unlike the NASDA officials who'd kept their hands in their laps during the meeting and their heads mostly bowed, she'd kept her hands clasped on the table, her eyes boring into mine. I suspected she was going to have something to say and I was correct. After the door closed, she said, "You must apologize."

I was confused as to who she was. "Excuse me. Have we met?"

"I am Hoshiko. I was hired by NASDA to be your assistant. I will give you the schedule with copies for the crew and will tell you what you need to know about the training. I will suggest to you hotels or houses for the crew to stay. And transportation, I will arrange. I will interpret documents. Anything you need." She cast her eyes toward the door where the training staff had disappeared into the hall. "Suzuki-san will go now to tell Director Osawa. Suzuki-san will lose his job. Director Osawa will apologize to Dr. Yamaguchi and to NASA and to prime minister. Prime minister will apologize to American ambassador."

I stammered, "Wait, wait, *what*?"

The situation had clearly spun out of control. If it kept spinning until NASA Headquarters heard about it, it would surely produce a large quantity of unfortunate excrement that would then slide downhill to Huntsville and then on top of the mission manager and then my lab and my supervisors and then, of course, *me*. "What can I do to fix this?" I frankly begged this young woman.

She rose from the table. "Wait," she said.

When she left the meeting room, I wasn't exactly sure what I was waiting for or for how long so I took the time to compose a note to the folks in Huntsville on what had happened. Before long, Hoshiko returned. "Director Osawa will see you," she said. "You apologize, Homer-san."

This sounded hopeful and I had a sudden idea on how to make things even better. "I want to give my apology in Japanese," I proposed to my unexpected NASDA assistant. "Will you teach me what to say?"

She looked doubtful but then sat beside me and wrote out the words. I struggled with them. There was nothing recognizable in them, no root words that helped me, just sounds I needed to make. *Moushiwake arimasen.* I first pronounced them "Mouse shi wake arry mason."

She gently corrected me. "Mo-she-wa-kay. Ah-ree-mah-sin."

The sounds were alien to my tongue and ears.

"Homer-san, we must hurry," she said urgently. Usually precise in her pronunciations, I would learn when she was anxious, Hoshiko tended to confuse her r's and l's, neither letter existing in Japanese. "Prease rook at me." I looked at this woman who was my lifeline. "Mo-she-wa-kay. Ah-ree-mah-sin. Prease say."

After I'd committed both words to memory, Hoshiko escorted me to an elevator and we rose to the top floor. A receptionist nodded to us and I entered the surprisingly small office of Dr. Hiroyuki Osawa, the director of NASDA. He was the same man who'd been so kind to Ken and me after the *Challenger* accident. He rose from behind his desk and walked around it and bowed deeply. I made an awkward bow back. When he didn't ask me to sit, I said, "Director Osawa, I apologize for me and my crew today. We did not mean to embarrass Dr. Yamaguchi. Please let him know that." I added, *"Moushiwake arimasen."*

He studied me for a moment and then said, "Welcome to Japan," and bowed again. I returned his bow and, since I sensed he was done with me, turned and left the office.

Hoshiko was waiting for me at the door. "Did I say it right?" I asked.

"Mr. Suzuki is waiting," she replied, which I took as somewhat noncommittal.

She led me into the elevator and back down to the third floor and into the big open bay where Mr. Suzuki and his training staff were working away at their desks. "Do they ever go home?" I whispered.

"To leave first is no good," she said. "They work late, come early. They are grateful for jobs. They love space." She stopped and looked at me. "You love space, too, Homer-san?"

Did I love space? At that moment, what I would have loved best was a good night's sleep. I repeated my memorized apology in Japanese to Mr. Suzuki who, after several bows, seemed to accept it. Still, I was honest with him about what might happen in the future. "Suzuki-san," I said, "in the United States, if astronauts don't like the training, they say so. I can't change that. That's their culture. But maybe if you let me review your lesson plans before they're given, I might be able to help keep anything like what happened today from ever happening again."

Mr. Suzuki, whose English was somewhat limited, and Hoshiko had a conversation in Japanese where she apparently explained my suggestion. "Training is Japanese to give," she said to me at the end of their talk. "Not NASA. That is our agreement."

"Of course," I said. "Training is your responsibility, but maybe I can be an advisor."

Hoshiko considered this. "You are saying you work for NASDA?"

"Absolutely."

"Does absolutely mean yes or no?"

"It means yes."

Hoshiko talked some more with Mr. Suzuki and then turned back to me. "Do you expect to be paid by NASDA?"

"No, no," I said. "For free."

"But you work for NASDA?"

"Sure. Absolutely. *Hai.*"

After Hoshiko relayed my answer, Mr. Suzuki arched an eyebrow and almost smiled. "You work for us," he said.

"Is this OK, Homer-san?" Hoshiko asked.

Was it OK? If I said yes, I was agreeing to at least partially cross over to the Japanese side, to be a player on their team, to be as loyal to them as NASA. This was outrageous, of course, because I was an American, a NASA engineer, and entirely devoted to our astronauts and my various bosses up and down and sideways in NASA. I used to laugh and say there wasn't anybody in NASA who didn't think they were my boss and, of course, I was entirely loyal to all of them. That's why I bowed to Mr. Suzuki and said, "*Hai.* I work for you, Suzuki-san!"

And so it was that I became the unpaid and secret advisor to the Japanese space agency. With great relief at avoiding an international incident and the loss of my neck, I asked to see the next day's lesson plans and sat down with Hoshiko to review them. It didn't take long before I had a major suggestion. When Hoshiko explained it to Mr. Suzuki, he sucked through his teeth but agreed and went off to make it happen. With that one suggestion given and taken, I felt as if I'd already earned every yen NASDA wasn't going to pay me.

Even though I'd sort of more or less kind of crossed over to the other side, I still had a responsibility to the folks in Huntsville so I called the mission manager to apprise him of the incident and to also let him know I thought I'd fixed things. He wasn't in, but I left a message and told him to look for my NASAMAIL note coming his way with more details.

If the situation wasn't already somewhat dire, it suddenly got direr when I heard from a fellow at the American Embassy. I knew who he was because he'd called me before I'd left the United States. I'd taken it as just a complimentary call, let us help if we can, yada yada, but it was clear by this call he was paying attention to Spacelab-J. Somehow, and I would never find out how, he'd heard about the incident with Dr. Yamaguchi and was more than a little agitated. He calmed somewhat when I told him about my apology but he was still plenty worried. "If the press gets hold of this," he said, "there's gonna be a stink right up to the White House."

To that I had no answer, but he did. "Here's what we're going to do. If there's anything that might cause bad press while your crew is over here, you get hold of me instantly. Understood? Don't go through your NASA channels. Come straight to me because from now until the end of this, you represent the ambassador. I also want you to call or write me at least once a week and tell me everything that's happening. Do you understand? It's important that you say yes."

So I not only said yes but "yes, sir!" meaning I was now not only on the Japanese team, I was on the American ambassador's team, both jobs without the slightest permission from NASA. I wasn't up the creek without a paddle. I was up the creek with about three paddles and no canoe because an astronaut wouldn't read aloud from a damn book, an astronaut I had zero authority over and, actually, kind of agreed with. We couldn't and shouldn't spend months in Japan with that kind of slow-motion training!

I sent my NASAMAIL note to the mission manager with a cc to Ken Smith and Chuck Lewis, my direct supervisors, which left off those parts about me doing this and that for NASDA and the embassy, don't ask me why. By then, it was approaching midnight and still there was scarcely an empty desk in the training team's office. Hoshiko was gone, so I walked to my hotel and waited for the telephone to ring with either Ken or Chuck or the mission manager or the ambassador or the NASA administrator or the president of the United States on the other end hopping mad. When it didn't ring, I took that as good news. In the morning, I went to Hoshiko's computer and checked my NASAMAIL. There were replies from both Ken and the mission manager, each in their own way saying, essentially, they were not thrilled by what had happened but glad it had been smoothed over and to keep them apprised.

Maybe I should have felt relieved but what I mostly felt was a sense of failure. I had seen the training schedule before coming to Japan, I had seen who was going to be giving the presentations, I had seen everything and yet I had seen nothing. Because I thought it wasn't my responsibility, I had made no attempt at all to familiarize myself with the way the Japanese had already trained their three astronaut candidates, no matter that their culture was entirely different from ours, that their educational system was different, that there were bound to be differences that might unsettle the crew. Why had I not done my research? What part of training manager didn't I get? I needed to manage training! On top of that, wasn't I a great researcher? I had, after all, unraveled the battle against the U-boats along our coasts during World War II in such a way and to such a depth that no one else had even come close. The technical library on Redstone Arsenal had floors lined with shelves laden with books about every subject under the sun, and the adjunct at Marshall Space Flight Center was also full of books about the space programs of the world. Didn't I say when I was a Rocket Boy in Coalwood that what I needed most of all was a book that would tell me what I needed to know? Why had I not done my research about the Japanese? In short, I had let the crew and the mission manager and my office down, and that realization settled in hard.

Hoshiko, just arriving, sat down beside me and slid across a mug with the NASDA logo on it. "Ease your bosoms," she said.

I wasn't sure I'd heard her right. At my raised eyebrows, she showed me the brand of coffee she'd used to make the cup. On the pouch, it said "Ease Your Bosoms."

With a sigh, I took the cup she offered. She gave me a sympathetic look. "It is OK, Homer-san."

It wasn't OK, but after nearly causing the mission to go down in flames, I was definitely ready to ease my bosoms.

You Are *Sensei*

The next day, oblivious to everything I'd done, the crew arrived and, unlike me, were all rested up after a good night's sleep. They went immediately to their classroom. Although the schedule showed two of Japan's top scientists as instructors, they were not there. Per my advice, these learned scientists were told that they would be asked to participate in classes at a later time because the Americans were too jet-lagged to appreciate how august the professors were at this early stage in their training. NASDA instructors, familiar with the experiments, were instead rushed down to Tokyo from Tsukuba, Japan's science city. Although I knew they had not gotten much sleep, the instructors did well. Their English was good and their descriptions of the experiments practical and not the least bit theoretical. If this button was pushed, that light came on, and that happened inside the device. Instead of eight hours of classes, it was reduced to four. This seemed to please all three of our astronauts, especially the squirmer, and meant they had an extra half day to explore Tokyo, nap, or whatever they wanted to do.

After the Americans were gone, I was asked to meet with the three Japanese astronaut candidates. In the meeting room with Hoshiko by my side, they were hesitant at first to tell me why they wanted to talk to me but then it came out. Why, they asked me, were the American astronauts fighting amongst themselves? Since I knew nothing of that, they told me that one of the astronauts had decided training in Japan was a waste of time, one wasn't sure, and the other thought it was their responsibility to stay in Japan and be trained in whatever manner the Japanese saw fit. Learning about the Japanese culture, that astronaut maintained, was as important as learning about the experiments.

I depended on Hoshiko to keep me from saying anything too stupid so with her there and translating as necessary, I assured the three upset future astronauts it didn't mean anything, that our crew were just tired, and, anyway, I would talk to them. After we all relaxed over some cups of Ease Your Bosoms, we began to talk about other things and as we did, I got the measure of them.

Mamoru Mohri outwardly seemed the most relaxed and confident, although I could sense an inner tension within him like a compressed spring. He did most of the talking in the meeting. Chiaki Mukai, the surgeon, stayed cheerful throughout. Although she was curious about why the Americans were arguing, I didn't get a sense from her that she really cared. All she wanted to do was go into space. Takao Doi and I immediately formed a bond. He was the most upset of the three that the Americans were arguing, and I learned he was the one who'd insisted on meeting with me about it. He had placed the Americans on a pedestal and they had fallen off hard, and it bothered him that they didn't seem to understand that there was no amount of suffering that was too much to be allowed to fly into space. After the two others left, he stayed behind to talk to me, to tell me why it was so important to go into space at all. "We must learn all we can about what is there," he said. "Now that we have the tools, it is our responsibility to use them."

Although our meeting ended with what I hoped was some reassurance, I knew I had not been entirely honest with the Japanese candidates. If there was bickering amongst the American crew, there was little I could do about it except to hope it wouldn't get worse. The problem was that they were three highly motivated individuals from completely different places geographically, educationally, and philosophically. If I had failed them, so had their office in Houston who apparently had not considered the type of people needed to fly on international missions, especially when that meant they would be separated for months from their friends, families, and fellow astronauts. It was a recipe for failure in a mission that couldn't fail.

One morning after a couple of weeks in Japan, Mr. Suzuki told me there was a call for me on his phone. When I picked up, it was a fellow from NASA Headquarters in Washington, DC, who was high enough in the chain of command that I instantly recognized his name. In fact, he was a retired astronaut who'd switched to management. After he asked me how I was doing, although I immediately sensed he didn't really care, he said, "The Astronaut Office wants you fired. There's been complaints from the crew." When I didn't say anything, mainly because I wasn't surprised, he went on. "I talked to your bosses in Huntsville. They said if that's what the crew wants, they will order you home and send another training manager. Frankly, Homer, that's what I think we should do."

Mentally, I started packing my bags but then the fellow went on. "But we're not going to do that just yet. I don't know how but the Japanese got wind of this and they called the administrator and told him they want you to stay. In fact, they insist on it. You've made some friends over there, so we're going to leave you for now. But, listen up, you've got to take care of this crew, OK?"

After I promised I would do my best, the former astronaut turned high-ranking NASA official hung up. Hoshiko had been watching and saw the blood drain from my face. She came over and I told her what had just happened. "Who took up for me?" I wondered.

Although she wouldn't say at first, I finally got her to admit she knew everything. One of the Japanese astronauts had heard one of the American astronauts say I was going to be fired and told Hoshiko who then told Mr. Suzuki who then told somebody high up in NASDA who then called NASA Headquarters. I was at least temporarily saved, but I knew I couldn't be completely comfortable. If one of the astronauts thought I was doing a poor job, enough to complain to Houston, then I probably was. I redoubled my efforts, poring over every lesson plan, compressing the training where I could, moving parts of it to later in Huntsville where I'd have more control, and did my best to be friendly to the crew, including the one who I knew tried to get me fired. The way I saw it, it wasn't me who was going to have to climb aboard that big, dangerous beast of a rocket known as the space shuttle. The astronauts were eventually going to put their lives on the line for this mission. Getting yelled at, even threatened with being sacked, was easy in comparison.

After classes in Tokyo, we moved to Tsukuba, there to train on the materials science experiments. The prime contractor for these experiments was Ishikawajima-Harima Heavy Industries, or IHI. After the astronauts were taken to IHI to see where they would train, they wanted to immediately go to their hotel. When I started to go with them, Hoshiko stopped me. "The director of the Tsukuba office wishes to meet you."

In his office, the director rose and bowed. By then, I was getting fairly good at bowing. A young woman wheeled in a cart with a fancy tea set. The director, Hoshiko, and I moved to a small table and delicately sipped our tea. After some polite conversation, he inquired of my background. Before I knew it, I was telling him about being raised in the little mining town of Coalwood and how my dad was a coal miner and then how some other boys and I built rockets. The story clearly amused him and he laughed heartily. After we talked some more, he said, "I hope you will enjoy your time here. We are honored to have you."

Hoshiko and I bowed and left his office. Puzzled, I asked, "What was that all about?"

"You are sensei, Homer-san. You are the teacher. You are respected in Japanese culture."

Although I appreciated the sentiment, I said, "Hoshiko, you know I'm just a NASA grunt. I do what I'm told."

Her almond eyes flashed. "You are a trained engineer. You have fought in a war. You have gone into the ocean. You have written a book. And you love space. I know that. It is why you are here. You have loved it since you were a little boy. You have much to teach us. You are sensei."

Doubtful, I said, "If you say so."

Her expression changed. She warmly took my arm. "I like your story. You are coal mine rocket boy! I will write you a song!"

And she did, too. Hoshiko was a woman of many talents. When she wasn't keeping NASDA and NASA and me straight, she was also in a Tokyo rock band, the lead singer who wrote many of the songs the group performed. When she told me her band's name was Zinc Sulfide, I was astonished. "When I built rockets in Coalwood," I told her, "we used zinc dust and sulfur as the propellant and zinc sulfide was the exhaust. Where did you get the name?"

"Because of you, Homer-san," she said in a tone that sounded as if she thought my question was stupid.

"But you formed the group three years ago. You didn't know me then."

She looked at me with concern. "We met long ago, Homer-san. And many times. Don't you know that?"

Being the sort of literal fellow I tend to be, especially when it comes to time and schedules, I was completely and utterly confused. "But when?"

She smiled. "Somewhen," she said.

"That's not a word."

"It's our word."

Of Frogs, Whales, and Cows

One of the most interesting experiments on Spacelab-J was the Frog Embryology Experiment, or FEE according to its acronym. It was not a Japanese experiment. The principal investigator was Dr. Ken Souza at Ames Research Center in San Jose, California, and most of the training was done there. Souza's team already had a good handle on the training, so I could relax when FEE was on the schedule. The frogs to be flown were female African clawed frogs, big girls who were about to be famous at least in the scientific world. It was my first time in the beautiful valley that would eventually become known as Silicon Valley. A lot of future billionaires were already there hard at work in their garages. Since I knew how to solder and weld, had knowledge of printed circuit boards, and could also program a computer in BASIC, FORTRAN, and COBAL, they might have found me useful. Oh, for a time machine! Instead, when in the midst of this new world hidden in plain sight around me, I concentrated on frogs, African frogs, frogs with an attitude, frogs that, like the soon to be billionaire nerds of Silicon Valley, were quite capable of taking over the world.

The experiment was to see what would happen with a fertilized frog egg in microgravity. The pertinent question was to discover if it would divide into a complex tissue system like it did on Earth or if gravity was necessary to make that happen. To find out required that an egg-bearing female frog be flown into orbit, stripped of her eggs in a glove box, and the eggs put into a petri dish along with the testes of a male frog, the latter "sacrificed" prior to launch to gain said testes. *Ouch!* After a number of fertilized eggs were produced by this procedure, one set was to be left in microgravity, another set in a centrifuge that simulated Earth's gravity, and kept there until tadpoles hatched. After that, we would see what we would see. It was a very complex experiment that required the astronauts to learn how to handle the frogs, strip them, and properly fertilize the eggs. In effect, the astronauts were sort of froggy midwives. One of them said it was like being a frog pimp. That was an awful joke but I laughed at it anyway.

One of the warnings Dr. Souza gave me was that the African clawed frog was a dangerous amphibian, especially to other amphibians. He said if they got released into the wild, they would go after the local frogs and kill every one of them. That was why he kept insisting that all the training be done at his secure lab facility in California. The crew, however, wanted training on the live frogs to go right up to the time of launch so I convinced Dr. Souza to send four of them to the PCTC, where I guaranteed him that all would be well. There'd be no escape for those evil froggies while Homer was on the job! Reluctantly, the Ames team sent us four hearty, plump girls and on the very first night we had them, one went missing.

I couldn't believe it! With visions of environmental disaster and yours truly run up the Greenpeace flagpole, I instituted a thorough search of the PCTC. Finally, after I had visions of the girls marching across Huntsville like green hellhounds snapping up other froggies, puppies, kittens, and perhaps small children along the way, the wily froggess was found underneath the refrigerator in the break room. She was a little dehydrated but I soon had her wetted down and she was fine. She became my favorite frog and I named her Sally. After the training, Sally went back to Ames to an uncertain future, but I hope she had a lot of tadpoles and a happy life. By the way, the result of FEE was the frog eggs developed just fine in space so we now know we can raise frogs in low Earth orbit. I could make a joke here about eating weightless frog legs but, out of respect for Dr. Souza and Sally, I'll leave it at that except to say it was very important research that will provide much insight to how organisms react as we move into space.

After returning to Japan with the three American astronauts, one still reluctant, one still enthusiastic, and one still in the middle, I kept recommending changes to Mr. Suzuki that compressed the training or eliminated some of it so there was little downtime for the crew. With Mr. Suzuki's permission, I also split the Americans up where I could, pairing them with the Japanese astronaut candidates instead of each other. It was my hope this would hold down on any arguments between them. Dr. Mohri seemed to fit in best with all of them and I made a mental note about that.

Hoshiko patiently taught me some typical touristy phrases in Japanese to help me when she wasn't around. The ones I most often used included:

Konnichiwa - Hello.

Ohayo gozaimas - Good morning.
Kudasai - Please.
Kampai! - Cheers!
Duomo - A handy, friendly word in any situation.
Arigato gozaimas - Thank you.
Hai - Yes.
Chotto - No, but thanks.
Ikura des ka? - How much?
Benjo - Toilet.
Benjo Benjo! - Where is it? I got to go!

Mischievously, she also taught me some Japanese slang:

Baka! - Stupid!
Baka-da - You're stupid.
Baka iwanai dayo - What you said was stupid.
Kono imo - Potato head.

You might have spotted a trend there.

One of my favorite movies when I was a teenager was *Sayonara* based on James Michener's novel. Thinking it would please her, I told Hoshiko I remembered the theme song from the movie and, in my best Coalwood Community Church choir voice at a karaoke bar, I sang the lyrics that went on about sayonara being a romantic word to say goodbye.

After I'd finished my poor rendition, it was instantly clear Hoshiko was not pleased. She knew about the movie and wanted nothing to do with it. "But in Coalwood all those years ago," I pointed out, "it taught me a Japanese word."

"It is stupid word," she said.

"You don't say sayonara?"

"It is a stupid word, Homer-san, used for a stupid movie. *Sayonara* for Japanese is not used."

"Never?"

She flashed scorn in my direction and then looked away. "Unless to say goodbye forever," she huffed and thus ended my Japanese lesson for the day.

Like the nonuse of sayonara, there were always surprises to be found in Japan, mysteries that somehow were never quite resolved. After work one day, Hoshiko and I were strolling along the streets of Kobe when we happened upon a statue of three turtles stacked on top of one another. It was in front of a police station.

"What does it mean?" I asked.

"I don't know," she answered. "I am hungry. Let's go."

"It must mean something," I said.

Hoshiko provided me with an unhappy face. "I don't care about these turtles. Let's eat."

I was rooted to the spot. "Maybe it's so they'd have a better view. The first turtle had a great view so the second turtle climbed up on him for a better view and then the third turtle climbed up for an even better one. But now they can't get down and the first turtle can't move because the others are too heavy."

"These turtles don't matter, Homer-san. They are just turtles."

"They have to mean something," I insisted.

Hoshiko allowed a long sigh. "Japanese people like turtle. One good, three better. Everything doesn't have to mean something. Some things just are."

As my time wound down in Japan, Hoshiko took it upon herself to show me the bright, sweaty lights of Tokyo as only someone born and raised in Tokyo would know it. She was thoroughly a woman of that city. We visited cabarets and clubs in the Shinjuku "High Touch" area and other districts that were rarely visited by Western tourists. To walk through these Tokyo areas is to move through streets filled with vast towers of neon cut through by dark alleys with crouching vending machines and murmuring bars lit by inviting lanterns. In a way, I think she was showing me off as she often brought out the owners and hosts and hostesses to meet me. Although it was typical for patrons to drop $500 for an evening in such bistros, I rarely spent more than $20. As Hoshiko's guest, fees were waived.

The few Westerners I saw in those places were usually tall blonde American women on the arms of Japanese businessmen. When they lowered themselves to talk to me, they were oddly pleased to tell me how much money they made, which was an astonishing amount. A few years in Japan and they'd never have to work again. One of them, a Canadian who could have easily won any beauty contest, told me she had a PhD in English literature and when she first started out in Japan, she tried to not only be sexy but intellectual, believing that a combination of beauty and brains would attract the best and richest men. To her surprise, after a few dates she was shunned and had to work hard to get back into the game. "Now, I use this voice," she said in a breathy Marilyn Monroe imitation, "and talk oh so sweet about how handsome my man looks and how oh so powerful he is and how I just love pearls and diamonds and gold."

Hoshiko told me the real value to the businessmen of taking these women out was not sex but to show them off to other businessmen, thus earning respect for the obvious wealth and influence it took to acquire one of these stunning beauties if only for a few hours in a club.

There were also Japanese women who were willing, if the price was right, to be shown off by these rich men. Although they did not make as much as Western women, they were able to have a larger clientele over a longer time. They were incredibly beautiful, impeccably groomed, and dressed in the latest fashions. Hoshiko never introduced me to them because, she said, to be seen with a Western man, even for a short time, diminished their value in the eyes of Japanese businessmen, most with wives and children at home. Hoshiko said usually the wives knew what their husbands were doing but took a "boys will be boys" attitude about it so they could stay home and raise the children without being bothered by their silly men.

One night, Hoshiko sang "The Rose" and dedicated it to me from on stage, which earned me stares from the Japanese men in the room, most of which were decidedly unfriendly. She was playing with fire by taking me to the places where she performed, but she did it because I think she wanted me to understand the society in which she lived and thrived. Although I enjoyed these places, I was never comfortable in them. When I rode the trains through the countryside and saw the quaint little towns passing by, that seemed to me a Japan I thought I was missing. When I mentioned that to her, Hoshiko said she would stay in the city, the countryside was not for her and anyway, her band had a gig nearly every weekend. I knew I'd hurt her feelings by not loving the city as much as she did but, as always, I was drawn to the hinterlands.

Training continued with long, long days. Before the classes, I talked to new Japanese trainers to make sure they knew how much I appreciated their work. Although the American crew and the Japanese trainers did well together for the most part, there was still a cultural gap that never quite closed. There were instances of the astronauts talking amongst themselves during the lessons, or leaving without notice to make a phone call, or, worst of all, laughing at a trainer's mispronunciation of an English word or making a joke about the Japanese way of doing things. They were small things and in the United States, our training personnel would have simply shrugged it off. In Japan, however, such actions were considered insults and took some smoothing over every time they happened.

After our return to Japan, I continued to send my contact at the American Embassy a weekly report on the training. Usually, the only method open to me was to fax it, which meant I didn't know who would see it first at the embassy. Accordingly, I tried to make these reports as interesting and entertaining as I could but always positive. One day, my contact called me and said I had fans all over the embassy who looked forward to my missives, including the ambassador himself. Since I had put my writing career on hold for the duration of SL-J, it was good to know I could still write entertaining copy!

In the evenings, when the astronauts went back to their hotel or out shopping or eating, I was quite often invited to the homes of the Japanese trainers and NASDA officials. Hoshiko told me this was a great honor. Japanese businessmen—for they were almost entirely men in NASDA management positions—rarely let foreigners—*gaijin* as we were called—in their homes. Yet I often found myself in these homes, which ranged from small tenement apartments to large houses in American-style suburbs. Whenever I went, I brought the gift that Hoshiko said would be most appropriate, usually wine or sake, and then did my best to sit at the low tables and eat correctly whatever was put before me. Although I had to hit the Wendy's on the way back to the hotel from time to time because the portions were small, the food presented to me was artistic in its preparation and delicious for the obvious time and effort put into it. I ate everything, even when it was sea urchin which, to my Western eyes, sort of looked like an eyeball floating in slime. Down it went with gusto and it tasted good, too.

Although there was invariably some shop talk about SL-J training during these visits, in almost every case I was also asked how I "felt" about space. This was a philosophical question that I never heard in the United States. To answer it, I began to tell the story about some Coalwood boys who built rockets and blew things up until they flew high. Every time I told it, I guess I got better at it and my gestures of the rockets exploding or flying got bigger. Children watching with huge eyes this crazy *gaijin* with curly hair and a West Virginia twang telling his stories would sometimes run and hide, giggling around the corner. When I asked Hoshiko why I kept getting invitations and not the crew, she said, "They wish to know you so you will know them." Personally, I think the real reason was because I got the reputation of being guaranteed entertainment for the kids!

By working so closely and socializing with the Japanese, I had the time to study and appreciate things that at first seemed odd but then understandable, at least as far as my Western mind could grasp. The strange English I saw on T-shirts such as "Don't Choice I Wicked Want Funny" or "Way the Bridges I Burn Light" didn't make sense, but Hoshiko explained it didn't really matter. The Japanese thought English was a modern language, one that was fun to play with, so using English words didn't have to make sense. This was difficult for my engineering brain to wrap itself around but that other side of my brain, the writer side, loved it. That words didn't have to make sense to still have meaning was a glorious concept.

Being careful not to say anything negative to my Japanese coworkers was also something I learned lest I get an overreaction.

When I said one time, "The classroom is too hot," in Tsukuba, it resulted in a redesign of the entire heating and cooling system for the building, several meetings to discuss the implementation, and a wish for me, the complainer, to approve everything before the work began. Not wanting to cause such a stampede of activity, I learned to keep everything as positive as possible or if I really thought something needed to be done, I told Hoshiko and she took care of it in her Japanese way. When she said it was too hot, the thermostat for the classroom was lowered and that was that.

The simple word—*hai*—also didn't always mean what I thought it did. Although in the Japanese language it means "yes" in a literal sense, it also had a lot of other meanings, including "I hear you" and even "no." Maybe the best way to explain it is it's similar to the American manner of using the expression "OK." OK has many meanings that most of us understand simply by the way it is said. A chirpy OK means compliance. A sharp utterance of both letters or an emphasis on the O followed by a lowered K is often a warning. Drawn out utterances of both letters means doubt and so on. *Hai* in Japanese is like that. Sometimes, when I laid out a plan to a Japanese trainer, I would get a staccato of "*Hai, hai, hai!*" followed by a comment that sounded to me like moosey-car-seat and then they would suck between their teeth. Hoshiko said the word was *muzukashi*, which meant "difficult," which also meant they weren't going to do what I was asking them to do, no matter how many times they said *hai*!

I also learned there were many normal expressions or convolutions in English that Americans take for granted that are best not to say to the Japanese. Double negatives was one of them. When one of the Japanese trainers worried to me that the astronauts would not like a lesson he had prepared, I replied, "I can't be sure they won't." This was a big mistake on my part. Since, as

Hoshiko explained to me, Japanese are so precise in their own language, double negatives in English often send them down a path of balancing the negatives against one another. I learned to avoid all double negatives.

The phrase "not yet" also caused some confusion. For instance, if my answer was "not yet" to the question on whether I had approved a lesson plan or schedule, the Japanese assumed I meant I was offended because of the negative imprecision of my reply. I learned to think through everything I said to avoid any misinterpretation. I'm certain, however, I made plenty of mistakes and left the poor training people scratching their heads, an idiom, by the way, that made them think of bloody skulls, not confusion.

When we watched television, I noticed on news shows that there were almost always two news readers at the desk, one male and one female. Nearly always, it was the man who would read the news while the woman would nod and erupt with an occasional "*hai!*" in affirmation. I called them "Hai-girls" and, just to get a rise out of her, told Hoshiko that she was my Hai-girl. "No, Homer-san," she laughed, "you are my hai-boy!" In that, she was more right than not. Usually, her advice was the best I received and, when I was smart, I took it.

Watching Japanese TV reality shows was also an introduction to a society I could appreciate but knew I would probably never fully understand. There were several shows where people were sent through mazes and across obstacles where they fell or were knocked senseless, which apparently was great fun as everyone laughed, even the people who were being tossed about like rag dolls. There was also a popular show where a man dressed up like a bumblebee went to a home or apartment and rang the doorbell. When it was answered, the man-bee would pass gas, which caused the poor man or woman who answered the door to throw their hands to their face in embarrassment or make any children inside laugh uncontrollably. After the embarrassment or mirth subsided, there would then be a long and apparently thoughtful discussion between the bumblebee and the family until the matter was resolved. And then there was sumo wrestling, which simply was bizarre to my eyes and yet Hoshiko, who often seemed more Western than Japanese in her attitudes, loved it. She also couldn't understand why I thought it was wrong to eat whales. "But you eat cows," she pointed out.

"Yes, but whales are intelligent."

"So are cows. Do they not get in the shade of the trees when it is hot? Do they not raise their calves? Do they not run when they are afraid?"

"Whales are different. They think."

"Cows think. They think please don't eat me, Homer-san!"

It was never an argument I would win. Anyway, I never ate whale meat in Japan and, actually, never saw Hoshiko eat it either. I think she just liked to pull my cow tail on that one.

Religion in Japan was also difficult to understand except that I understood it wasn't anything like I knew from my Appalachian Christian culture of allegiance to a particular denomination. Most Japanese were spiritual but were, in general, not religious in terms of everyone of a certain sect believing exactly the same thing. One peculiarity of the Japanese was, from my observation, that they didn't seem to worry much about what happened after they died. What was important was the good or bad accomplished in the life they were presently living.

Hoshiko believed in predestination and past and future lives. The predestination part I agreed with, as that was much like Kismet, that great river I believe that flows through our lives, but

I wasn't sure about being alive in the past or the future. Hoshiko said that the matter of the Creator was too big for anyone to understand but that life was too precious to only be given once. "That is why I know you, Homer-san. We have been together in past lives."

"In what way?"

"That I do not know." She smiled impishly. "Maybe you were my cat."

"Or your husband?"

"Or my wife. These lives we are given to live are like fabric that can be twisted. There is not just one side. There are many sides according to the twist we are on and some lives become intertwined. That is why I used that word somewhen for us."

She had come back to that. "Is that really our word?" I asked.

For a moment, she looked sad and then, her eyes lowered, she quietly answered. "Yes, if it must be."

Coalwood, Japan

After the training in Tsukuba, we took the bullet train from Tokyo to Kobe for the life sciences subset of our training. The train was comfortable, modern, and amazingly fast, the countryside going past in a blur. We were going to train at Mitsubishi Heavy Industries, or MHI as it was called. Because the MHI grounds required a long drive from the hotels in Kobe, I agreed we would stay at the company hotel, a bare-bones six-story building with sparse rooms, hard beds, a simple table, a sink, a commode, and a shower as an afterthought. Close by the MHI hotel was the MHI store, a low brick building where nearly anything and everything could be bought from groceries to clothes to work boots to sandals to pharmaceuticals to hats. Along the same street as the hotel was an MHI hospital and also apartments and houses for the MHI workers. There was also an MHI school for the children and MHI playgrounds, gyms, and soccer fields.

At the high bays and clean rooms where we trained, the MHI workers all had the MHI insignia on their blue coveralls and ball caps and were clearly proud of their company and who they were. They were also efficient and knowledgeable and tolerant. When some of our American crew arrived late, they were patient. When the crew left early or was inattentive or made jokes, the MHI training folks plowed on. It was obvious to me they had dealt with Westerners before. In Kobe, I could relax a little.

Despite its spartan setup, I slept well in the MHI hotel, the best sleep I had in Japan. I went to the MHI store and strolled past the MHI houses and apartments and watched the different shift changes, the men and women streaming back and forth and talking to one another as they passed. I felt a sense of peace come over me that seemed odd until it hit me why. The company hotel, the company store, the company doctor and dentist, the lines of workers passing one another in shifts, the schoolchildren walking to school from their company houses. I had seen this all before. *I was in Coalwood, Japan!*

When Hoshiko came down from Tokyo, she steered me away from the crew to visit with the MHI superintendent of the shipyard who, after I told him about my diving experiences on the great wrecks off the Outer Banks, opened it up for me and allowed me to go where few outsiders were allowed, to where they were building nuclear submarines and vast container ships and deep ocean submersibles. At the end of it, the MHI superintendent, whose English was excellent, asked if I would consider working for them, that he'd looked into my record, and perhaps I might join the company in Japan and then later, if I wished, at an affiliate in the United States. I tactfully declined, saying I had a job at NASA that I needed to finish and I wasn't quite ready to leave it. My refusal was accepted with a bow and a wish that I might reconsider. I said I would give it some thought. That evening, Hoshiko urged me to take the offer, that MHI really wanted me, and I would make many times more money than I was making for NASA. Anyway, she said, didn't I like Japan? The truth was I did. I liked it a lot. But I had also put down deep roots in Huntsville and loved my work with NASA. Hoshiko was asking me to give that up and come live in Japan. It was a decision I decided to put off, to let things work out as they should, at least until the mission flew. I rationalized this by telling myself I was putting my trust in Kismet but I also knew very well I was avoiding making any decision at all.

Over the months in Japan, when I had some free time, I traveled across the country. Once outside the big cities, I found calm and peaceful little towns and farmers in the fields and children who, upon seeing me, were enthralled at the big round-eyed Westerner who returned their V finger sign for peace or victory or hello or this is fun or whatever it meant. On one of those weekends, I joined the tourists and, after working my way through all the souvenir shops, trekked up to the last platform on the side of Mount Fuji. It was worth the climb but I knew there were better mountains in Japan to explore, ones that were covered with lush forests, and I wanted to climb them, too. The next mountain I climbed was Mount Takao, which was a long climb with a glorious view and left me breathless both by the altitude and the beauty of all that lay below.

My favorite mountain, however, proved to be Mitake, just a couple of hours outside Tokyo by train. Its steep path led through a beautiful forest and there was a shrine on top where prayers could be written on paper slips and given over to the gods for hopes and dreams and also to honor loved ones who had passed. Thinking of my dad, whose loss was still fresh, I climbed the mountain in his honor and wrote his name down plus a message: "Dad, the brass from your mine was in the Skipper. I'm sorry I never told you that. I love you. Sonny."

When the schedule stretched out because of shuttle launch delays, I went back and forth to Japan for training and meetings. When I added it all up, I had spent nearly a year there across three years. Once the training was over and the Japanese simulators were packed up and shipped to Huntsville to be installed in the PCTC, there was no reason for me to stay in Japan. I spent a couple of weeks wrapping up Spacelab-J business at NASDA headquarters in Tokyo and wrote a paper for them that listed my recommendations on future training and operations not only on Spacelab but the future International Space Station. Before I headed back to the States, I thought first to climb Mitake-san one more time, there to ask that Spacelab-J be a success. Hoshiko and several other NASDA trainers climbed it with me.

The last night in Japan, I was surprised when Mr. Suzuki and his team threw me a party in their office to thank me for my work. It was even more of a surprise when the NASDA director, Dr. Osawa, also showed up. He took me aside and asked who I thought should be the chosen Japanese candidate. "Any of the three would do a great job," I told him, "but I think Dr. Mohri because he works best with the Americans." With a slight smile, Osawa-san bowed. A week later, it was announced that Dr. Mohri was the candidate picked to fly on Spacelab-J.

The day I was to leave, Hoshiko insisted on driving me to the airport even though it was after dark and Tokyo traffic was always a little scary to her at night. She clenched the steering wheel and was mostly silent all the way to the airport at Narita. When we were at my gate, she hugged me and said, "Sayonara, Homer-san."

This was a surprise. "I thought you didn't use that word," I said.

"This is the time we must use it," she answered. "Say it to me."

"Why?"

"Homer-san, you will not come back. I know you think you will but you will not. I am twenty-nine and will be married by thirty. It is what my family wants. It is time for us to use this word."

I shook my head. "I'll come back. You'll see."

When I got home, the training in the United States was in full swing, which required me to bounce all over the country to various American PI sites and pull long hours to keep the training on track. Weeks went by and then months. One of my favorite people was Lorna Onizuka, the widow of *Challenger* astronaut Ellison Onizuka, who worked in the NASDA office in Houston. She was a voice of wisdom that I often relied on during the years of Spacelab-J. When she heard I was coming to observe training on two JSC experiments, she called and asked me to come by her office, that she had a letter for me. When I did, she handed me a small envelope. To my surprise, it was from Hoshiko. How she knew I was coming to Houston I didn't know, except our training schedule was no secret to anyone at NASDA. I opened the envelope and read:

> *Homer-san*
> *I am married.*
> *Somewhen.*
> *Your hai-girl forever,*
> *Hoshiko-san*

I guess I looked stricken. Gently, Lorna took the note and read it. She looked up at me. "Somewhen? Is that a word?"

"It's our word," I replied while my heart accepted its truth.

More Space Stuff and...Olivia!

Throughout the training in Japan and the United States, I was ably assisted by others in my branch and our Teledyne Brown contractors. George Norris and Julie Sanchez, both young NASA engineers, performed splendidly to support crew training and then later in their roles as Crew Interface Coordinators (CIC) that had them talking directly with the crew during the flight. I was also a CIC on the same shift as Dr. Stan Koszelak, who served as a backup for the American crew members.

Two of the Johnson Space Center medical doctors who worked on Spacelab-J were Dr. John Charles and Dr. Chuck Lloyd. Both were terrific fellows and I enjoyed working with them. Dr. Charles had an experiment called Lower Body Negative Pressure that put an astronaut into a bag that was cinched around their waist and had the air sucked out of it. The idea was to avoid space adaptation syndrome or space sickness—thought to be caused by blood pooling in the head and trunk—by using low pressure to pull blood down into the lower extremities. I made a joke that if it didn't work for astronauts, it should be advertised in men's magazines (wink, wink) but Dr. Charles didn't hold that against me...much.

Dr. Lloyd was also great in that he decided to let me test his experiment called the Fluid Therapy System (FTS) by sending me off on a wild ride aboard the KC-135 plane called the Vomit Comet. The VC flew over the ocean and then in up-and-down parabolas. While it fell, it created weightlessness. Eagerly, I headed for Houston and my date with the famous aircraft.

From the very start of the day when I flew on the KC-135, it was clear that nausea was something that the flight crew dealt with every time they went aloft, so the briefing was filled with information on what to do when your stomach rebelled, which was mainly to make sure its contents went into the supplied bags because otherwise the crew had to clean it up. Once on board the aircraft, it was hot and smelled of old vomit. Some of the others on board said they felt like puking just from the odor but off we went, zooming over the Gulf of Mexico and thence into our parabolas, about fifty of them, while we set about doing whatever it was we were going to do. For me, that was putting my feet into foot loops and operating Chuck's experiment, which consisted of turning on and monitoring a fluid IV pump while it moved a saline solution from a bag into an artificial arm. I loved every minute of it and never felt the least bit sick. Over and down and bottoming out was interesting as at the lowest dip in the parabolas we pulled two g's or twice normal gravity. All around me, people were hurling into bags but I just laughed every time we went up and over, fell, and bottomed out. Yes, I was well hated, but I had been on a lot of bouncy dive boats so the Vomit Comet didn't get to me at all.

When I was able to get back to my office at Marshall Space Flight Center, it was always stacked high with documents pertaining to upcoming Spacelab flights. Wernher von Braun once said that no rocket ever flew that didn't have paperwork piled as high as the rocket. My experience was it was about ten times as high. My job was to go through the boxes of documentation and comment if I saw anything that didn't match our training plans and simulators. It was tedious but necessary.

When I walked in after being away for a few weeks, I found not only stacks of documents piled everywhere but, to my astonishment, a young man occupying more than half my already too small office with a big gray steel federal issue desk, filing cabinet, computer and all. Although I griped at first about all his stuff taking up so much room, the tall, ungainly youth was so naturally cheerful he soon won me over. His name was Mike Massimino and he was a student from MIT come to learn the ins and outs of NASA. To my amusement, he kept saying that he was going to be an astronaut which I took as highly unlikely. Because of my attitude, I missed an amazing opportunity for a great quote: "Mike," I could have said, "you have about as much chance of being an astronaut as I have of writing a number-one bestseller." Sadly, I didn't say it but Mike, of course, not only became an astronaut but, after retirement, a featured performer on the long-running television series *The Big Bang Theory*.

As more SL-J experiments were integrated into the Spacelab module, I flew down to Kennedy Space Center to observe the progress and compare flight hardware with our simulators to make sure our training was correct. It was wonderful to be at Cape Canaveral. In the mornings when I was there, I usually jogged down the old, cracked asphalt roads that led to the launch pads used during the early days of spaceflight that meant so much to Sonny Hickam and the Rocket Boys back in Coalwood. There was little security in 1992 at these old launch sites, and I could get very close to where Jupiter-C and Vanguard had launched our first satellites. All the old pads were in sorry shape, even the more recent Apollo complexes, and painted across most of them was the sad message: "Abandon in Place." Yet it thrilled me to see them and imagine them as they were in the 1950s and '60s.

In September 1992, Spacelab-J flew, the crew performed perfectly, all the experiments were accomplished, and the three years of my life spent on it were over and done in seven days. The thing I remember the most about the flight itself was when one of the American astronauts who liked my cat Paco got a little space sick, I taped Paco meowing and played it so a little cat power was there in orbit. Paco was a great meower and, from what I heard later, the astronaut felt better almost immediately. Paco's meow had gone up without permission so I fully expected the space police to descend on me and drag me out of Payload Control, which, at that point, wouldn't have mattered much. Instead, a NASA public relations person called and said she had looked it up and Paco was the first cat to meow in space. So, in an ironic development, it wasn't all the work I'd done on behalf of Spacelab-J that I was remembered for in the space business but because I was the owner of a famous space cat. Eventually, I wrote a book about it in a lot more detail and titled it *Paco: The Cat Who Meowed in Space.*

As for the American astronauts who were trained in Japan, all went on to have great careers in and out of the aerospace business. They were and are good people who were dropped into Japan without any attempt by NASA to properly prepare them to take on their tasks. If there was any blame to be had for the problems we had there, it was mine as the training manager for not anticipating what could happen in a heady stew of travel, training, and a clash of cultures.

All three Japanese astronaut candidates would reach space. After Spacelab-J, Dr. Mohri flew once more in 1999. Ironically, during that flight, one of his fellow crew members, Janet Voss, took my memoir *Rocket Boys* with her to read. Mohri-san presently heads up Tokyo's National Museum of Emerging Science and Innovation. Dr. Doi would also go into space twice, once in 1997 and again in 2004. He would be the first Japanese to go outside in a spacewalk. After retirement from the Astronaut Corps, he became a professor at Kyoto University and, while still avidly pursuing astronomy, discovered two super novae. Dr. Mukai would fly twice as well, once on a Spacelab flight in 1994 and on John Glenn's flight in 1998. She remains active in the space business.

For most of us, the truth was after *Endeavour* touched down on September 20, 1992, Spacelab-J was promptly forgotten except for the good science that was brought back for our principal investigators, which would give them years of data to work with and write papers about. When I look back on the entire tri-year episode of my life, the only thing that really mattered is the people I met along the way. They were all marvelous human beings, especially the Japanese, who reminded me of something I had forgotten: my love for space that began with Sputnik flying overhead in my little mining town of Coalwood, West Virginia. Vietnam and my scuba adventures and all the other things had scrubbed much of that out of my head, but the Japanese with their love of space brought it back. Upon reflection, I think they were at least partially responsible for me eventually writing *Rocket Boys*.

After writing a final report on the training of SL-J, I returned to the Man-Systems Integration branch of the Mission Operations Laboratory. Because of all my travels to Japan and the American PI sites, I was a bit of a stranger to the office so it took me a while to fit back in. Since I was forty-nine years old, I was also one of the oldest people in a branch filled with dynamic young people that included Sue Boyd Rainwater, who would eventually oversee NASA's space suit designs, Patti Moore, who would be the primary crew interface in Russia during the early International Space Station years, and other luminaries in crew training such as Angie Stewart, Alice Dorries, Debra Underwood, Chuck Lewis, Carole McLemore, Janet Dowdy, Kimberly Robinson, Jessica Osborne, Dave Scott, George Hamilton, and many others. Everyone who was in that lab kind of stood out and would go on to have great careers.

My first order of business when I got back was to meet with Ken Smith, still my direct supervisor. "Well, Homer," he said, "what do you want to do next?"

My answer was, "Well, Ken, whatever you want me to do."

"You've heard about the space station, I guess," he said.

Of course I had and said so. President Reagan's Space Station Freedom had morphed into Vice President Al Gore's International Space Station, which would include as an equal partner the Russians who were, to me, still our Cold War enemies. Had I not, like all Americans, faced nuclear holocaust from them during the Cuban Missile Crisis? Had I not almost lost my life fighting against them in that proxy war in Vietnam? Had they not cost us trillions of dollars in building all kinds of war machines and flinging our troops all over the world to keep them at bay? Now, according to Al Gore, we were going to build a space station with them? After I gave it some thought,

I decided it was a great idea. Except for their radical politics at the top, I'd always suspicioned the Russian people weren't that much different from us.

"We need somebody to figure out how to train crews on payloads aboard the station," Ken went on. "The Russians have their ways and we've got ours, but somehow we need to pull them together. We'll have to make the Europeans and the Japanese happy, too. How about it? You up to taking that on?"

Since it was a good assignment, I instantly agreed. "Don't screw it up," Ken said as I left his office, which was always good advice, especially for me.

Before the space station got going, I helped the other training managers as best I could with their Spacelab missions, occasionally filling in as a CIC or checking out a simulator in the PCTC. After SL-J, it was something of a relief to just roll with what was happening. One day, Ken burst into my office. "Homer, there's some singer wants a tour of the PCTC. Name's Olive or Olivia something-something. You got time to do it?"

For a split second, I almost pled the "I'm really kinda busy" excuse but then something clicked in my head. "Olivia Newton-John?"

"Yeah, I think. Something like that."

"Well, I guess I could make the time. You know, if I have to."

"Great! She'll be there at 3:00 p.m."

Kismet was at work! I tossed up a prayer of thanks that Ken didn't keep up with beautiful, famous Australian singers and instantly got up and walked to the PCTC where I nonchalantly hung around until here this most amazing woman came with a little girl who proved to be her daughter. They were both blue-eyed, blonde, gorgeous, and bright. The public relations guy handed her and her daughter off to me. "Miss Newton-John, Homer Hickam."

She extended her hand to me and I think I melted into the floor. I don't remember too much about the tour I gave her except I was in full flower with lots of stories that made her laugh and her daughter giggle. At the end of it, a NASA photographer detailed to follow us around took our picture in the Spacelab mockup. She leaned into me and I naturally put my arm around her slim waist. After the photo, she kissed me on my cheek and thanked me. "You are an interesting fellow, Homer Hickam," she said.

There are some moments in every life where if it would all end at that moment, it would be perfect. That was one of mine, the moment I got kissed by Olivia Newton-John. Swept away by the public relations guy, she was suddenly gone but I stared at the Spacelab hatch where I'd last seen her for what I recall was a somewhat longish time.

While waiting for the ISS to gear up, I also had time to do something else that had been bouncing around in my head for a while and that was to rattle NASA's cage about going back to the moon. At the time, NASA was decidedly focused on operations in low Earth orbit with the shuttle. Not only were there no plans to go back to the moon ever again but to even bring it up was to invite the ire of the big guys in Washington, DC, who didn't want to hear about it. We'd gone to the moon and we were not going back and that was all there was to it.

Cindy Fry was the payload training manager I most often turned to when I was considering going off on a tangent. When I sat down with her at lunch one day and told her we should go back to the moon, she asked me, very simply and cogently, "Why?"

Why, indeed? I thought it over and said, "Because I think the moon is the best place to go if people are going to actually live in space. Not just astronauts but everybody. There's work to do on the moon, blue-collar kind of work. For one thing, we could just go up there and mine the blame thing."

Cindy had her thinking cap on. She'd also just finished a difficult mission and I think we were both looking to break out a little and shake things up. She said, "You know what, Homer? I bet if we pitched it right, we could get a trip to the South Pole Station to study it as an analog for a moon base! Why don't we go after some contingency funds?"

The idea of going to Antarctica on a boondoggle appealed to me, so Cindy and I submitted our proposal to the center director. After a few weeks, the answer came back. It was a disappointment but no surprise: *Disapproved*. As an addendum, however, we were told we could pursue the idea on our own and write a paper of the results if we could get somebody to send us to Antarctica for the study. Cindy soon after decided to move to Texas and go to work for Baylor University so if anything was to be done, I would have to do it. I ditched the idea of actually going to the South Pole and decided to write a paper instead on why and how we could go back to the moon. Since I'd received some funds for a study of the South Pole as it related to the moon, I would have to disguise my real intent of writing the piece. That was really no problem.

The National Science Foundation (NSF) was my first stop. The NSF is an interesting organization, a federal agency like NASA but with very different goals and organization. One of the responsibilities given it is to operate the Amundsen-Scott South Pole Station. When I made a call to the NSF, I was shuffled around until I finally found someone there willing to talk to me, a fellow I'll call Bill. Bill didn't have a lot to say except to tell me the only NASA people the NSF was allowed to talk to about the South Pole Station were in Houston. After I prodded him a little bit, Bill gave me the number of someone in Houston, a fellow I'll call Bob. I therefore called Bob and told him what I wanted to do. "Good luck," he replied.

After waiting for him to say something else, which he didn't seem inclined to do, I asked, "What have you done so far?"

"Nothing." He hesitated for a long second and then said, "Look, Homer, we're not going to the moon again. Just drop this thing, that's my recommendation. They'll burn you alive at Headquarters if you start talking about the moon. It's the space shuttle and the space station and that's it."

And there it was. I thanked Bob and hung up and just shook my head in exasperation. What was wrong with these people? Were we to be stuck in low Earth orbit forever? After pouting for a while, I got back on the phone to Bill at the NSF. "Look, you've got to help me," I begged.

"OK, I'll help you," Bill said, "but it'll have to be unofficial. I've wintered over there so what do you want to know?"

"Everything," I said and, to his credit, Bill provided me with a vast amount of detail about the station. With that information even without going there, I was able to design a moon base that reflected the Antarctic station while sneaking in all the other stuff on how and why we should go. I titled my piece "A Study of the National Science Foundation's South Pole Station as an Analogous Data Base for the Logistical Support of a Moon Laboratory." When it was published, I had done what I could for the moon and so went on to other things. Time would have to pass for NASA to catch up. When it did, a road map was there, right where I left it.

And then along came the Hubble Space Telescope and its spherical aberration. When it was launched after years of NASA hype, the Hubble had a flaw: it couldn't focus on distant faint objects such as stars and galaxies, which was, after all, its primary purpose. My old seatmate in first class to New York, Jay Leno, made a joke about it on his *Tonight Show* by calling it the Hubble Space Paperweight, and very quickly the media piled on with articles and comments on news shows on how it was an enormous failure and a waste of good money. NASA Headquarters managers hid under their desks for a while until a few brave souls at Goddard Space Flight Center raised their hands and said, "Hey, we can fix this!" After some dithering, they were given some funding and told to go ahead and see if it was really possible. As soon as we heard about it in Huntsville, we knew we were bound to get a piece of this work because we had the Neutral Buoyancy Simulator, the only water tank large enough to hold both a mockup of the shuttle cargo bay and a high-fidelity Hubble model. Since I was active on the NBS diver's list and also had lots of experience in the Extravehicular Mobility Unit (EMU) space suit, I was soon into the thick of it.

After Goddard convinced Headquarters and Congress agreed to put it in the budget, the Hubble repair mission was on. Four astronauts were assigned: Story Musgrave, Kathy Thornton, Jeff Hoffman, and Tom Akers. Story had done quite a few tests in our tank but had never spent more than a day or two there. With this momentous assignment now laid on him, Story flew up to Huntsville, dug into the capabilities of our tank, and told its managers that the NBS was inadequate to the task. What he needed, he told them, were end-to-end runs, meaning if the repairs on the Hubble were planned to take six hours in space, he wanted six hours underwater with no breaks. That sounded good, but there was a big problem and that was the possibility of decompression sickness for that long at forty feet, the depth of the NBS. Vyga Kulpa, the lead engineer and manager of the NBS, scrambled to design a system to let Story have his end-to-end runs. His solution was to pump into their suits and helmets a gas called nitrox that had a higher content of oxygen and less nitrogen. This solved one problem but created another. With such a high content of oxygen under pressure inside the suits, there was a chance that a spark would cause the astronauts to catch on fire.

Since Story and the other astronauts were willing to risk it, everyone on Vyga's active diver list was called to show up at the NBS for extra training on what to do in the event of fire in the suit. This consisted mostly of being prepared to get the astronaut to the surface as quickly as possible and a willingness to get burned ourselves to help them out of their suits. We were also told that we divers would still be breathing compressed air, not nitrox, so that meant during those long runs, we'd be pushing right up to the edge of the decompression limits ourselves before being relieved by another set of divers. Although we were essentially being warned that we could die or be crippled in support of Story's plan, not a single diver refused to be a part of the Hubble repair mission. Our paramedics, Brenda Bradford and Lori Kegley, both veterans of my Deep Space company that supported Space Camp's Underwater Astronaut Trainer, stood by to assist or patch us up as required and, of course, the decompression chamber located topside of the NBS was always ready to go.

The lead from Goddard for the Extra Vehicular Activity (EVA) development and training was Dr. Russ Werneth, who came to Huntsville with his team to show us and the crew what needed to be done. Russ and his team fit well with us and we were soon socializing with them at the local restaurants and in our homes. We spoke the same language and we all had the same determination to fix the Hubble. The Goddard engineers developed not only the procedures but also some unique wrenches and drills. The plan to correct the optics was to insert a big clumsy-shaped box called the Corrective Optics Space Telescope Axial Replacement (also known as COSTAR) inside the Hubble while also replacing the Wide Field Planetary Camera (WF/PC pronounced Wiff-Pick). Designed by Ball Aerospace engineer Jim Crocker, COSTAR could be installed only after other instruments were removed. No matter how you looked at it, we ran the risk of not only failure to get the COSTAR and WF/PC installed but damaging the Hubble beyond repair. By implication, NASA might be left beyond repair if we failed. Lots of dice were being rolled.

Before the training began, I was one of several suited subjects who went underwater with the new nitrox system, our job to go through some of the initial procedures the team from Goddard had developed and also to make sure we didn't catch on fire. When we didn't, the crew was brought up from Houston.

We all gathered around the NBS conference table. For those of us who'd been around for a while, we knew the Hubble repair crew all fairly well, as they were all experienced astronauts who'd been in our tank quite a few times. Their leader we knew to be one part mad scientist, one part adventurer, one part philosopher, and all parts space flier. In other words, Story was an interesting fellow but also somewhat intimidating. It was well known he didn't suffer fools, so most of us kept our mouths shut around him.

Ron Sheffield, the Huntsville test director, asked Story to start the meeting. Uncertain of what was coming, we were all tense as he spoke for the first time. What he wanted, he said, was the Hubble mockup to be as nearly like the real Hubble as possible and that the repairs he and his crew would do on it should be as close to real as could be accomplished underwater. There were to be no shortcuts and what he was looking for was not so much a set of typical NASA procedures but a choreography similar to what ice skaters like Dorothy Hamill performed so flawlessly in the Olympics. Story, a farmboy as well as a medical doctor, said in his nasal Kansas twang, "She makes it look easy but it ain't. That's because she's trained her muscle memory through practice, practice, and more practice. That's what we gotta do."

While we remained respectfully silent to this tall order, Story went on to say that everybody needed to set their egos aside, including him, and that anybody and everybody had an equal voice on the team. "If you see something that's wrong, say it." He looked around the room and spotted our janitor leaning on his mop. "That includes this man," he said. "You tell me if you see me do anything wrong."

The janitor, born and raised in Alabama, pondered that and said, "Well, you could start by picking up your dang towels off the dang floor in the dang shower room!"

There was a shocked silence and then Story erupted with a huge guffaw that broke the ice. It was just what we needed. From that moment on, we were truly a team. After hours and hours of underwater practice combined with the work of the Marshall and Goddard and Johnson engineers plus the crew's courage and dedication, the Hubble was fixed. It would go on to revolutionize what we know about the universe and, to an extent, our place in it. After Apollo, it is my opinion that the first Hubble repair mission was NASA's finest hour.

Tiny Bubbles in My Brain

Once more, I headed down to Guanaja to make another dream come true and that was to build a house on that enchanted island. Although I'd given up building on the beautiful beach I'd purchased from Verne Hyde because of its remoteness, I now had another plan which was to purchase a hundred-year lease on a little seamount, otherwise known as a patch, which was charmingly pronounced "potch" by the Guanajans.

That's right.

I bought underwater property, although to be precise, and in my defense, it was only a few feet beneath the sea.

My plan was to build a house on pilings sunk down through the sand into the bedrock underneath. The locals quickly dubbed my new property "Homer Potch." My first goal was to purchase large-diameter PVC tubes that I would drive into the sand and fill with concrete to form the pilings. I would also need to rent a barge with a pile driver to dig the holes in the sand. Once the pilings were in, I saw it taking a couple of years but I would do it, little by little. Dreams, it seems, can not only light up the sky but can also dig holes in the sand underwater.

After the flight out from La Ceiba, I climbed off the DC-3 with the other passengers, their chickens and their pigs, and a few dogs and walked down to the dock where my friend Ivey Garrett was waiting for me. There was also a boy who tried to sell me a dead iguana. "Good eats, mister," he said, holding up the reptilian carcass.

With an apologetic expression, I turned down the offer but it was OK since one of the other passengers quickly gave two limps for the thing, which I've been told tastes—wait for it—just like chicken. Anyway, off we sped in Ivey's runabout to his house, which he called Casa Sobre Del Mar, which in Spanish means House Over the Sea. It was an apt name, as Ivey's house was built entirely over the water except for a few feet that rested on the edge of the little island called Pond Caye. He'd leased those few feet from the owner years back and then proceeded to build his house the same way I hoped to build mine, by digging holes into the underlying limestone, placing concrete posts in the holes, and building atop them. The house was beautifully laid out with two floors and covered decks that went all the way around. Downstairs, there was a giant aquarium that was fed seawater directly from the sea underneath by a series of pumps. Beautiful reef fish and eels and crabs lived in the aquarium. At night with the moon and stars filling the room with their heavenly light, the aquarium glowed a translucent, magical blue.

After a nice dinner cooked by Ivey's gracious wife, Betty, I read for a while before going to sleep to the sound of the gentle lapping of a placid sea. The next morning over breakfast, Ivey told me he needed to collect some fish for the aquarium. Would I go along? I was glad to do it and we put on scuba gear and went off his dock, descending rapidly to eighty feet. After so many hours and hours underwater in the sterile NBS, the tropical water felt warm and alive. There was an old wreck of a wooden ship called *Springtide* on the bottom just off the deck and she was our destination. Fish swam in and out of its exposed ribs, including some huge groupers and barracuda. Ivey wasn't interested in the big fish. He was after smaller ones. Using a net, he sneaked up on some colorful wrasse, swept them into his net, and put them in a plastic bag attached to his waist. It didn't take more than fifteen minutes before he had enough fish and signaled me he was going up.

Although Ivey quickly rose to the surface, I followed him slowly and safely. The rule of thumb is to rise more slowly than the bubbles you exhale but I kept well below them, just a nice leisurely trip up through the water column. When I reached the sandy bank below Ivey's dock, I stopped in about twelve feet of water. Ivy had already gotten out but I wanted to add a little more decompression time, not to mention just to enjoy the undersea splendor. When I turned to watch a cloud of silverside sprat under Ivy's house, what felt like a stiletto blade was plunged into the back of my head just above my neck. Gasping with pain, I saw a burst of red light followed by a weird sensation. It was as if my skin was no longer part of me but instantly turned into a wet, creepy, crawling cocoon.

Uncertain what was causing the pain and creepy feeling, I kicked for the dock ladder and dragged myself up on it, where I pulled off my scuba gear and then knelt with my head down as the fiery dagger kept jabbing. When I realized I couldn't feel my knees on the wooden planks, I stood up and almost passed out from the pain in my head. I couldn't feel my feet so I lurched along, as if on stilts, and made my way upstairs to my bedroom, where I collapsed on my bed. Inside my mind was a raging storm, mostly one denial after the other. Did I have decompression sickness? That was impossible. I hadn't been down long enough. I had come up slowly. I was at a decompression stop! *Impossible, impossible, impossible!*

Deadness crawled up my legs inch by inch as the skin went numb. Above the numbness line, it felt as if I were on fire. I crawled off the bed and got a bottle of aspirin from my bag and took two of them. Sometimes, so the dive lore went, aspirin could make the blood slippery and send a lodged nitrogen bubble on its way to the lungs to be breathed off. It was worth a try. I also took a decongestant. Maybe, so my thoughts went, this was all some weird ear problem, a result of pressure inside that made my brain go haywire. The next thing I tried was lying on my back on the floor with my feet up on the bed. This was an approximation of the Trendelenburg position, another part of diving lore, that by putting the feet and legs higher than the head, a bubble in the spinal cord or brain might move to a less damaging spot.

In about an hour the headache went away, but I was weak and wobbly. I kept to myself, refusing to come down for meals, and spent the night fretting as my skin stayed numb from the waist down and from the waist up felt like hot worms crawling across me. Somewhere in the night, I realized I couldn't feel my bladder and when I tried to urinate, I couldn't. There was no sensation there at all. If I wasn't certain before, I realized now I was in real trouble. It was one thing to try to persevere through numbness and pain, quite another to not be able to pass water. Uremic poisoning was on its way and I was on an island without a hospital, clinic, pharmacy, or doctor. Death was staring at me with its bony face.

In the morning, I had to confess to Ivey that I had a problem I couldn't solve myself and I needed help. Ivey wore a patch over a weak eye so he stared at me with his good one. "Maybe all you need is a drink," he said. "There's rum in the cabinet."

"I don't think rum is going to solve my problem," I said.

Ivey shrugged. "Tell me what to do because I sure don't know."

What was there to do? It wasn't as if Ivey could pick up a phone and call for help. Phones didn't exist on Guanaja. All he had was a ship-to-shore radio with about the range of a CB radio that he used to call people on the island. "How about the fish plant?" I asked. "Can they contact the States?"

The fish plant, a small cannery that was only occasionally open, was located on Low Caye in Bonacca town. With some difficulty since I still couldn't feel my feet, I managed to get into Ivey's little boat and we sped over there. Fortunately, it was open. The manager heard me out and took me inside his office where he had a radio-telephone. He dialed the number of the Divers Alert Network that I always kept with me. DAN was a group of diving physicians in North Carolina that had a hotline for divers in trouble. I got on the phone with one of the doctors who heard me out and then said, "I think you've got a Type 2 decompression hit, which means a bubble lodged either in your spinal cord or your brain stem. The best thing to do is to go on pure oxygen immediately and then get yourself to a decompression chamber."

The closest one, he went on to say, was in the Republic of Panama and that's where I needed to go. "But don't fly," he added. "Flying might cause the bubble to expand."

Confused and conflicted, I thanked him and hung up. How could I get to Panama without flying? That was two countries away. Go by shrimp boat? That would take days, even if I could find such a boat to take me. I dismissed the idea of going there and focused on the oxygen. The fish plant manager scratched his head at my question on where pure oxygen could be found. "Well, we've got some for welding but I'm not sure how you'd breathe it."

I knew how. By hook or crook, we needed to get the oxygen from the welding tank into a scuba tank so I could breathe off a normal diving regulator. But how to do it? Their valves were completely different. There needed to be an interface between the two different sizes of hoses. "Do you have shop equipment?" I asked. "And aluminum or steel or copper tubing?"

The manager said he had a lathe, drill press, a milling machine, and plenty of tubing of all kinds. After looking over what he had, I sketched a design on the back of an envelope and showed it to the manager. "This is what I need," I told him.

"It might work," he said after a few seconds of study. "I'll get a machinist."

I sent Ivey racing back to get an empty tank, cautioning him to empty it completely and inspect it. Compressors on Guanaja were often dirty and pumped in oil vapor along with air and Ivey's was no exception. "Inspect it and flush it out," I told him. "It has to be absolutely clean. Pure oxygen mixed with oil under pressure and we've got a bomb. And bring back the filling yoke from your compressor, please."

When Ivey came back, I sat in a chair beside the machinist and we went over what was needed. After studying and measuring the attachment at the end of the hose from the oxy tank and the one from Ivey's compressor filling yoke, he tapped threads on the ends of tubes that fit each, then brazed them together. Holding our breath, we put our jury-rigged system to the test and it worked perfectly. After opening both valves, the scuba tank sighed as pure oxygen flowed into it. After pumping it up as much as possible, I attached my regulator on the scuba tank and began breathing in the crisp-tasting lifesaving gas. After two hours of pure oxygen, I felt much better and then came a welcome urge to urinate. I lurched into the fish plant toilet and, with some great relief of both body and mind, let the poison in my bladder leak out.

When Ivey took me back to his house, the divemaster at the Posada del Sol resort was waiting there. His name was Tino and he was a big barrel-chested mainland Honduran. He had heard of my plight and thought he could help. We sat down at Ivey's dining table and went over a manual from Australia that outlined an emergency in-water decompression technique that required going down to a depth of thirty-three feet for thirty minutes, then rising one foot every four minutes on a two-and-a-half-hour schedule. To do in-water decompression went against everything I'd been taught. The rule was never, never, *never* go back into the water after being bent. Every certifying agency, including the United States Navy, preached this.

"The Aussies claim it works, Homer," Tino said, "but it's your choice."

The one choice I figured I couldn't take was to do nothing. Breathing oxygen had caused some of the numbness and weakness to be relieved, but if there was still a bubble anywhere near my brain or spinal cord, it had to be dissolved. "Let's do it," I said. And so we did.

Tino dropped a line with an anchor attached to it from the dock and I crawled down it while breathing pure oxygen from a scuba tank. Oxygen breathed at pressures greater than two atmospheres is poison to humans and at thirty-three feet, I was exactly at twice normal atmospheric pressure so I had to be careful not to go any deeper. During my time in the water, Tino dived down and brought water in an upside down Coca-Cola bottle for me to suck from and bananas to eat. Even though the water was warm, probably around eighty-five degrees, there was a lot more of it than there was of me. An hour in, I began to shiver as my inner core cooled. Before long, I was shaking as I moved toward hypothermia. Although I knew that I was risking a shock to my heart on top of everything else, I kept at it. At the intervals called out by the Australian manual with Tino diving down and showing me what was required on a notepad, I gradually moved up the anchor line.

Three hours after beginning the emergency procedure, Tino helped me up the ladder where I collapsed on the dock and let the hot Central American sun beat down on me. After I warmed and stopped shivering, I realized I felt better. The weakness had subsided, although the skin numbness was still there.

After thanking Tino profusely, I had Ivey take me back to the fish plant and called DAN again, this time talking to Dr. Deere, the head of the network who'd heard about me and taken an interest. After I told him what I'd done, he scolded me but then asked, "Did it work?"

"I think so," I answered. "At least I feel better."

He chewed that over and then said, "Look, Homer, you've got to get to a decompression chamber."

"But the last doctor said I couldn't fly," I said.

"That's true. You need an air ambulance pressurized to one atmosphere."

"Sounds expensive."

"I'm sure it is."

"Can you get me one?"

"I can recommend several."

It was time to call for help from somebody back in the good old USA, but who? Since she had been a divemaster for Deep Space way back in 1987, I had developed a deeper relationship with Linda Terry, whom I called LT. In fact, we had become partners in just about everything. Using the fish plant's telephone, I connected through a ship at sea that in turn called a fish store in Tampa that then in turn called LT's parents with whom she lived.

When LT heard about my plight from her mom, she started calling the air ambulance numbers Dr. Deere passed along. She found one in Houston that was willing to come and get me. The cost? Only $13,500. LT gave them her American Express number. A few hours passed and a woman from Amex called and politely asked, "How do you plan on paying this bill, Miss Terry?"

"I've always paid my bill on time," LT answered.

"Yes," the Amex rep replied dryly, "but it's never been more than $150."

LT thought about that and then reminded them that this was an emergency situation. The nice lady said she knew that but she had a corporate responsibility not to allow the charge unless it could be paid. LT mentioned I had an Amex card, too. This was checked. Since apparently I'd paid off some larger bills, the American Express lady allowed the charge to go through.

The next morning, the jet arrived on Guanaja's crushed-coral runway, I climbed into it, and off we went, destination Huntsville, Alabama. When LT told the managers of the Neutral Buoyancy Simulator what had happened, they were prepared to pop me in their decompression chamber. We landed at the Redstone Army airfield where paramedic and fellow Deep Space/Shallow Diver Brenda Bradford was waiting for me with her ambulance. Off I went to the chamber, where Dr. Dye and Dr.

Lee, MSFC physicians, took over. Over four days, I was put on a decompression schedule, the first day five hours, then for three more days at two-and-a-half hours. During my sessions, volunteer NBS divers entered the chamber with me. Between sessions, I occupied a room at Huntsville Hospital. After all the procedures, I was left slightly numb from the waist down and couldn't feel either the soles of my feet or the tips of my fingers.

After a visit with my friends at DAN and a number of tests at Duke University, the medical opinion was that I had suffered a bubble probably near the brain stem. What had caused it, however, was unknown. There was some thought that it was the result of a hole in my heart that was so small it never showed up on any examination. Another theory was all the hours I spent underwater working on the Hubble had built up "invisible bubbles" that caused the decompression tables to no longer work for me, at least at that time. There was even the idea that I had so much nitrogen in my blood from diving that it was attacked by antibodies that caused something like little beads in my blood vessels that got stuck near my brain.

No matter how I rationalized it, I knew in my heart God had let me off easy but my deep, long dives were over and my days as a scuba instructor were numbered as well. I was grateful to Ivey, the fish plant people, Tino, LT, the MSFC doctors, the NBS divers, and Brenda and the other paramedics in Huntsville who worked hard to save me. Even afflicted, I knew I was blessed and maybe kept alive for some good reason. At least, I hoped so.

After about six months, I convinced NASA to let me go back to work in the NBS but, like the miners who refused to let my dad go into the mine with his black lung, Bobby Beavers, the NBS scheduler, cut my hours back so as to protect another obsessed Hickam from himself. As for the $13,500 bill to American

Express, it got paid month by month, little by little until one day, somebody at the office said I should check with my congressman, one Ronnie Flippo, and ask him to intercede with my medical insurance carrier. After one phone call from Flippo's office, the carrier promptly paid all that was left in the bill. As I came to learn at that moment, it never hurts to ask your local politician for help.

Sputnik Again

In *Rocket Boys*, I tell the tale of the night that little Sonny Hickam saw Sputnik, the world's first artificial satellite, and was so impressed he decided to build his own rocket, which led him to form his own missile agency right there in Coalwood, West Virginia, and ultimately win a gold medal at the National Science Fair. Astonishingly, even though the Russian moon crashed into the atmosphere decades before, there came a day when little Sonny, now big Homer, would actually see Sputnik again and vodka would only have a little to do with it.

When you work for NASA, it isn't all astronauts and rocket ships. In many ways, the space agency is just another federal agency staffed by federal employees with all the rules, regulations, and other nonsense that such implies. To meet congressional directives, the NASA administrator and the directors and managers at the various field centers must contend with an onslaught of financial, personnel, administrative, and organizational imperatives that sometimes overlap and don't always make complete sense but have to be documented in one way or another on paper or on a computer or, preferably, both.

As mentioned before, Dr. von Braun famously said that no NASA rocket ever flew unless the paperwork was stacked as high as the rocket but even when no rocket is involved, the documentation is still enormous. To meet every task and see that it is all accomplished properly and recorded as required, the space agency has developed intricate bureaucracies in all its field centers that range from administrative to supremely technical. The Mission Operations Lab where I worked during the Spacelab era was kind of in-between in that we trained the astronauts on very technical experiments and operated the Payload Operations Control Center during flights, but we also had an administrative side where we provided a service, per various agreements, to the other field centers and our international partners. To accomplish these tasks, we had a full complement of civil service and contractor personnel. When the International Space Station came along, however, everything we were responsible for on Spacelab was up for grabs. As the point man for the Marshall Space Flight Center on payload training and knowing full well that the Johnson Space Center coveted our role, it was necessary that I sharpen my mental sword, prime my mental musket, don my mental armor, and turn into one of the most vicious creatures known to mankind, a United States government bureaucratic in-fighter.

Since Chuck Lewis, Debra Underwood, Ken Smith, and I in the training office were very aware of Houston's wish to take over our role, it was necessary to get ahead of them by first simply accepting the fact that they were in a strong position and doing what we could to bring them into direct negotiations. Their strength lay in the fact that the astronauts lived and worked in Houston. We Huntsvillians preferred that the astronauts travel to the PCTC or to the PI sites for payload training, but the crews preferred to stay in Houston for all their training. Although my allegiance was to Huntsville, my SL-J experience made me sympathetic toward the astronauts in that regard because they deserved to have a reasonable family life, too. This left me with a dilemma only a certain amount of delicate diplomacy at the middle-management level could resolve.

It took a lot of travel to Houston and many meetings and not a little angst for all parties to finally hammer out an agreement. Fortunately, I had some great folks at JSC to work with, including Frank Hughes, Ronnie Lanier, and Willie Williams. Ultimately, we knew we had to find a compromise and we did. In our final agreement, Huntsville kept responsibility for the payload science training but the training itself would be mostly performed in Houston. The upside to that was our experienced Spacelab training people could transition over to the ISS. The biggest downside was that we no longer had a need for the PCTC, and it was closed after the last Spacelab flight. Nobody was completely happy with our agreement, which usually means there's been a fair compromise. To my credit or perhaps to place blame where it belonged, the agreement was called the Hickam Paradigm for Payload Training, and a version of it is still in use to this day.

With our disagreements settled, Huntsville and Houston could present a united front to the Russians, our new partners on the ISS, on how to train our crews. Unfortunately, the Russian approach was radically different from ours. While we did whatever we could to make our astronauts happy with their training, Russian cosmonauts were shown a training schedule and ordered to comply or else they were booted out of the program. From what I could tell, a lot of times they were treated not much better than lab rats.

A NASA team was formed in 1994 to negotiate how we were going to work with the Russians on the new space station and, along with others in our lab, I was assigned to it and visited Russia for a variety of meetings. Very quickly, we realized it wasn't just a matter of signing agreements between two space agencies. We were dealing with a people in a state of shock after the collapse of their country. Although NASA contracted with a German-operated luxury hotel on the outskirts of Moscow that offered some protection from the reality of the situation, I wanted to see what was to be seen and, when I could get away from our meetings, took off on my own to poke into as many neighborhoods as I could.

The poverty and misery I saw on the streets away from Red Square was shocking. In deep winter, many people, both men and women, were sleeping outside. They lay on grates in the street or on park benches or just huddled near shop doors that might offer a slight rush of heat whenever they were opened. At the subway entrances, beggars clustered. When I climbed the steps of the subway one Sunday morning, I saw a number of policemen rousting an old man lying on the cold concrete. He was wearing a tattered brown overcoat, black boots, and a wool cap with a red star on it and I wondered if he was a World War II veteran. It didn't seem to matter. The police were clearly a rough lot with an awful job, to keep order in a crumbling city filled with a lot of people who had lost everything. The vast concrete Olympic stadium that Jimmy Carter famously boycotted by not allowing our team to participate in 1980 was abandoned and, within the dingy recesses of its rubble, I saw cooking and warming fires with people huddled around them. It was Rome the day after being sacked by the Vandals except in subzero weather.

It is perhaps curious that someone from an isolated coal town in West Virginia can be comfortable wherever he is across the world but, for me, that is the usual case. Despite the language barrier, for some reason I am usually welcomed or at least accepted in foreign lands. Maybe it's because I don't wear expensive clothes and I try my best to fit in. For the most part, I was treated casually on the Russian streets as I walked around, although it must have been obvious that I was observing everything with intense curiosity. I was also trying to wrap my brain around not only what I was seeing but what I was feeling. After all, I had spent a major portion of my life either fighting against the Russians in the proxy war in Vietnam or working for the military throughout the height of the Cold War. Even NASA had come into existence because of the Russians beating the United States in space and our need to form an organization to catch up with them. Yet, in a matter of minutes, all that animosity I had accrued in my heart for these people simply vanished and my heart went out to them with a prayer that they prosper.

A very sad spectacle was families selling their household goods on the streets. They looked so pathetic, these proud men and women holding up what must have been something they had once enjoyed, perhaps a ceramic statue, some good china, an old clock, some small luxury now handed over for a few kopeks to buy food. During the summer of 1994 and winter of 1995, the times when I was there with the negotiating teams, Moscow was truly a city under siege by not only a collapsing infrastructure but by starving animals. One morning, I passed through a gate in the fence around my hotel to take a run around the park close by. After the first curve, wild dogs came out of the trees and started chasing me. A man in tattered clothes sprung from somewhere—maybe he'd been sleeping on a park bench; I was never sure—and fended them off long enough for me to run back inside the barrier. When I turned to thank him, he gave me an exaggerated bow and walked away. The dogs, their ribs showing, gathered forlornly and howled. When I mentioned the dogs to a Russian with the idea that maybe I could buy some food for them, I was told in no uncertain terms not to do it unless I wanted to lose an arm. To compound the misery of the situation, he went on to say that hunters had been hired by the government to shoot the wild dogs and even wolves that were within city limits and many pets had been shot by mistake. Once more as I had done often during my life but less than I should have, I thanked God I lived where I did.

On weekends when I had more time, I took the subway line to its end because I thought that might be the best way to see what was happening outside the city. The Moscow subway was amazing in its architecture and artistic treasures. Clearly, Muscovites were proud of it, as it was pristine. Following a guidebook, I found a memorial to space on the northeastern boundary of the city. A magnificent titanium structure that swooped upward like a rocket's fiery plume, it was heavily vandalized and covered with graffiti and was also being used as a skateboard track. It all felt very sad. A society that destroys its statues and memorials is one surely in decline. Yet, for all this, I sensed a dour determination among the Russians. Their proud country had failed, but they were going to get back up one way or the other.

We would eventually reach an agreement with the Russians on how to train our astronauts and their cosmonauts, which was a compromise that required a little more travel by our crews to Russia than we liked and a little more travel by theirs to Houston than they liked. To help break the ice between bouts of negotiating, I told the Russians across the table how important Sputnik was to my career and my life. To my surprise, many of them were part of the team that actually launched it! One evening, at a party that featured vodka and, well, more vodka, one of those men through an interpreter said since I had seen Sputnik as a youth, would I like to see it again as a man? I was sure the translation was in error. After all, that magnificent orb had burned up in the atmosphere long ago and that's what I pointed out. "That is true," he responded, "but we built two."

Several days later, several members of the Russian space agency took me to a warehouse that looked like something straight out of Indiana Jones. There, a wooden box was opened to reveal a shiny spherical ball with recesses for antennae, the precise twin of Sputnik. After an excited barrage of Russian erupted from my hosts, the interpreter said, "There were two Sputniks and the one that went into space was chosen randomly. This one could have been the one you saw. It could have been the one *everybody* saw."

It was difficult to imagine that moment as being anything other than what it was—Godsent. Some things are just meant to be, and all I could do was enjoy the moment and thank my new Russian friends and the angels who had arranged me to see Sputnik twice, once in the October sky as teenaged Sonny Hickam and once within arm's reach as Homer, the grown-up NASA guy.

Courtesy of Don Howard

5

That Author Feller

The Article That Started It All

Just before Christmas 1994, my phone rang and I found myself talking to Pat Trenner, editor of *Air & Space/Smithsonian* magazine. I'd written a couple of articles previously for Pat and she had liked my work so I wasn't too surprised when she said, "Homer, I need a short article as a filler for our February issue and I thought of you. Do you have anything?"

Because of all the travel I was doing to Russia and elsewhere for NASA, I didn't have an article in my hopper but before I could tell Pat that sad fact, my eyes strayed to a paperweight I had on my desk. It was, in fact, a steel de Laval rocket nozzle built in the Coalwood machine shop during my days of building rockets as a teenager. The reason I had it was because just before my dad died, he convinced my mom to help him box up all the toys and other artifacts that belonged to me and my brother from childhood and ship them off to us. When I received a dozen or so boxes with a note from Mom explaining this was all my "stuff" and I could keep it or throw it away, I carelessly stacked the boxes in the garage and avoided looking at them until 1994 when water seeped inside and got them wet. Pondering the collapsing mess, I noticed that unlike the other boxes that had my mom's handwriting on it, one of them, a shoebox, was marked by my dad, his scrawl easily recognized. He had written but one word on it—"SONNY." When I opened the box, I found two things: the medal I'd won at the 1960 National Science Fair and a perfectly crafted steel rocket nozzle. My father had saved those things for me! But why? Into my head popped an image, the final day when we Rocket Boys had launched our last, great rocket. Dad pushed the button that sent our missile skyward and then we had shared a moment of understanding that I thought was enough to last me a lifetime. Were these mementos his way of telling me that this moment was important to him, too?

The medal went into a drawer, the nozzle became the paperweight on my desk that I saw when I was talking to Pat Trenner. "Pat," I said, "when I was a boy in a West Virginia coal town, some other boys and I built rockets. How about an article about that?"

Pat was completely, totally, and utterly underwhelmed by my proposal but she graciously replied, "Write it and I'll take a look."

Maybe the story had always been pent up inside me, or maybe the artifacts Dad saved for me caused me to recall it, or maybe me telling the story to the Japanese had kept it fresh in my mind, or perhaps seeing the second Sputnik in Moscow was what did it. Whatever it was, when I started to write, the words flowed out of me like a literary flood. I recalled the five other boys who made up our rocket club: randy Roy Lee, excitable O'Dell, polio-afflicted Sherman, studious Billy, and genius Quentin. I recalled Miss Riley, our marvelous physics and chemistry teacher, and how she encouraged us to take our chances with the science fairs, and how my mom backed us up against my dad and how the town disliked us at first but then came to embrace us. It only took me two hours to write the article and fax it to Pat. The next morning, she called. "Half the people in my office are laughing at your article, Homer," she said, "and the other half are crying. I think you're onto something special. I need photos of those boys and your medal. We're publishing it!"

The article came out in *Air & Space*'s February 1995 issue. Within a few days, I was swamped with letters from people telling me they wanted to hear more about those feisty Rocket Boys. When I got letters from two independent movie producers who thought my story might make a good film, I knew I needed help. Although they seemed honest, there was always the possibility my story might be fictionalized or otherwise ripped off. But where to go for help? I didn't know anybody in Hollywood. All I knew was I'd better find somebody—and fast!

The Cowboy of Hollywood

In 1996, the Olympics were held in Atlanta and I was honored to be selected to carry the Olympic torch through part of Huntsville. I was put in for it by LT's parents, who cited my part in the *SCItanic* tragedy. At first, I didn't think too much about it and kind of laughed it off by telling my friends that I had limited goals: (1) not to drop the torch, and (2) not to set my hair on fire. When the time came, however, as I waited dressed in my special white Olympics shorts and shirt, I discovered I was absolutely thrilled. The mile I ran at night while carrying the flaming torch seemed to go by in a heartbeat and I don't recall once taking a breath. It was one of the best times in my life and it solidified in my mind how much I loved my adopted city, Rocket City, Huntsville, Alabama.

Soon after, I received a contract from Kawasaki Heavy Industries to build two EMU space suit simulators for the new Japanese neutral buoyancy simulator. After getting permission from NASA to do it under my Deep Space company banner, LT and I, with the help of her mom, her brothers, Carl Spurlock, Al English, and others, built two high-fidelity versions of the EMU suit we called the Underwater Spacesuit Trainer (UST). After testing the UST in Space Camp's UAT with Al English and none other than my old friend Japanese astronaut Takao Doi as test subjects, we shipped the suits off to Japan. Deep Space didn't make much money (we probably lost a little), but we surely had fun building those suits. From all reports, they were exactly what the Japanese needed to train their astronauts before they were able to buy a couple of the real EMU suits.

Although these sideline activities were fun, and I was still working on the training for the ISS, I still needed to figure out what to do with the movie offers for my *Air & Space* article. After giving it some thought, I recalled that I actually did know someone in Hollywood. In 1989, after *Torpedo Junction* came out, I was called by Neil Russell, an established producer who was interested in the book. Nothing came of it but I still had his phone number, so I gave Neil a call and told him my situation. His answer was immediate: "Don't sign anything. I think I know an agent who might be interested."

About a week later, I got a call from a fellow named Mickey Freiberg. Mickey, I would come to learn, was a legend among Hollywood agents. Nicknamed "the Cowboy," he was a relentless salesman on behalf of his clients. "Tell me about your property," he said, and I did. He was silent for a moment before asking, "What do you expect to get out of this?"

"Well," I said, "my girlfriend and I could use a new microwave."

This earned me a chuckle, followed by another question. "Can you write a treatment?"

"Sure," I said. "What's a treatment?"

"A treatment is just telling the story like it was a movie. Can you do that?"

I said I could and worked on it all weekend, ending up with ten pages that told the story of how the Coalwood Rocket Boys were inspired by Sputnik to build rockets and how we had gone on to win a gold medal at the 1960 National Science Fair. Within hours of faxing the treatment to Mickey, he called back. "If I can't sell this," he said, "I shouldn't be an agent."

Quite frankly thrilled, I asked, "What should I do now?"

"I think you should pick out that microwave because you and I are going to make some money. And I hope you're writing a book. Are you?"

I was now. But what kind of book? The concept I came up with was to write a memoir that contrasted my boyhood life in Coalwood with my life as a NASA engineer. A lot of pages got written along that track before I realized it didn't work. Looking for a fresh start, I talked to Emily Sue Buckberry, a high school friend who was then a speech therapy professor at Ohio University. After hearing me out, she provided me with some valuable insight. "Let Sonny tell it," she said. "I always loved that boy."

After giving her advice some thought, I realized she was right. The story should be told as if it were written by the boy who experienced it. To do that, I would have to find that boy and get inside his head because, after all, Sonny Hickam wasn't me. He was a boy whose life had been spent in Coalwood, a boy who'd not fought in a war, a boy who hadn't gone to engineering school, a boy who hadn't dived on U-boat wrecks and written a book and worked for NASA. He was a boy for whom nearly everything in the world was a mystery. The search for Sonny began by opening myself up to him to tell me the story. In the process, I like to say I got a million dollars of psychotherapy I didn't even know I needed.

My work at NASA still required long days, so I got up in the dark and wrote until I had to go to work. When I got home, I ran a couple of miles to recharge my batteries and then, after a quick dinner, wrote until I couldn't keep my eyes open. Four or five hours of sleep a night became normal, but it didn't matter. I was obsessed with telling the story and gradually, the little town of Coalwood started to come alive again through my fingers on the computer keyboard. The miners, their lunch pails clunking against their legs, trudged up the old path to the mine. The people of the town bustled in and out of the company store and gathered on the church steps after Sunday services to gossip. My mother was in her kitchen, in her refuge in front of the big portrait she was painting of the beach and the ocean. Our dogs, Dandy and Poteet, waited in my basement laboratory, their tails wagging, and lounging on the couch was Daisy Mae our calico cat and Chipper the squirrel hanging on the living room curtains. In my room, there was my old desk and the rocket design book Miss Riley bought for us with her own money. Everything and everyone were still there, all in their places, defining the path, urging me along as I wrote.

But there was someone else there, too. Every time I tried to turn away from him, he moved like a phantom to stay in my view. He was there, standing on that old slack dump we called Cape Coalwood while our last, great rocket soared overhead. More than anyone else, I needed my dad to be found, too. And it was then I remembered Mom telling me before Dad died that I should write him a letter. That was another key to writing the memoir that became *Rocket Boys*. It was Sonny's letter to tell his dad, at long last, how much he loved and appreciated him.

Writing *Rocket Boys*

Astonishment was my natural reaction when, less than a year later, Mickey negotiated a deal with Universal Studios with Charles (Chuck) Gordon as the producer. Mickey said Gordon had produced *Field of Dreams* and had a solid reputation in the movie industry. When Mickey began to go through the contract terms, I listened with my jaw unhinged. Listening in, LT tried to take notes but the names, rights, representations, warranties, and indemnities were coming like bullets from a machine gun. When she showed me the last dollar number she'd written down, we stared at each other and shook our heads in wonder. As amazing as it all sounded, it simply did not seem real. When I said this out loud, Mickey said, "It's real but it isn't everything. Universal has taken an option but many options are taken, few movies are made. It's the only money we'll get for now. The rest won't be paid until we get a green light. Don't worry. Worry is my job. You just write your book! The movie may depend on it."

When the option money arrived, LT and I bought our new microwave but it still seemed like gossamer moonbeams. Deep in my heart, I couldn't believe anybody would want to make a movie about the Coalwood Rocket Boys, but then the phone rang and I found myself talking to Chuck Gordon himself. He told me how much he'd enjoyed my treatment and handed the conversation over to Mark Sternberg, an associate, who asked if I would talk to Lewis Colick, an A-list writer. "If we can get Lewis on board," Mark said, "that would go a long way to getting the movie made."

A few days later, Lewis Colick called. He was very friendly but told me up front that he was only calling as a favor to Chuck. He was pretty sure he wasn't the right person to pen a screenplay set in rural West Virginia. After all, he'd grown up in Brooklyn and knew nothing about small towns! When I asked him about his boyhood friends, he described them as kids who liked to play outside. "We got in trouble lots of times," he confessed, "but we always felt safe. Everybody in the neighborhood looked after us. We couldn't get away with much because our parents would hear about it before we got home."

Picking up on that, I said, "That doesn't sound much different from Coalwood. You had streets and tenements, I had mountains and company houses. I bet you also wanted to get out of Brooklyn as soon as you could but now you sometimes wish you could go back."

Lewis laughed and agreed maybe I was right. We talked a little more and then, after cordial goodbyes, hung up. Mickey called a week later and said Lewis was in. "You did really good, Homer," he said. "Chuck and Mark are grateful. You're a player!"

Being a "player" sounded fine and I agreed to send Lewis what I'd written of the memoir to date, which was about ten chapters. Before long, Mickey called and said everybody agreed the chapters were wonderful. He also had an interested editor at Putnam. This all left me feeling good about everything but a couple of months later, Mickey told me the editor at Putnam had passed on the book. When I asked what was wrong with it, Mickey said there was nothing wrong, that it was just the wrong editor. This worried me a lot. The movie Lewis was writing was going to be based on a treatment and an incomplete book manuscript for which I had no publisher. Everything seemed out of kilter.

When I finished the first draft of the complete manuscript, I had LT read it and she thought it was great, but friends and loved ones aren't necessarily the best judge of unpublished books so I hired a college English professor to read it with the proviso he tell me exactly what he thought and not spare the criticism. His report was almost entirely extravagant in its praise. Feeling more confident, I decided the time had come for me to share the manuscript with the other Rocket Boys. Although they'd read my *Air & Space* article, this was the first time I'd told them anything about a book or a movie. Roy Lee, O'Dell, Billy, and Quentin (Sherman had passed away) all reported back that they admired what I'd written, although none of them thought anything was ever going to come of it, especially not a movie. After a good laugh at my expense, O'Dell said, "Be sure to invite us to the premiere!" Roy Lee was bemused, wondering, "Sonny, who would care about what we did back in high school?"

I let the boys think what they wanted to think. For all I knew, they were right, and for months afterward, it seemed they were. Mickey had no news on either the movie or any interested publishers. All I could do was sharpen the manuscript and ponder the main character. I still didn't think I'd entirely found the real Sonny Hickam. *Who was that boy?* Intuitively, I kept peeling away Sonny's character layer by layer. Some of the things he did I understood but at other times, I was uncertain about his motivation. Then came the day when the boy finally presented himself.

Hey, old man, he said. *Stop putting words in my mouth and making me do things I wouldn't do. I was a sneaky little brat and was lazy as a cloud in the sky. After I started building rockets, you think I went to Mr. Bykovski because he was the best mechanic in town? No, I asked for his help because I knew I could get to him, make him feel sorry for me.* He wiped his nose with the back of his dirty hand. *And that's what got him killed.*

That explains why you stopped building your rockets after the accident! I exclaimed silently in my mind. *I wondered about that. You were ashamed!*

The boy I once was laughed a bitter laugh. *I wasn't ashamed. Something far worse. I felt* nothing!

Nothing! And there it was. At last, I realized what I had missed in the first draft. Sonny Hickam was quite capable of being sneaky and selfish and what he did with his rockets and chasing girls and making trouble for his brother and his parents was just part of his many plans to get his own way, plans that often fell apart. Sonny could also be noble, but it wasn't his nobility that made him an interesting narrator. It was because of how he'd been molded by the people of Coalwood and his teachers to do the right thing even though his inclination often took him in the opposite direction. He was always struggling, and there is no more interesting character than one who struggles with himself! With this insight, I thought: *Got you, you little rat! I know who you are!* Sonny just laughed.

Eagerly, I settled in behind my computer and rewrote vast parts of the book, this time bringing in the comedy and tragedy of the real Sonny telling his story. In the midst of the rewrite, Mickey called with an update on Hollywood. "Something you should know," he said. "They've decided to compress everything into one school year."

This was terrible news. The story had occurred over a three-year period during which so many things happened that a few months couldn't possibly encompass the sweep of the story Sonny was telling. "You've got to trust Chuck and Lewis," Mickey said. "They know what they're doing."

Whether I trusted them or not wasn't the point. I knew Lewis was still working off the treatment and the first chapters of an old draft. When I told Mickey I wanted to send them my latest, he said, "It would only confuse things. Oh, by the way, you're going to be called Homer in the movie, not Sonny. They think Homer sounds more West Virginian. They've also changed your dad's name to John." I was still sputtering when he hung up. My dad's name was, of course, Homer. I was named after him. It seemed like a double insult for both our names to be changed.

In November 1996, LT and I flew to Kenya and then traveled on to Tanzania for two and a half weeks of tent camping on safari. We saw everything: lions, cheetahs, rhinos, hippos, wildebeests, water buffalo, hyenas, even leopards. When we returned, there were phone messages from Mickey telling me to call an editor at St. Martin's and also an editor at Pocket Books. He also left a warning: the movie was probably not going to be made unless there was a book behind it.

When I called the editor at St. Martin's, he said, "I thought this was supposed to be a kid's book. You've got all this stuff about teenage girls built like brick shithouses. What the hell does that mean? One of the boys even has a rubber. And you got so much about the town and how it was founded and how it was built and who runs it. Nobody cares about that. And coal miners getting killed? Downer. And there's this drunk you find passed out. And that colored preacher. You don't need all that. This is about kids building rockets."

"No, it isn't," I argued. "It's first about growing up in a coal camp and second about some teenage boys there who get it in their heads to build rockets, and…"

"Just write that. Nothing else. Use the town as background but I wouldn't otherwise get into it. Write about boys who build rockets and maybe we'll publish it."

I hung up and called Pocket Books. "It's slow. It drags," that editor said. "You have way too much about your parents. Just write about building rockets. Anything else, nobody will care."

"Without Mom and Dad, the story doesn't make sense," I said. "Mom challenged me to build the rockets and I did it for Dad so he'd notice me."

"Leave all that stuff out. Make it inspirational. You built your rockets so you could work for NASA."

"There was no NASA in 1957."

"You know what I mean. This is a young adult novel. You've got to inspire the kids."

That made my blood boil. "That's like saying *To Kill a Mockingbird* is a young adult novel."

He laughed. "If you think you can write anything like *Mockingbird*, come up here and let me sell you a bridge. Oh, and you need to make that town a lot nastier than you wrote it. Have you ever seen *Coal Miner's Daughter*? Like that."

I was polite but still hung up rather soon. Confused, I reread the manuscript. What was I supposed to do? Simplify it? Take out the big words? Eliminate the struggle and sexual tension between my parents, dilute the lust Sonny had for the unattainable

Dorothy Plunk, and leave out the wiles of Valentine Carmina who was destined to steal the boy's virginity in the back seat of her boyfriend's car? Was I supposed to take out Miss Riley's Hodgkin's disease that was killing her day by day? Did I need to throw out Jake Mosby, the great womanizer and drunk who Sonny admired? No more Little Richard, the black preacher who was so often my mentor? Should I change Sonny back to being all noble again? Did they want me to remove my dad from the story? And should I make Coalwood into a stereotypical nasty coal camp filled with starving people dressed in rags and kids running around without shoes? All those things seemed to be what the publishers wanted and, for all I knew, what Hollywood was crafting in secret.

After running these questions through my mind, I concluded that I wasn't going to do any of those things. This was not only Sonny's story or the story of the Rocket Boys; this was the story of Coalwood as I had lived it and its people as I had known them. If that meant the book wasn't going to be published and the movie wasn't going to be made, I could live with that.

One day, Mickey called and said, "Listen, I'm working with an agent in New York. His name is Frank Weimann. He's got great connections. Give him a call. He wants to talk to you."

Reluctantly, expecting the same thing I'd heard from the publishers, I called Frank. After telling him what I was doing with the book and also how much Mickey wanted the movie to be made, he said, "Don't worry about the movie. Movies are movies but books are books. I've read your manuscript. It's magic and I'm going to find it a publisher."

"You mean that?"

"Absolutely. I couldn't put it down."

"Thank you," I kept saying. "Thank you, thank you."

"There's just one thing…"

Uh-oh was my thought.

"I want someone else to look at it. To help you a little."

"I'm a published writer," I said through gritted teeth. "Nobody helped me with *Torpedo Junction* and I don't need anybody to help me with *Rocket Boys*."

"Maybe not," Frank replied. "But I want you to talk to this fellow. See if you hit it off."

"No way" was my answer.

"Expect his call," Frank replied and hung up.

A sleepless week later, I got a call from a young man who identified himself as David Groff. "I read your book," he said. "It's great. It could be published the way it is now, but I think I can help you make it better."

"Let me think it over," I said.

"Sure," David replied. "Just let me know."

I thought it over, got in touch with my better angels (who were startled to hear from me), and then called him back. "I'm going to go through the manuscript again and then send you a chapter at a time. When will you be ready?"

"I'm ready now."

To my surprise, I loved what happened next. It turned into an intellectual exercise, mainly because I knew David was waiting to see what I'd written, and I knew his commentary would be on the money. Chapter by chapter, he became my touchstone, rarely changing a word but suggesting places where my writing could be better. I was still really busy with NASA but kept at the memoir. There was a snowstorm chapter that nearly got Sonny frozen to death that I wrote in Moscow while a Russian snowstorm was raging. By going outside the hotel and walking to clear my mind, I remembered what Sonny felt in that fearsome blizzard and what it was like to be really cold. David and I kept honing *Rocket Boys* until it was the best both of us thought it could be. Frank read the result and then called. "It's brilliant, Homer, and everybody up here is going to think the same thing."

Within a month, Frank had gotten so many accolades about my manuscript from editors, he decided to put it up for auction. When it was held, the winner was Tom Spain, a senior editor for Delacorte, a publishing house in the Bantam Doubleday Dell Random House empire. I called Frank. "Thank you," I said. "It wouldn't have happened without you."

"It's nice to be thanked," Frank said, "and you're welcome."

With a book contract secured, Chuck Gordon called and said he had a director for the movie. His name was Joe Johnston and he'd directed *Honey, I Shrunk the Kids*, *The Rocketeer*, and *Jumanji*. Not long after, we had a green light from Universal Studios. The movie was going to be made!

I called Mickey. "Thank you," I said. "It wouldn't have happened without you."

"You're right," he said and then laughed. "This is fun, isn't it?"

It was, but I also sensed there was something coming my way, something that was good but not good. Whatever it was, it meant change and I wasn't absolutely convinced that change was something I needed or wanted.

But that no longer mattered. It was out of my hands. *Rocket Boys* the book and *October Sky* the movie were both coming at me like twin guided missiles. For some reason, I thought back to that time on the Slick heading up to Dak To and wished somebody would hand me some ammunition and tell me to stay low and never try to be a hero.

Making *October Sky*

With the book sold and the movie greenlit and also my negotiations finished on the International Space Station, I gave it some thought and decided it was time to retire from NASA. It was not an easy decision. Every day when I worked for the space agency, I loved my job. But if I was going to be a writer, and I had in mind many other books, I thought I should dedicate myself to it. Accordingly, I submitted my retirement papers, my branch gave me a fine going-away party, and, after one last nostalgic visit to the NBS and the PCTC to allow myself a little time to be grateful for all the friends and colleagues I had made during my years with NASA, I drove away from Marshall Space Flight Center into another life.

Filming for the movie was scheduled to begin in February 1998 and was supposed to last a month. Primarily because of the weather and the schedules of some of the actors, it lasted three. Since I'd been hired as a consultant, I worked with set designer Barry Robison to make certain that every nuance of the film was accurate to the times. Director Joe Johnston also asked lots of questions about what things looked like back in 1950s West Virginia.

Most of the film was made near Oak Ridge, Tennessee. Since that was only about a three-hour drive from Huntsville, I was on the set quite a lot. LT went with me most of the time, and she was a big hit with the cast and crew. As to the cast, we got to meet some of them before the movie was shot. My high school friend Emily Sue Buckberry, the speech therapy professor at Ohio University who had recommended I write the book as teenager Sonny, was hired to teach the actors our West Virginia dialect. Larry Franco, the assistant director, introduced the four young actors playing the Rocket Boys to us between their classes. Chad Lindberg, a tall youth with Jimmy Stewart looks, played Sherman O'Dell, a character that combined Rocket Boys Jimmie O'Dell Carroll and Sherman Siers. Will Lee Scott played Roy Lee Cooke. Will exuded toughness and maturity, which was perfect for the Rocket Boy who loved the girls. Chris Owen was Quentin Wilson, the genius of our group who also lived a desperate life of poverty he tried to keep hidden. With his shock of red hair and goofy expressions, Chris didn't look much like the real Quentin, who was sharp-faced with slick black hair, but I could see why he was cast. He had about him the air of the quintessential nerd that decidedly defined our Quentin.

Last to be introduced was Jake Gyllenhaal who was playing me, or at least the Hollywood version of Sonny/Homer. Jake was a handsome young man—sixteen at the time and still in high school—with deep blue eyes (mine are brown) that twinkled with mischief. He vigorously shook my hand. "I hope I can do you justice," he said.

"I think you'll be great," I replied, although I had no idea if he would or not.

The Tennessee Film Commission had promised the director and producers that the weather was mostly good in February but as soon as they set up shop, one of the worst winters in the state's history descended on the area. This was a problem since almost all of the movie was set outside. One of the locations was on a huge slack coal dump near Wartburg, which was standing in for our Cape Coalwood rocket range. Slack is excess coal waiting to be sold and is nasty and raw. When we visited, there was a frozen wind blowing across the vast layers of coal and spitting rain and snow. Crew members circulated amongst us, handing out chemical hand and boot warmers. Scott Miles, the young actor playing my brother Jim, came over to say hello. His hair was fashioned into a 1950s-style flattop and he was wearing a Big Creek High School jacket. He and I had a little talk about Jim and how he was one of the best football players in the state. Although "Jim" was only in a limited number of scenes, Scott did a great job with his character. Whenever I watched the dailies, Joe invariably admired out loud Scott's work.

After a couple of days on the dump, many of the actors and crew came down with flu-like symptoms including headaches and nausea that I called slack dump fever. It was probably caused by the methane seeping out of the raw coal. Jake's mother was Naomi Foner, a screenwriter, who became one of my best friends on location. When Naomi said she wasn't feeling well on the dump, I told her she should leave for the day. She shook her head and said she would stick it out because she wanted to support her boy. As for Jake, Chad, Will, or Chris, they were having fun in their 1950s clothes running around atop the exotic material known as coal. Jake came over to me with a big grin and asked, "Did you really have a rocket range on this stuff?"

I assured him that we did. Jake wrinkled his nose. "It's nasty," he said, pointing at his shoes, which were coated with ebony grime.

"Now, you're a real Coalwood boy," I said, which made him laugh. I could tell he had more questions but before he could voice them, he was called to makeup. Although having your hair combed and lipstick applied by a pretty woman wasn't much like being a Coalwood boy, it was all part of the movie process.

As the filming went on over the weeks, it kept getting colder and wetter. Natalie Canerday, who was playing my mom, shivered in her light housedress costume but hung in there day after day. She was playing the role as strong as my mother was. I never once heard her complain.

Between takes, I often talked to the special effects folks. Joey Digaetano, affectionately called Joey D, headed up the team. His two vans held a complete machine shop, a supply of steel and aluminum bar stock and cylinders, various chemicals, and a group of talented and skilled men and women who loved to fly rockets and blow things up. Just my kind of people! Although I didn't notice it at the time, Joey D looked a lot like a young Wernher von Braun, but our director had noticed the similarity very well. Toward the end of the making of the movie, Joe put Joey D in the movie as the rocket scientist and had him shake my hand. I didn't know the scene existed until after I'd seen the first edit. Joe's response when I thanked him was, "I wanted you to finally meet Wernher von Braun." One aside: to play the part, Joey D had to dye his normally light brown hair to nearly black. His fiancée was not happy about that since it hadn't grown out in time for their wedding!

It was an exciting day when Laura Dern showed up to play Miss Riley although the weather, as usual, didn't cooperate. It was snowing, the wind was blowing hard, and ice covered the roads. She was undaunted and played her scenes. Later, she asked to see me in her trailer. We talked while she was getting her hair done, mostly about Miss Riley and what she was really like. When she arrived late for a scene after our talk, I was admonished by Larry Franco to perhaps be a little more aware of the schedule. He was right. Time is definitely money on a film shoot.

When I lightly complained about something in the script, Joe Johnston delivered a funny and classic line. "You know, Homer," he said, "we're just trying to sell popcorn here." He didn't mean it, of course, but I understood what he was saying. Movies ultimately need to please their audiences so the writer and director arrange the stories they tell to do just that. The makeup of the audience for this film, however, was an unknown. For his part, Joe was determined that it wouldn't be considered a kid's film. That's why he allowed some cursing and shot a torrid make-out scene between Jake and Kaili Hollister, the delightful actress playing the movie version of Valentine. Although the cursing would remain in the final version, the scene of Jake and Kaili kissing and cuddling hit the cutting room floor after test audiences said they didn't like it.

The drivers who brought out the cast and crew each day from their hotels were all Teamster union members and since I was a former member of the United Mine Workers and still at heart just a Coalwood boy, we got along great. They kept sneaking me Tennessee moonshine in fruit jars, which I had no intention of drinking, mainly because I'd gotten truly sick on it when I was a Rocket Boy. To get pure alcohol for our rockets, John Eye the bootlegger insisted we drink a good portion. Other than when I had scarlet fever as a boy, I was never so sick in my life.

When the temperatures dropped well below freezing, Joe kept filming even though, for continuity's sake, Jake and the boys wore light clothing. To stay warm between takes, they gathered around heat blowers and sucked down coffee and hot chocolate until Joe ordered them back outside. Shivering, Naomi stood beside me, her voice raspy. "I just hope Jake doesn't get sick," she said.

"He seems like a tough kid," I replied.

"Until this movie, I didn't know how tough," she said and went on to explain how much she and his film director father wanted him to go to college rather than become an actor. "It's opposite the way it was with you and your dad," she added. "You wanted to go to college but he wanted you to stay in the family business."

"It's hard to tell your dad you want to do something with your life," I replied, "that's different from what he wants."

"That's what this story is really about," Naomi said. "It's about you and your dad." Of course, she was absolutely right.

For the school scenes, Chris Ellis, the actor playing Principal Turner, often consulted with me about who his character really was and what he was like. I was glad for Chris's presence on the set. It seemed anytime he was there, everything went smoothly due to his competency and fine portrayal of the irascible Mr. Turner.

When Iva Dean, Miss Riley's sister, came on set, Laura walked over and listened attentively while Iva spoke lovingly about her older sister. "I will do my best to bring Freida to the screen," Laura vowed. "Homer and I have been talking about how strong she was and I'm working to get more of that in the script!"

We soon learned Joe Johnston was a train buff. He lobbied long and hard with Chuck Gordon, who in turn lobbied Universal Studios to bring in a steam locomotive and a line of coal cars. The Tennessee Film Commission jumped in to help and the Tennessee Valley Railway Museum in Chattanooga agreed to send a 1950s-era Southern Railway steam locomotive—old 4501—with several coal cars, all dressed out in Norfolk and Western livery just as in Coalwood so long ago. The real Roy Lee Cooke turned up to see the train scene. It was great to see Roy Lee team up with Will Lee Scott, the actor playing him. Both of them were good at telling funny (and often dirty) stories, and they soon had the crew laughing.

The setup for the railroad part was two scenes. In the first one, the boys are shown stealing the track from an abandoned rail spur. In the second, after hearing a train whistle, they run to stop it from running off the rails. The punch line was it wasn't going down the spur at all but past a switch on the main line. The first scene went well, but the second required Jake and the other boys to run down the track. Jake had an awkward gait and tended to hold his hands together in front of him like the rabbit in Disney's *Alice in Wonderland*. During a pause to wait for a stubborn cloud to move, I called Jake over and asked him if he wanted to run like a West Virginia boy. When he nodded—albeit uncertainly—I demonstrated by sprinting away and back again. "You see how I held my arms? Tuck your elbows in and pump your arms with closed fists. That's how a West Virginia boy runs." Jake tried it a couple of times and used my form in the next takes.

As for our director, he was nearly giddy when old 4501 chuffed onto the scene. Joe had somehow managed to cast the locomotive engineer to be none other than O. Winston Link, the famous photographer whose series on steam locomotives made him an icon in the world of train afficionados. The trouble with that was the sad fact that Mr. Link was in the second stage of Alzheimer's disease, but on that day it didn't matter. Joe let him fulfill a dream to actually operate one of the locomotives he had so lovingly photographed.

With Joe's permission, I rode in the cab with the real engineer, a fireman, and Mr. Link. For the rest of the day, we ran up and down the track. Link's job was to wave at the cameras as we ground by while also pulling the whistle chain. When that proved too difficult for him to master, the engineer, who was actually operating the train from the floor, decided he would pull the whistle, leaving only the wave to be performed. When Link kept missing his wave, I said, "Tell you what, Mr. Link, how about I pull your pants leg when you're supposed to wave. Would that be OK?"

Link nodded and I laid down on the cab deck where I could just glimpse the cameras as they came into view. When they did, I tugged Link's pants leg and he waved. The shot was deemed perfect. LT, who was photographing that day, got the perfect shot of the four boys together on the tracks that was later used in the media packets for the film.

When the filming moved to an exterior shot of the Dugout dance hall, it was for a scene between Jake and Kaili. The interior scene was shot earlier in as near an exact replica of the basement dance hall I described in *Rocket Boys* as possible. For my part, I was pleased that the song the kids slow-danced to was Tommy Edwards's "It's All in the Game." It was the song that was actually played when my beloved Dorothy Plunk fell into my brother's arms and danced while my heart broke into a million pieces.

Chris Cooper's scenes were quickly shot. Chris, who was playing my dad, was available only for a short time because of another role in a movie titled *American Beauty*. I knew him from two previous movies: *Matewan*, the story of a union mine organizer, and *Lone Star*, in which he'd played a Texas sheriff. Ironically, the last movie my dad saw before his death was *Matewan*.

My mother chose to visit on the day when Chris played an intense scene with Natalie. Before the shot, I brought Mom around to say hello. Chris stepped out of his trailer dressed in the same kind of khakis Dad preferred for his work clothes. He was also carrying a silver dollar that Dad had as a good luck charm and was wearing Dad's Masonic ring, both items I had given him. When Chris showed them to Mom, it was one of the few times I ever knew her to be astonished beyond words.

It was another cold day, so I gave Mom my jacket so she could watch a scene being filmed in the little town of Petros. The crew rushed over a chair for her and there she perched, queen for the day. The wonderful actor Randy Stripling, who was playing the machinist Leon Bolden, came over to say hello. "I'm Leon Bolden the machinist," he said with a big grin. Mom puzzled over him for a few seconds and then said, "I'm sorry I don't remember you."

I rushed to explain. "Mom, there's the book reality, the movie reality, and the real reality. Try not to get them mixed up."

Mom gave me a warning look. "I'd say that's more your problem," she snapped and I knew it was time for me to back off.

When Natalie came over for a word and a hug, Mom looked her over and said, "I told Sonny I wanted Kathy Bates to play me, but I guess you'll do."

Natalie didn't blink an eye. "Kathy would have made a great you," she replied. Although Mom's remark to Natalie made me grit my teeth, it was just her way and, once they got past her directness, everybody loved her.

Throughout the book, I wrote how young Sonny craved not only the attention of his father but his touch. At the final launch, I wrote that Sonny had hoped that his dad would put his arm around his shoulders and tell him he'd done something good.

Instead, during a coughing fit by his father, I wrote Sonny put his arm around his dad and told him he was the one who'd done something good. Although I knew he was under a lot of pressure to wrap things up, I went to Joe to convince him to do it my way, not the way Lewis had written it where the father puts his arm around the boy. Joe heard me out and then said, "I think we'll film it my way, Homer," and that was that.

In some ways, the filming of the final launch was as thrilling as the real one back in Coalwood in 1960. I could tell the extras were pumped up, as were Jake and the boys. This was the climactic moment of the entire movie. Joey D and his team prepared several "Miss Rileys," big rockets designed by Ky Michaelson, the famous rocket builder, and I was given the honor of pushing the launch button. They all flew perfectly.

With the rocket launches in the can, what had been a lovely day turned sour with the wind picking up and low clouds packing in overhead. When somebody yelled "Tornado!" I saw a swirl of gray air drop from the clouds and start dancing along the edge of the coal dump. People started running while Chuck, LT, and I sought shelter beneath a canvas canopy meant to protect the cameras. Another whirlwind appeared, turned black from the coal it was sucking up inside its guts, and hurtled toward us. With nowhere to run, we grabbed the spars of the canopy and held on even when we were lifted a foot off the ground. Fortunately, as suddenly as they had appeared, the mini tornadoes vanished, we were dropped back to Earth, the clouds scudded away, the sun came out and, to our astonishment, a rainbow formed over the vast coal dump. The movie was made.

Back Home

After the book and the movie came out, there was a slight pause while the world decided what it was going to do about it, and then a lot of wonderful craziness began. There were tons of fan letters and emails. Massive requests for interviews. Demands for appearances and speeches from every state and nearly every country around the world. Everyone, it seemed, was in love with the Rocket Boys. Frank Weimann took me across New York to the offices of Greater Talent Network, a lecture agency, and signed me up. Before long, I was on the road to make speeches, tell stories, and sign books. It soon became clear what people wanted to hear most from me were tales of Coalwood, the people who lived there, what my parents were really like, and my boyhood dreams of building rockets. Happily, I discovered my West Virginia roots had provided me with the ability to tell a good story in front of a crowd. When people came to see me, I think many of them thought I would be technical and dry and were pleasantly surprised to find I soon had them laughing and sometimes shedding a nostalgic tear.

Gradually, I realized that *Rocket Boys* (or its mass market paperback version retitled *October Sky*) was being read and studied in science, English, and literature classrooms. When so many emails came in from students asking for detailed information about the book, LT and I finally figured out they were asking for help with their homework!

A lot of the mail was, of course, about the movie, which was being shown in schools everywhere. I began to use the line that "every substitute teacher in the world shows *October Sky*," and I believe it. Some schools had *Rocket Boys* celebrations where the students dressed up like characters in the book. At one school where I visited, I was delighted to be met by a huddle of "Dorothy Plunks" and "Valentines," dressed in poodle skirts and sweaters!

Awards began to roll in, so many I began to lose track, even including an honorary doctorate from West Virginia's Marshall University. *Rocket Boys/October Sky* also began to be picked by communities and libraries across the country as their annual read. So many of them picked the book, a search on the internet revealed that it was the most selected book for these reads during the first decade of the twenty-first century, ahead of even *To Kill a Mockingbird*. My memoir was being hailed as a classic.

I was savvy enough to know that writers who write classics are sometimes pigeonholed by that work and, sure enough, I was. Even though I was writing about one book a year, people who met me invariably said, "Oh, Mr. Hickam, I love your book!" and I needed no explanation as to which book they were talking about. Of course, most writers would be delighted to write a book that is beloved by millions and I am no exception. In a Texas bookstore when I was on tour for another book I'd written, I was introduced as that "author feller who wrote himself a great book about some boys building rockets they made that movie about." It was at that exact moment I realized there was no escaping it and that was also OK.

One of the best things that happened because of the popularity of the book and the movie was the worldwide interest that turned toward little Coalwood. After the mine closed in 1978, houses there were abandoned or torn down, the old school was burned to the ground by vandals, the company offices and machine shops were left to fall down, and the people in the town found themselves mostly unemployed. With a new spirit provided by the story of their Rocket Boys, Coalwood rallied and began to put on an annual October Sky/Rocket Boys Festival. For thirteen years, the remaining Rocket Boys and I went to Coalwood and signed books and gave autographs all day while people flocked from everywhere to celebrate our story and the history of the coalfields. When there were too few people left in Coalwood to put the festival on, the city of Beckley, West Virginia, picked it up and the other Rocket Boys and I continued to support it, mainly because it brought people to West Virginia to celebrate its history and way of life.

The October Sky/Rocket Boys Festival I remember best and with the most fondness was the one held in 2000. The first one in 1999 I was unable to attend because of my mad schedule of book tours and speeches, but I promised to be there for the second one and I was bound and determined to do it. It was my first time back in many years, and I was devastated by the abandoned homes, schools, and businesses in Coalwood and McDowell County. A lot of the old places where I was raised looked like combat zones, but there was still a spirit there and life trudged on because people that tough dig in and do what they can and hope for a better day. I was glad my book and the movie helped remind everyone how important the coalfields were to the nation and how very special were the people who lived, worked, and sometimes died there to provide the nation with abundant energy and the ability to make steel.

For the festival in 2000, West Virginia's governor, Cecil Underwood, volunteered to come down from Charleston to meet and honor the Rocket Boys and the people of Coalwood. Attending also were thousands of visitors from all over, including my mom, come up from Myrtle Beach to enjoy a day of well-deserved accolades. We gathered at the gas station across the street from the house where I'd spent my teenage years. While we waited for the governor to arrive, I took a moment to look at the house and remember not just that boy who built rockets but that time when he'd passed through the back gate heading for college while his mother stood in the yard to watch him go. That was in 1960 and now here it was the year 2000, forty years and Blacksburg and Utah and Vietnam and Guanaja and Germany and NASA and Japan and all the other things and places and people later. I looked around and discovered they were all there with me, at least in my heart. Somehow, perhaps according to some purely cosmic plan, that boy riding off to college had finally and properly worked his way back home.

Epilogue

And so ends this account of a period of my life that begins and ends in my hometown of Coalwood, West Virginia, with a space of almost exactly forty years between them. After that, no matter what else I might do or say or be, I was the man who wrote that book about the boy who was in that movie. Since this perception affected nearly everything I did afterward, it seems best to wrap up these stories with a bow around it and call it a memoir.

And yet there were so many things to see and feel and do. My life wasn't over, but it was decidedly different. After *Rocket Boys*, my literary career was in gear and I would write many more books, including this one, nearly all of them well received and some falling into that coveted category of bestseller.

During subsequent years, I also became an avid amateur paleontologist. Because Joe Johnston, the director of *October Sky*, was a friend of Dr. John "Jack" Horner, the famous dinosaur hunter, I got to know Dr. Horner and visited his field camp the summer of 2000. This began two decades of work in the Montana badlands where my little team of fossil hunters and I have found to date five T. rexes and numerous triceratops, hadrosaurs, and other species of the Cretaceous in the Hell Creek Formation. While doing this work, I have suffered scrapes and sprains and passed out once from heat exhaustion but, as the writer and poet Charles Bukowski famously said, "Find what you love and let it kill you." I've also formed friendships with paleontologists and their students from the world over as well as becoming friends with the wonderful, amazing people in the Montana ranchlands. My adventures out there might be worthy of another memoir, but we shall see.

Rocket Boys the Musical was a remarkable creation by the talented Tramon siblings of Broadway, Carl, Dan, and Diana. After listening to a tape of their proposed musical based on *Rocket Boys*, I loved it so much I joined as a cowriter. Ultimately, we would have some great productions in New York, Atlanta, and West Virginia, only to be shut down by a multinational corporation claiming ownership of my story. This began a terrible interlude in my life filled with lawsuits and lawyers that saw our wonderful musical crushed. But it is too good to stay down forever, and I have hope yet to see it once more on stage and thence around the world.

Although I never built a place on my beloved island of Guanaja, I was able to purchase for LT and me (we are now married) a wonderful home we call Skyridge high on a mountain overlooking the sea in St. John, US Virgin Islands. This was in 2002, and we enjoyed the house with good friends for fifteen years before it was destroyed by Hurricanes Irma and Maria in back-to-back punches. After these horrible storms, the island looked as if a nuclear weapon had blasted it. Scarcely a leaf was left on a tree and the people who endured it were left, often hungry and thirsty, to wander across an awful landscape. With two friends, Al English and my brother-in-law Chris Terry, we arrived three weeks later to tear down what was left of Skyridge. Over many harrowing, dangerous days, when heaven wept for what it had done, we lived amongst the ruins. After that came the decision whether to rebuild. Ultimately we did, but it was a long, frustrating project that saw consternation, great expense, but a challenge met.

It has also been my honor to be appointed to the boards of two magnificent organizations, the United States Space & Rocket Center, home of the world-famous Space Camp, and the Museum of the Rockies, one of the finest paleontological museums and dinosaur research centers on our planet.

Sadly, we lost Mom, Elsie Hickam, in 2010 at the age of ninety-eight. She did not die so much as she stopped living. Nearly everyone she knew had gone on ahead, and I think she was lonely for them and decided to join them whether the rest of us liked it or not. Her ashes went on the beach she loved and there, I believe, she walks forever with the sky above eternally blue and the sea spread out to a heavenly shore covered with shells and, her favorite to find, fossilized shark's teeth.

Although retired from NASA, I've kept my hand somewhat in the space business. A great honor was being appointed to an advisory group of the National Space Council by Vice President Mike Pence, where I was able to encourage our return to the moon, this time to stay. The vice president told me that he had read both *Rocket Boys* and my novel *Back to the Moon* and their influence, along with his own studies and talks with space professionals, had caused him to revitalize NASA and the commercial space industry. I was proud to sit beside moonwalker Buzz Aldrin when Vice President Pence stood up at a National Space Council meeting at the US Space & Rocket Center in Huntsville and announced we were going back to the moon in a program that was eventually named Artemis. I watched and listened through the eyes and ears of Sonny and let him enjoy the moment.

LT and I have traveled the world. In Australia, we lived beneath the stars in the outback to watch and celebrate amateur rocketeers as they lit up the sky with their whooshing creations in a gathering called Thunda Down Under. After an invitation from the International Institute of Education, we traveled to Vietnam to speak to students about furthering their education. Remarkably and coincidentally, it turned out that the Vietnamese version of *Rocket Boys* was published the same time we were there. After traveling so far, I felt it necessary to go back to the old battlefields in the Central Highlands to recall those days with such brave men. There was hardly anything I recognized there, but I was so glad to see the country at peace. Everywhere we went, we were treated with overwhelming love and hospitality.

For leisure trips, we have sailed around the Galapagos Islands and dived along its storied shores, vacationed in Italy where we explored and hiked along the Amalfi Coast, poked into the ancient towns of Pompeii and Herculaneum, saw a deceased pope and a live pope the same day in Rome, walked amongst the vineyards and wineries and artistic triumphs of Tuscany, and dawdled along the canals of Venice. We drove the entire circumference of Iceland and snorkeled in a glacier pond and were mesmerized by one little town named Siglufjördour that I called Coalwood, Iceland, because it, too, was a company town except the product was herring, not coal.

A cruise aboard the good ship *Sikumi* in Alaska's Inside Passage was an amazing voyage where we caught barn-door-sized halibut, kayaked amongst blue icebergs, gloried in the flights of eagles, and danced amongst the whales. This time, I also got to visit another Coalwood, also known as Petersburg, Alaska, where a "slime line" was still active, where men and mostly women plucked out the fish guts and junk through the mass of fish going by on a conveyer much like the old coal pickers in Coalwood plucked out rock from the coal.

There were other wonderful trips to Germany and France for LT and me, especially Paris to visit the French publisher of my novel *Carrying Albert Home*, and elsewhere in the world. LT and I have had so much fun during our travels. No matter what Kismet has in store for me in the future, I am grateful to family and friends and to my Creator for nudging me along and keeping me around, and to everyone and everything that still makes life interesting and alive. As long as I can, I hope to keep writing and thinking and doing and, like Sonny Hickam on his motor scooter off to VPI, I am eager to see what comes next.